DATE DUE			

Lavigerie in Tunisia

J. DEAN O'DONNELL, JR.

Lavigerie in Tunisia

The Interplay
of Imperialist and Missionary

THE UNIVERSITY OF GEORGIA PRESS
ATHENS

Copyright © 1979 by the University of Georgia Press
Athens 30602

Printed in the United States of America

Library of Congress Cataloging in Publication Data

O'Donnell, Joseph Dean, 1943-

Lavigerie in Tunisia.

Bibliography.

Includes index.

1. Lavigerie, Charles Martial Allemand, Cardinal, 1825-1892.
2. Church and state in Tunisia - History. 3. Tunisia - Politics
and government. I. Title.

BX4705.L4036   266'.2'0924 [B]   78-9041

ISBN 0-8203-0456-5

In Memory of

W. Linwood Thompson

Contents

Acknowledgments

Financial support for this research came from a Rutgers University
Fellowship, the Trustees of the Student Loan Fund of the Rotary
Club of Baltimore, and a Small Project Grant from the College of
Arts and Sciences of Virginia Polytechnic Institute and State Uni-
versity.

Many friends provided moral support during my work, but those
who contributed to my understanding of the topic deserve mention
by name. Professor A. Carter Jefferson supervised my first year of
doctoral research at Rutgers, and Professor Peter N. Stearns's editorial criticism thereafter has been as prompt as it was helpful.
The earlier personal influence of Professor Eugene O. Golob at
Wesleyan University must rank with theirs. Professors David Ringrose,
Michael Curtis, and Herbert H. Rowen at Rutgers provided many helpful comments. Professors C. Alfred Perkins of Upsala College, James
E. Ward of Notre Dame University, and Alexander Sedgwick of the University of Virginia gave encouraging advice through correspondence.
Fr. Joseph N. Moody of Boston College and Catholic University was
particularly helpful with suggestions during the summer which we
both spent working at the Archives Nationales. He has provided
encouragement ever since then.

The basic documents for my research were in the Archives Lavigerie
at the White Fathers' headquarters in Rome. Fr. René Dionne at
Washington arranged for me to live in the Mother House in 1969 while
I worked there. Fr. Dionne worked in the Archives Lavigerie during
my second visit in 1972, and he was very helpful with his advice.
Fr. René Lamey of the Service Historique opened these archives
to me without reservation and helped me find the documents I needed.
The White Fathers are proud of their founder, but they have no il-
lusions about getting him canonized. Several of them have done thèses

d'Etat at the Sorbonne. During my months at Rome Fr. François
Renault was finishing his study of Lavigerie's Oeuvrage Antiesclav-
agiste, and Fr. Jacques Durant was investigating the activity of
Lavigerie in Algeria. Both men gave me advice and guidance based on
their work in Lavigerie's papers. The superior general of the White
Fathers, Théo Van Asten, and the procurator of the Society, Fr. Ver
Haag, endorsed my requests for access to the Vatican and Propaganda
Archives. Other veteran missionaries befriended me during my total
of five months in Rome, and their knowledge of the Society added to
my awareness of its evolution. Frs. Gerald Lachance, Anthony Coolen,
and Leonard Marchant deserve special thanks. Since in their early
days some of these priests knew Lavigerie's younger associates,
their first-hand anecdotes of the Society helped me to understand
the founder's personality, particularly his violent temper.

Although the Vatican Archives do not permit researchers to cull
material after the pontificate of Pius IX, Fr. Charles Burns kindly
searched later material and obtained permission for me to examine
relevant documents. Mgr. Joseph Metzler, O.M.I., of the Propaganda
Fide archives and library, likewise was most generous with his time.
For these courtesies I must also thank the Americans who helped pro-
vide the indispensable references which open doors in Rome: Lawrence
Cardinal Shehan of Baltimore; his secretary, Miss Elizabeth Sweeney;
Mr. Alphonso Di Meo of New York; and Fr. Henry Browne and Mgr.
Eugene V. Clark of the Archdiocese of New York.

During a research trip to Tunis in June 1972 the Prelate of Tunis,
Mgr. Michel Callens, and his private secretary, Mgr. Paul Labbe,
were hospitable and gracious in opening their archives to me.
Dr. Abdeljelil Temimi at the Archives Nationales was also very helpful. Special thanks must go to Professor Pierre Soumille and to
Mr. John Crockett, the American cultural attaché. The Soumilles welcomed me into their home, and Pierre spent hours sharing his insights
about Tunisia and its history. Mr. Crockett's warm personal interest
in American scholars is remembered appreciately by anyone who worked
in Tunis during his tour there.

During my second research trip to Paris in December 1972 several people helped me finish my work there in a short period of time. I wish to thank individually M. Degros at the Quai d'Orsay, Mlle Sueur at the Archives de l'Armée de Terre, and Fr. Guillaume de Bertier de Sauvigny, the patron of many American researchers in Paris.

Laurence Michalak of the University of California at Berkeley courteously showed me a manuscript of his work on the French protectorate in Tunisia. Professor James McNab of Virginia Tech helped me translate some phrases in French. My colleague Michael Hurst gave numerous suggestions on improving the manuscript, and I benefitted from the advice of others in Virginia Tech's Department of History: William Mackie, Thomas Adriance, Thomas Howard, and William Ochsenwald. Other colleagues and administrators provided indispensable moral and practical support, particularly Professor Daniel Frederick. Professor James B. Campbell advised Mr. Darrell G. Nolton in preparing the maps.

Mrs. Carolyn P. Alls, Mrs. Donna B. Pugh, and Mrs. Dianne S. Cannaday worked hours typing the illegible into clean drafts. The final copy was prepared at the College of Arts and Sciences typing pool by Mrs. Regina Lewis.

I owe a great debt of gratitude to many people for help in this project, although its shortcomings are my own responsibility. Most of my sources were in French, and I have therefore followed a French transliteration for Muslim names. Some of these arbitrary choices may not seem the best, but lacking a command of Arabic I decided to stay on solid ground and strive for consistency. This applies also to questions of capitalization in English. In the 1970s books seem to favor the upper case as little as tennis players favor white. Purists may commiserate with my friend Bev Brinlee: "e. e. cummings saw it coming."

Words can not express my feelings for some of the friends who encouraged me in this project, except to say that they were there when I needed them. Gertrude S. Thompson has been there since 1957.

Preface

In the minds of many Europeans of the late nineteenth century,
Charles Cardinal Lavigerie was the Catholic Church in French North
Africa. He personified the Church's dual ministry to Europeans
and natives. The Archbishop of Carthage and Algiers supervised his
diocesan clergy with the particular purpose of making Italians,
Maltese, and other foreigners submit docilely to French authority.
To carry out his long-range program of preparing the native populations of Africa for conversion to Christianity, Lavigerie founded
the Society of Missionaries of Algiers. Although his technique in
dealing with Europeans was sometimes heavy-handed, the apostolate
of his White Fathers was indirect for fear of offending Muslim
sensibilities. Yet his secret memoirs to French officials regarding the desert nomads' capacity for rebellion were blunt, and some
of his confidential suggestions on ways to maintain and increase
French control were merciless. Notwithstanding the government's
program against the Church in the métropole, Jules Ferry, Léon
Gambetta, and other French leaders followed Lavigerie's recommendations so closely in establishing the Tunisian protectorate that
they took pains to conceal this source of advice from less pragmatic anticlericals. At Tunis Lavigerie worked so intimately with
officials that he became, in effect, one of the French authorities.
The personal gratitude and admiration of Third Republic leaders,
which enabled him to mediate the bitter struggle between church
and state in the métropole, was one dividend of Lavigerie's crucial support for French power in Tunisia.

   The "new imperialism" of this period followed different patterns
among the countries which competed for overseas territories, and

its complexity of causation still fosters historical debate. The
precise influence of Christian motives is hard to define, but the
importance of the missionary factor in imperialism is evident.
The rank and file of missionaries carried on their work with a
sense of sacrifice and duty, concerned with the practical advantages which European power offered to their ministry in undeveloped
territories. Colonialists applauded their "civilizing influence"
on the peoples under European control, while the clergy's participation seemed to sanctify and ennoble overseas conquests. Charles
Cardinal Lavigerie shared the views of both missionaries and imperialists, but he had a very sophisticated understanding of the
relationship between the apostolate and overseas expansion. In
spite of all his political machinations, Lavigerie was essentially
a pastor and missionary. His religious vocation was fundamentally
in harmony with his nationalist commitment. He realistically considered the two activities in their diplomatic, political, and
military contexts. A study of his role in the establishment of the
1881 French protectorate of Tunisia discloses the importance of
religion in the high politics of overseas expansion, and it sin-
gles out the personality who linked the issue of imperialism with
clerical affairs in the Third Republic.

The French government's traditional role as the Western protector of Turkish Christians in communion with the Holy See was a
resilient bond between Paris and Rome even during the bitterest
rounds of the anticlerical struggle. But impersonal diplomatic
calculations alone cannot fully explain the steadiness with which
French ministers and Curia officials maintained this cooperation
during the 1880s. To be sure, the missionary boundaries of Chris-
tendom and the borders of French power were in many places the
same line, manned by priests, consuls, and soldiers. But one
Frenchman especially personified the relationship that kept them
all in tandem. He provided the confidential brokerage between the
Quai d'Orsay and Rome which preserved the overseas tie between

church and state at a time when domestic bonds were systematically
severed. In fact, Lavigerie's personal participation in the ecclesiastical affairs of Asia Minor on behalf of the Eastern Religious
Protectorate had much to do with revitalizing this agency of
French influence there. The "prisoner of the Vatican," Leo XIII,
with no Catholic power but France to rely on, leaned heavily on
the advice of his beloved "Apostle of Africa."[1]

Lavigerie's cooperation with the government of the Third Republic was inspired by a view of politics and the apostolate formed
during his early years of work in overseas relief, the Vatican
bureaucracy, and the court of Napoleon III. Thereafter, his perspective of the domestic and overseas interests of the Church and
of France was broader and subtler than that of the royalists,
most of his episcopal colleagues, and many republican leaders.
Politicians of both extremes attacked him for his service as a
mediator in domestic clerical affairs and for his support of overseas expansion. Monarchists like Paul de Cassagnac, grieved by
his allegiance to the republic, criticized his acceptance of a
cardinal's hat in 1882 for services rendered. Lavigerie received
a torrent of abuse from conservative Catholics in 1890 for his
Toast of Algiers, which called for their ralliement to the legal
government of France. The radicals, on the other hand, condemned
him and the government annually for every credit recommended to
fund his North African projects. They especially opposed government subsidies for Lavigerie's work in Tunisia as an indirect
means of attacking the moderate republicans' colonial policy.[2]
But Lavigerie worked above the narrower interests of French political factions and remained for many years the trusted servant and
colleague of such a diverse array as Leo XIII, Jules Ferry, Léon
Gambetta, and others.

Lavigerie was one of the most ubiquitous figures of the nineteenth century, to borrow an adjective from Arthur Marsden.[3] His
fine hand appears repeatedly, sometimes quite unexpectedly, in

the history of France, Europe, Africa, the Eastern Mediterranean,
and the Church. It is impossible to treat his role in Tunisia
without relating it to other matters concerning French domestic
politics and diplomacy, European colonialism, and Catholicism.
Tunisia was only one part of Lavigerie's nationalistic and apostolic design.

An understanding of this larger view requires references to
areas of his activity beyond Tunisia at the risk of overlapping
recent research by other scholars. White Fathers of the Society's
Service Historique have produced several studies, including
François Renault's two volumes on the Oeuvrage Antiesclavagiste
and Xavier de Montclos's works on the Toast of Algiers and on
Lavigerie's ecclesiology. An American, Professor James E. Ward,
discussed Lavigerie's importance in a dissertation on "Franco-
Vatican Relations, 1878-1892: The Diplomatic Origins of the
Ralliement."[4]

These monographs supplement the biographies and memoirs published in the decades following Lavigerie's death. Mgr. Louis
Baunard, Abbé Jules Tournier, and Fr. J. Mercui based their metic-
ulous studies on documents conserved by the Society.[5] These biographies emphasized the cardinal's apostolic commitment and did
not relate Lavigerie's work in North Africa to the larger historical issues of imperialism and its causes which have broader
interest today. The authors did not have access to Quai d'Orsay,
Cults Ministry, nor War Ministry archives, which disclose many
details concerning Lavigerie's cooperation with the government.
The centenary of Lavigerie's birth, in 1925, occasioned testi-
monials and memorials from Jules Cambon, Georges Goyau, and others,
expressing the gratitude and esteem felt by members of colonialist
groups who knew the importance of his contribution.[6] Despite the
value of these earlier publications, they were written by men
who took for granted the assumptions of their ecclesiastical or

colonialist milieus and who did not have the perspective of the
post-colonial period. None of them adequately treats the story of
Lavigerie's collaboration in the French protectorate of the 1880s,
and the Tunisian ralliement of his clergy to the policy of the
Third Republic.

Lavigerie's support in Tunisia was vital to French policy. When
a few of his White Fathers took custody of the Chapelle Saint-
Louis at Carthage in 1875, their quiet presence among the country's
clergy of Italian Capuchins hardly seemed like the beginning of a
"work of Gallicization." But Lavigerie obtained the Vatican's appointment as apostolic administrator of the Vicariate of Tunis in
the spring of 1881, right after the Treaty of Bardo (12 May) imposed French rule on the beylic. Three years later he persuaded
the Pope to restore the ancient Christian See of Carthage, whose
archbishop enjoyed the title of Primate of Africa. Within the
European colony, religion was the key to assimilating the Italian
vicariate into a French diocese. The cardinal's "religious protectorate" was the cornerstone of French influence on the Europeans
in Tunisia.

Lavigerie was devoted to both the national interests of France
and the propagation of the Catholic faith. The sincerity of both
loyalties was evident to churchmen and politicians who had known
and watched him for many years. Believing that the best interests,
"rightly understood," of both church and state overseas were in
accord, he had no difficulty defining his policy. Precisely for
this reason, the historian faces considerable difficulty dissecting
the anatomy of his motives.

Lavigerie took seriously the notion of France's civilizing mission, in which religion had an important part. When he accepted
the See of Algiers in 1866, his first thought had been to Chris-
tianize the native population of Africa. The White Fathers whom
Lavigerie sent to central Africa made numerous conversions in

areas where Islam had not established itself first. But French
officials opposed proselytizing in Algeria, and Lavigerie himself
quickly realized that the profound faith of the Muslims could not
be changed in one generation. His policy in Algeria and Tunisia
was therefore one of indirection: a ministry of education, medi-
cine, and charity, which would earn the natives' good will and
prepare for the conversion of their descendants. Although a
nationalist, Lavigerie argued forcefully during the 1880s for a
protectorate regime in Tunisia which would provide justice for
the natives. He was severe in his warnings to the Paris government
during the first days of the protectorate when the army had to
pacify insurgent tribesmen, but he worked thereafter to prevent
the establishment of a regime of officers and annexationists which
would repeat the mistakes made in Algeria.

Lavigerie approached North African problems with great political acumen and finesse. He also had a shrewd sense of conditions
in the rest of the Mediterranean area and in the African interior.
The opportunities he saw for the Church and for France gave him
great hopes for the future. Yet Lavigerie's vision was set in the
context of his time. It was the age of imperialism, and today such
a man would be denounced as a racist, no matter how generous and
protective his paternalism. This treatment of Cardinal Lavigerie's
involvement in French overseas expansion therefore puts the writer
at pains to correct any mistaken inference regarding the present
activities of the White Fathers.

The Society has long since outgrown the founder's nationalism,
and in this century the French minority of its members fully share
its primary commitment to the peoples of Africa. A council of five
men from as many countries coordinates the work of more than three
thousand priests and brothers enlisted from ten provinces on both
sides of the Atlantic. In recent decades of anticolonial and post-

colonial tensions, their sympathies have been with the aspirations
of the Africans.

During the Algerian War White Fathers provided medical
sanctuary - and by one pied-noir's allegation a few of them stored
arms - for members of the National Liberation Front. Later in
Mozambique they denounced forced labor conditions and military
atrocities while Portuguese bishops there looked the other way.
The Society's Dutch father general, Théo Van Asten, went to Lisbon
to protest to the minister of colonies, who refused to see him.
The forty White Fathers in Mozambique faced a choice between keeping silent or speaking out and again provoking colonial authorities into torturing black hostages taken from their parishes. At
a meeting they agreed that their position was impossible. In 1971
the White Fathers left Mozambique, not with a whimper, but with a
well-orchestrated bang.

Today in North Africa a small number of White Fathers minister
to the Catholics remaining there. Some teach or serve in other
capacities where they are welcome. In the Arab world the White
Fathers have renounced all proselytizing. A number of them are
Arab scholars, whose deep respect for the Muslims' faith and culture differs totally from Lavigerie's prejudice. The Institut des
Belles-Lettres Arabes at Tunis is internationally known for its
journal IBLA. White Fathers at Rome have for some time held key
positions in the Pontifical Institute for Arab Studies and in the
Vatican offices which seek ecumenical dialogue with all mono-
theists.

Among the Christian populations of sub-Saharan Africa the
Society is the junior partner of black bishops. They welcome the
Society's help because in their second century the White Fathers
still follow Lavigerie's fundamental principle of Adaptation - to
the needs of those they serve.

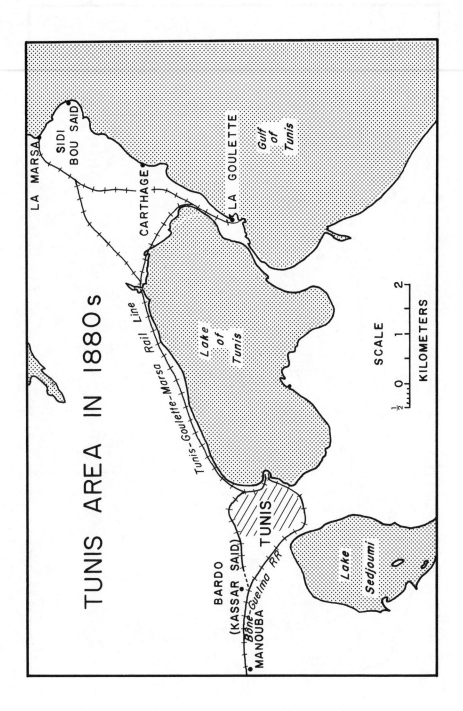

TUNIS AREA IN 1880s

REGENCY OF TUNIS IN 1880s

Strait of
Sicily

BIZERTA

Cape
Bon

DJEDEIDEH

BÔNE   Khroumiria   TUNIS

Bône-Guelma Rail Line   NABEUL

• THIBAR

ENFIDA•

ALGERIA   SOUSSE•   •MONASTIR
TUNISIA
                    • KAIROUAN
                                        MAHDIA•

TUNISIA

SFAX•

GABÈS•   DJERBA

Chott Djerid

SCALE

10 0   50   100

KILOMETERS

I

Introduction

Charles-Martial Allemand-Lavigerie was born in Bayonne on 31
October 1825, the son of a customs collector in comfortable circumstances (he used the family name Allemand until the Franco-
Prussian War). His missionary zeal appeared in an early incident
when he forced Jewish playmates under a fountain in order to
baptize them. Lavigerie's father, not remarkably devout, provided
him with a Catholic education but initially resisted his determination to enter the seminary. Ordained in 1849, Lavigerie continued his studies for the doctorate. He published an Essai
historique sur l'école chrétienne d'Edesse in 1850 and joined
the Sorbonne faculty as a professor of ecclesiastical history.[1]

Lavigerie's participation in overseas affairs began in 1856
when he accepted the leadership of the Oeuvre des Ecoles d'Orient.
During the Crimean War a group including Montalembert, Falloux,
and other members of the French intellectual elite founded a
society for the establishment of French schools on the eastern
shores of the Mediterranean. The Turkish alliance against Russia
had opened the way, and by means of this wedge the group hoped
to continue the promotion of French culture in the Muslim world
after the war.[2] Another goal was to prepare Eastern Christians
for a return to communion with Rome.[3] France was not able to
rival British naval power in the Mediterranean, but for the rest
of the century she competed with Italy for influence on the lit-
toral by means of schools as well as the favor which her citizens
acquired as physicians, secretaries, and advisers to Turkish
officials. An intense rivalry developed between those promoting
French and those promoting Italian as the "lingua franca" of the

Mediterranean. Schools were the key, subsidized in later decades
by both Paris and Rome.[4]

Lavigerie was well suited for the chairmanship of the Oeuvre
des Ecoles; drumming up contributions provided an outlet for his
activist temperament. The Druse massacres of Maronite Christians
in the Levant required him to travel overseas in 1860. One hundred thousand survivors were left homeless by the time the French
fleet and expeditionary force arrived to maintain order. On behalf of the Ecoles Lavigerie distributed 2 million francs among
orphanages and refugee shelters in Syria. There he first met
several of the French officers and diplomats with whom he later
worked in North Africa, including General Antoine Chanzy and
Théodore Roustan. Lavigerie returned to Europe at the end of 1860
with a vivid, if unsympathetic, impression of the Muslim world.

Lavigerie's work in the Levant had earned the respect of
churchmen he visited at the Vatican as well as French officials
of the Second Empire. He turned down the See of Vannes in order
to move to Rome in 1861 as French auditor of the Rota, a position
which involved personal contact with Pius IX. Like Richelieu two
centuries before, Lavigerie profited from the opportunity to cultivate papal favor. Remaining active in the Ecoles, Lavigerie
coordinated the establishment of French schools, hospitals, and
shelters from Cairo to Constantinople, and he set up a council
of the organization at Rome.

In 1863 the French government again offered Lavigerie a dio-
cese, and he became Bishop of Nancy.[5] Although this was Lavigerie's
first full-time pastoral assignment, his brief administration of
Nancy was a conspicuous success. Within the French hierarchy
Lavigerie was part of a reformist faction which included Maret,
Dean of the Faculty of Theology of the Sorbonne, and Archbishop
Darboy of Paris - a group described by Bernard de Lacombe as

"a bit liberal, a bit academic, and if one may say, a bit
administrative."[6] During the mid-sixties Lavigerie and his old
teacher Darboy served as unofficial ecclesiastical advisers to
the imperial court. Friends in the hierarchy and the government
planned to move Lavigerie to Lyons, the second most prestigious
see in France. But the young bishop's outspokenness irritated
many of his episcopal colleagues, who criticized him for ambition.

The See of Algiers offered a way out of an uncomfortable situation in 1866. Coincidentally, Algiers became the metropolitan
see of an ecclesiastical province, with suffragan sees created
at Oran and Constantine. When Mgr. Pavy died in November 1866,
Lavigerie's celebrity within France appealed to Governor General
Patrice MacMahon. MacMahon was eager to enhance his administration of Algeria in the eyes of the métropole, and at first
Lavigerie seemed the ideal choice for first chaplain to the
French community. MacMahon disregarded Napoleon III's warning
that Lavigerie would rock the boat. The minister of cults was
reluctant to send overseas one of his best supporters in the
hierarchy, but Lavigerie wrote to Jules Baroche that he was the
only French bishop who had experience with Muslims or who concerned himself with evangelizing them.[7] Lavigerie's correspondence
with General MacMahon soon revealed the bishop's disagreement with
the colonial policy of restricting Catholic ministry to Europeans:
"Algeria is only the door opened by Providence on a barbaric continent of two hundred million souls. It is especially there that
we must bring the Catholic apostolate."[8] MacMahon realized his
mistake, but Lavigerie's acceptance was so widely known that
Napoleon had to proceed with the formalities of nominating him
to Algiers. MacMahon persuaded the emperor to buy him off with
the coadjutorship of Lyons. Lavigerie declined the offer,
announcing that "it would be nicer to live at Lyons, but it

would be easier to die in Algiers."[9] His friends at the Vatican
expedited approval of the appointment before the emperor could
have it shelved.

Lavigerie and MacMahon soon found themselves in a bitter conflict which reopened the issue of what role Catholic missionaries
were to play in French North Africa. The Archbishop of Algiers's
first pastoral letter in the spring of 1867 declared his goal of
converting the natives into Christian offspring of the mother
country.[10] Hence from the start he challenged the government's
traditional policy. Four years after the French seizure of Algeria
in 1830, the interim governor, General Voirol, had forbidden all
proselytizing on the grounds that questions of religion were,
for the natives, questions of nationality. The first Bishop of
Algiers, Mgr. Dupuch, fought this policy until his forced retirement in 1845. Bishop Pavy tried to familiarize his clergy with
Muslim culture, but official restrictions on clerical contacts
with natives remained in effect until his death.[11] Lavigerie had
known both of his predecessors, and he realized the difficulties
he faced with the military regime in Algeria.

The French army had governed the territory since the invasion
of 1830. In order to supervise the Muslim population the army in
1844 created a special agency of 50 officers. By 1864 it had
grown to a peak of 190 officers in 56 bureaus. These military
authorities were known as the Arab Bureaus, although properly
speaking, Berbers rather than Arabs predominated in the interior
region of Kabylia. These officers exercised the real power behind
the tribal chiefs. Some officers relied heavily on force of arms,
while others encouraged mutual respect and assistance; most of
them were dedicated and conscientious. They sought to prevent
extensive contact with Europeans from disrupting the traditional
tribal society, and they tried paternalistically to protect the
natives' land from covetous French colons. Many civilians wanted

to trade and settle in tribal territory, and they bitterly resented the Arab Bureaus' assertion that premature changes in
tribal society would jeopardize French control. In terms of public relations the Arab Bureaus failed to address squarely the
question of how fast and how far the colons should rightly be
permitted to settle in tribal lands. Rather, they justified pro-
longing the segregation of natives from the French as necessary
in order to keep the tribes tranquil, and they exaggerated the
spectre of rebellion in defending the maintenance of military
control.[12] Lavigerie had his own objections to a policy of segregation, and he sided with the colons in their increasingly
bitter dispute with the Arab Bureaus.

Patrice MacMahon worked in the middle of all this as governor
general from 1864 to 1870. He prevented mass spoilation of native
lands, but he ignored a lesser degree of exploitation. MacMahon
gave priority to the maintenance of order. For this reason he
resented the emperor's criticism of injustices in Algeria, which
undermined the military regime's prestige; and he opposed Catholic proselytizing for fear of provoking "fanatical" Muslims to
revolt.[13]

The attitude of Napoleon himself toward Algeria was gallant
and protective: "I am as much the Emperor of the Arabs as the
Emperor of the French."[14] He dreamed of constructing an "Arab
nation" to replace traditional Turkish influence in North Africa.
Army officers in Algeria followed a middle course, in a sense.
Resisting colons' efforts to seize native land, at the same time
they also opposed the gradual evolution of an "Arab Kingdom,"
the emperor's phrase for his policy of permanent segregation.
Napoleon had to tolerate passive disobedience throughout his two
decades of vacillating policy for Algeria. By the late 1860s his
attention to these issues was distracted by bad health as well
as Bismarck's challenge in Europe.[15]

Archbishop Lavigerie's letters and actions soon gave Napoleon
more distress. Lavigerie criticized forthrightly the notion that
an "Arab Kingdom" could coexist in harmony with the French colony.
If the barrier between Muslims and Christians were maintained,
"there will be . . . neither a single native who is not Muslim,
nor a single Muslim who is not still an enemy of France at
heart."[16] Lavigerie agreed that an aggressive apostolate risked
provoking the fanaticism of tribal populations subdued in 1848
by French arms. But he insisted that gradual assimilation was
necessary and fully practical by means of charitable works for
all and French schools for Muslim children.[17]

MacMahon completely opposed Lavigerie's goal, although they
reached an apparent and brief compromise in 1867, restricting the
clergy to works of charity. Against the military regime Lavigerie
exploited the discontent of French civilians. His speech to a
group of them in November 1867 was an open affront to the authorities: "I ask of France larger liberties [for the colons] out of
the justice of the mother country. . . . I ask of you the spirit
of initiative . . . for all that is useful, fruitful, Christian."[18]
Lavigerie subsequently pulled back somewhat from meddling in administrative affairs, but the break with MacMahon was irremediable.

A series of natural disasters led to a bitter confrontation in
1868. Cholera, locusts, drought, and famine literally decimated
the native population. Lavigerie established orphanages and other
extensive relief measures, drawing renewed opposition from the
authorities. He appealed to Napoleon: "I ask for the Church in
our African land the same liberty as in Turkey."[19] Both MacMahon
and Lavigerie travelled to Paris. The archbishop stressed the
importance of winning the Muslims' respect for Christians, and
he warned Napoleon of the bitterness of those orphans who survived
if MacMahon succeeded in turning them out. Lavigerie blamed the
authorities for much of the loss of life, and he threatened to

expose MacMahon's negligence publicly. Napoleon had privately
reprimanded General MacMahon's indifference, but the emperor did
not wish to see his administration in Algeria publicly attacked
by an archbishop. Catholics were an important component of the
Second Empire's political base. Napoleon knew that Lavigerie
knew how to win that kind of fight, so he gave in. Lavigerie
detested MacMahon to the end of his days, and as President of the
Republic from 1873 to 1879, MacMahon treated the archbishop as
an enemy.[20]

But Lavigerie obtained in 1868 the basic liberty for an apostolate of charity. He established for his orphans two agricultural hamlets, otherwise called Christian villages, in the Chélif
Valley west of Algiers. In 1868 he persuaded the Pope to make him
Apostolic Delegate to the Sahara and the Soudan, providing a
future mission territory in the North African interior. In the
same year he founded his Society of Missionaries of Algiers, the
White Fathers.[21]

The outbreak of the Franco-Prussian War interrupted the work
of Lavigerie's clergy in 1870. He hurried home from the Vatican
Council to rally their support for France. The archbishop offered,
at his own expense, to place at the disposal of the minister of
war half of his priests for service as chaplains and medics. Two
of them, later consecrated bishops, were wounded.[22]

The war of 1870 reversed the political situation in Algeria.
The destruction of the Arab Bureaus' power in 1872 gave much
satisfaction to Lavigerie and the colons; but it destroyed their
alliance, which had been based on opposition to the empire's
policy of military government. The Second Empire's collapse
brought turmoil to the colony and unleashed a wave of anticlericalism. A mob turned out the colonial administration, and the
municipal council of Algiers invited Garibaldi to lead a seces-
sion from the mother country. Freemasons in Algiers had been

trying for several years to laicize municipal schools; immediately after the proclamation of the French Republic in September 1870, Algiers and Bône (Annaba) voted such laic measures. The following year Algeria's colons elected deputies to represent their interests at Paris. Lavigerie lamented the state of affairs in January 1872: "All our elective councils are revolutionary. . . . The entire press of the colony is in the hands of radicals. . . . The Commune of Paris is the ideal of a great number."[23]

In the Algerian interior the Kabylian tribes took advantage of the army's withdrawal to France and revolted in 1871. The colons accused the military of inciting the rebellion in order to justify their regime, although later a parliamentary commission posthumously exonerated the Arab Bureaus of that slander. Lavigerie interpreted the rebellion as vindicating his criticism of the "Arab Kingdom" policy of segregating the natives from French or Christian influence. MacMahon's successor, Admiral Louis-Henri de Gueydon, put the rebellion down, and thereafter Gueydon supported Lavigerie's charitable works for the natives. But his replacement, General Antoine Chanzy, tried to revive the policy of the Arab Bureaus. Then in December 1873 Chanzy's son died. At the funeral the archbishop delivered a sermon which dissolved the Chanzys in tears. It also dissolved Lavigerie's problem with the military authorities, although he still had to bear attacks from anticlerical colons. Sixteen months after Lavigerie's eulogy for her child, Mme Chanzy helped him get a foothold in Tunisia.[24]

Lavigerie first became concerned with the Regency of Tunis in 1873. He took the initiative, proposing to the foreign minister, Duc de Broglie, that the government assign several priests to the French enclave at Saint-Louis de Carthage.[25] Lavigerie's interest was twofold. He realized, of course, the political value of reestablishing a French presence at Carthage, however

indefinite the government's design in Tunisia may have been at
the start. He likewise wished eventually to revive the ancient
memories of Africa's primal see, just as he emphasized the chapel's
medieval associations with the French king who had fought to recover Barbary from the infidels. Lavigerie recommended in his
letter of 1873 to Broglie that the Chapelle Saint-Louis once again
be attended by French priests, specifically by White Fathers.[26]

The shrine was built on land ceded to France in 1830 by a
secret treaty between Hussein Bey and Consul General Matthieu de
Lesseps. An emplacement on the ruins of Carthage, a dozen miles
from Tunis, was chosen for a religious monument to the memory of
St. Louis, who died there in 1270 during the Eighth Crusade.
Guided to the likely place by historical accounts of the crusader's
death, the French selected the plateau of Byrsa at the center of
the Punic acropolis, the site of an ancient temple. Eleven years
passed before the French broke ground for a small oratory, which
was consecrated in 1845 by Mgr. Fedele Sutter, titular (in partibus)
Bishop of Rosea. A Capuchin of German-Swiss origin, Sutter headed
the small group of Italians who served the Catholics of Tunisia.
A Frenchman, the Abbé Bourgade, took charge of the Chapelle Saint-
Louis from 1843 to 1855, but thereafter it fell into neglect.

For lack of French personnel to maintain the shrine, it fell
under Mgr. Sutter's complete control. On one occasion he denied
a French bishop the privilege of saying Mass there on the feast
of St. Louis. He likewise rejected suggestions that another
Frenchman be appointed to the post, although he offered to have
one of his Capuchins say Mass there on appropriate occasions - for
a suitable stipend.[27] Bishop Sutter served as Apostolic Vicar of
Tunisia from 1843 until his replacement in 1881 by the Archbishop
of Algiers. As an Italian Capuchin he was not likely to welcome
the appointment of Frenchmen to his jurisdiction. Broglie was
cautious in his reply to Lavigerie's suggestion of 1873; the

foreign minister left it to Lavigerie's initiative to persuade the Holy See to compel the admission of White Fathers.[28]

The project took two years to ripen. Théodore Roustan, Lavigerie's friend in Beyrouth and the man who joined with him to impose French political and ecclesiastical control on Tunisia, became Consul General of the Republic at Tunis in December 1874. In early 1875 Roustan wrote to Lavigerie that he would like to see French priests restore the Chapelle Saint-Louis; its neglect was a national disgrace.[29] The decision was artfully publicized in connection with the April visit of Mme Chanzy. She asked Roustan to accompany her to the shrine. Expressing dismay at its deterioration, she hastily wrote Lavigerie to ask that it be fittingly served and maintained by French priests. Lavigerie quickly obtained custody of the chapel from Pius IX.[30] He wrote to the Sacred Congregation of the Propaganda Fide, mission arm of the Curia, requesting that Mgr. Sutter be informed that new personnel were assigned within his jurisdiction.[31] Lavigerie had arranged with the French government that two White Fathers sent there should receive salaries under the budget of cults for the Archdiocese of Algiers. Their sole obligation was to offer Mass and pray for France.[32]

Frs. Bresson and Molles arrived on 13 June at the Tunis port of La Goulette with a letter informing Sutter of their assignment. Their instructions were to install themselves at Carthage, presenting the Capuchins with an accomplished fact. Bresson carried another letter to Roustan assuring him that if Mgr. Sutter should protest Lavigerie would have Rome transfer the chapel itself to the jurisdiction of the See of Algiers. "The Secretary of the Propaganda has proposed this to me, I am certain of obtaining it, and I think it is good that Mgr. Sutter not be unaware of this."[33]

Once the scenario with Mme Chanzy and Roustan had been played, Lavigerie restrained his characteristic flair for public relations.

During the first two years his letters to the chapel urged caution
in every respect. It was important to avoid giving provocation to
Muslim authorities by proselytizing, or to the Capuchin vicariate
by any competitive ministry. Lavigerie instructed Bresson, the
first superior at Carthage, to provide the Mass and sacraments
only at the chapel or at the French consulate. He urged them to
avoid outsiders and to follow the advice of Roustan.[34] This was
the beginning in Tunisia of a _ralliement_ to the support of the
Third Republic by French clergy, much more enthusiastic and durable than the one which Lavigerie signalled fifteen years later
at Algiers.

Eighteen months after the first White Fathers arrived at
Carthage, Lavigerie tried to move his own residence there. He
announced this on 1 January 1877 to the Missionaries of Algiers
at their Maison-Carrée headquarters. At the time of this meeting
the Society numbered three hundred. Lavigerie was exasperated by
new difficulties with Algerian authorities and saddened by the
recent murder of several White Fathers in the Sahara. He dramat-
ically told his missionaries that, for reasons of health, he had
asked the Pope "to let me leave my archepiscopal see, to take
your habit and your rule, to share your life and, if necessary,
your death."[35] He intended to keep his mission title of Apostolic
Delegate to the Sahara and the Soudan, withdrawing to Saint-Louis
de Carthage. As an African prelate he could act completely on his
own, without the restrictions imposed on French bishops by the
Napoleonic Concordat. Rome had recently named an American cardinal, and Lavigerie expected also to be elevated in recognition
of his adopted continent. But the French government would not
provide a pension for his retirement from Algiers, and the Pope
refused him permission to resign any of his responsibilities.[36]
The government and the Holy See did, however, consider giving
Lavigerie a coadjutor to reduce the burden of administration.[37]

Later in 1877 Lavigerie sent the Pope a memoir which outlined
his master plan for the African continent. He aimed to consolidate his position in Tunisia, and ultimately to restore the See
of Carthage. He also proposed getting a foothold in Jerusalem,
where White Fathers could promote reunion of Orthodox Christians
with Rome. This would also increase French influence in the
Levant. He suggested to the Pope that European activities against
the slave trade within Africa should be gathered under Catholic
auspices. Lavigerie himself planned a school for ransomed slaves;
this was to prepare native medical and teaching personnel for the
African Church.[38] He recommended an ecclesiastical counterpart to
the Belgian King Leopold's program of colonizing central Africa;
Lavigerie asked the Pope to establish two mission jurisdictions
there under his own direction. Regarding this last project,
Lavigerie faced competition from Jesuits and from Fathers of the
Holy Spirit, who also sought mission fields in central Africa.
At the very moment when Pius IX was preparing to give jurisdiction
there to the White Fathers, he died in early February 1878.

Lavigerie met the new Pope soon after election, and they began
a friendship which Leo XIII once compared to Peter's love for
Andrew. One of Pope Leo's first acts was to approve the appointment of Frs. Linvinhac and Pascal as apostolic delegates in
equatorial Africa.[39] The Vatican and the government soon agreed
to give Lavigerie custody of the Church of St. Anne of Jerusalem,
where White Fathers eventually established a seminary to train
priests of the Greek Melchite Rite in their own language and
liturgy. Later in 1878 the Pope instructed Mgr. Wladimir Czacki
at the Sacred Congregation of Extraordinary Ecclesiastical Affairs
to inform the French government that Mgr. Lavigerie's name would
be persona grata for nomination to the cardinalate. But there was
no possibility of this while MacMahon remained president.[40]

The end of 1878 is a point at which to pause in this narrative. The European sanction just given at the Congress of Berlin to the French desire for Tunisia brought the Third Republic one step closer to placing a French bishop at Carthage. In Paris republicans were contemplating measures to take against the Catholic Church in France once they wrested the presidency from MacMahon. Some of these anticlericals become lifelong partners of an archbishop whom the monarchist president detested. It is useful here to consider the personality, world view, and method of the man who inspired such strong affection and hatred among French leaders.

In several ways Lavigerie resembled another great colonialist, Marshal Hubert Lyautey. Both coped with chronic medical problems. Both of these devout Catholics inherited strong royalist sympathies, although they accepted the republic. They became disillusioned and bored with routine careers in France; restlessness drew these men of action to initial assignments in Algeria. They shared enlightened views on colonial administration, always remembering the connection between military and political considerations. Formulating policy for their respective protectorates of Tunisia and Morocco, Lavigerie and Lyautey favored governing through a native framework. In disputes with Paris each was a proud man willing occasionally to put his job on the line.[41]

Lavigerie's biography would tantalize a psychohistorian, for he left no intimate record of personal relationships. With regard to his emotional life he had intense feelings of love for institutions like church and country; he had strong friendship for associates like Leo XIII, Roustan, Ferry, and Gambetta. Lavigerie's hostile feelings focussed on Islam, certain Curia cardinals, and other political enemies. French relatives never appear in available correspondence, and he bequeathed no real wealth to them. Lavigerie felt a father's affection for younger priests. Several times the murders of White Fathers in the mission field shattered him like the loss of sons. He treated many of the other men who worked around him like children, but in a different sense, as characterized by this report in the Cults Ministry archives: "He guides his clergy with a quite military discipline. His iron hand is not even covered with a velvet glove. The least breach of conduct is severely reprimanded. Sober, of a private life beyond all criticism, he demands the same line of conduct from his priests. His clergy admire and fear him perhaps more than they love him."[42]

Several factors made Lavigerie extremely high-strung. With regard to external pressure, he had burdens and enemies more formidable than those which vexed other bishops. Ailments made him a hypochondriac. For most of his years in North Africa Lavigerie suffered from rheumatism, arthritis, and sciatica. He would not slow down, and in the 1880s his health began to break; a series of strokes crippled him at the end. Regarding Lavigerie's middle years one can speculate how much his illnesses were a cause or the result of the tension under which he worked. In any event, they shortened his temper.

He had no patience, to begin with, for mediocrity or independent action of the part of subordinates. He was a stickler for formalities like daily meditation and the breviary. His chief lieutenants implemented orders and programs; he did not depend on their advice. Pastors and superiors had to write or wire for permission to reschedule church services or move furniture around. Aides had to jump to keep up with him; in his morning office sessions a team of secretaries took dictation fired at them in alternating paragraphs. Occasionally he physically slapped a priest into shape to get the kind of performance he wanted, and an egregious blunder could precipitate a storm which lasted for days. In tears he might later beg the priest's forgiveness for

losing his temper, but usually his tantrums were calculated
chastisements.[43]

On the larger stage of politics Lavigerie was a comediante.
To quote Fr. Jacques Durant's assessment: "He was an impresario
at overstating things histrionically." Lavigerie had a gift for
sarcasm which politicians found trenchant and subordinates found
devastating. The ham actor sometimes combatted an adversary for
the sport as much as the strategy. Durant thinks that Lavigerie's
southern French temperament made him simpatico with the Italians
he encountered at Rome. Some associates, like Napoleon III and
Propaganda Cardinal-Prefect Simeoni, recognized the Latin in him,
perhaps because it took one to know one. Popes Pius and Leo played
their cards close enough to the chest to keep the upper hand.
Marshal MacMahon, Cults Ministry officials, and the North African
clergy learned from experience how Lavigerie could rampage out of
all proportion to a tactical setback. This tendency to overreact
led Fr. Durant to describe him as a "cyclothymic."[44]

Despite these ups and downs Lavigerie had the self-confidence
and relentless will to stay functional. His drive sprang from
apostolic zeal, deep patriotism, and personal ambition. He un-
questionably sought to extend his personal power; some contempor-
aries saw megalomania in Lavigerie's visionary schemes and majestic
personal style.[45] All of his projects were part of a complete
design, and he cultivated the people who could help him achieve
his apostolic and patriotic objectives. Lavigerie was a keen
judge of human nature as it governed public opinion and individuals. He knew what themes to play in the pulpit and the press; he
had an instinct for manipulation. In some of his machinations
this political sense appears more intuitive than calculating. He
could turn an antagonist's attack around on him, and he knew how
to exploit a person's susceptibilities. He usually applied these
talents constructively, as he did when he spoke the eulogy for

General Chanzy's son that prompted Mme Chanzy's subsequent role
in dramatizing the need for sending White Fathers to Carthage.
Critics noted his demagogy as a promoter and politician, his author-
itarianism as an administrator, and his shrewdness as a financier.
His clergy and his political allies recognized a pragmatic dedication to high ideals. They revered his ability to get things
done.

The strongest drive within Lavigerie was his love of the
Church. His ecclesiology was an exceptional combination of ideas
and practice. The Abbé Lavigerie had never run a parish, but as
a bishop and missionary his concern was essentially pastoral.[46]
Despite his personal scorn for Pius IX he was devoted to the
spiritual sovereignty of the Holy See.[47] But he loathed the Italian
cardinals' monopoly of power in the Curia, blaming their Latin
attacks on the ancient traditions of the Eastern Rite for creating
the great obstacle to bringing Orthodox Christians into communion
with the Holy See. Roman primacy, he thought, should be a paternal
principle of unity, not cultural uniformity. He believed that
the governance of the Universal Church was in great need of reform. He particularly desired the internationalization of the
Sacred College of Cardinals.[48]

Accomplishment of such a reform "takes a man of destiny, and,
believe me, I am he."[49] Since 1863 he had urged the government
in Paris to dilute Italian influence in the Vatican by assigning
French cardinals to work there, just as non-Italian cardinals
resident at Rome had helped govern the Church in the Middle Ages.
In order to promote reform of the Curia Lavigerie tried on several
occasions in the mid-seventies to obtain a cardinal's hat for
himself, but he would not go so far as to seek a major see in
France for fear of becoming embroiled in episcopal factions there.
Lavigerie's African base enabled him to play a more general role
in the Church "which only I can realize."[50] He spoke fluent Italian,

and his missionary activities could always be used to camouflage
visits to Paris or Rome on more delicate business concerning
French overseas expansion or the anticlerical struggle. He continued also to promote the reunion of Eastern Christians with
Rome. Lavigerie finally got his red hat in 1882, but he failed
in his efforts to internationalize the Curia. The "little Italian
coterie" which Lavigerie detested dominated the Sacred College
for many more decades. These <u>curiali</u> knew how he felt about them,
and some became troublesome enemies.[51] But with Leo XIII's confidence and support Lavigerie advanced the other aspects of his
ecclesiastical program, in particular the mission apostolate in
Africa.

The agency for this work was the Society of Missionaries of
Algiers, founded in 1868. These White Fathers wore Arab dress in
keeping with the founder's first principle of Adaptation to the
culture around them. Lavigerie soon organized the White Sisters
as well. Seminarians were required to study Arabic and the Qu'ran
as part of their training. The first White Fathers took their
life vows in 1872 and set up schools in the Kabylian highlands.
Lavigerie's rules prescribed an apostolate of three stages. In
the preparatory period there was to be no baptism or preaching
which might offend or threaten local leaders. Only after cultivating good will by teaching, medical care, and alms, were the
missionaries allowed to discuss religion individually with in-
quirers; because Lavigerie feared apostasy among hasty converts,
he insisted on four years of instruction before baptism. When a
few conversions solidly established the mission in the community,
open evangelism would be appropriate.[52]

Here on the mission frontier Lavigerie saw the purest expression of the Church's apostolate. The central principle inspiring
this effort was the mystery of Charity, the motto on Lavigerie's
episcopal coat of arms. This love of one's fellow man for the

love of Christ was the core of his theology.[53] In its practical
application charity was also a missionary strategy of winning
the respect of North Africans, reconciling them to French rule,
and preparing for the conversion of their descendants. As
Abdeljelil Temimi notes, Lavigerie planned "a new style of
Crusade."[54]

Lavigerie's zeal was fortified by an intense prejudice against
the Muslim faith. He had no appreciation of its important place
in the Hebrew-Greek tradition, considering Islam an evil to be
weakened slowly and overcome en bloc.[55] Lavigerie's understanding
of the Muslim faith was one-sided and negative in both the historical and the contemporary perspectives. Letters to mission
journals perhaps exaggerated his feelings in order to inspire
the reader's generosity, but they expressed his basic views:

> Armed apostles of a sensual religion, . . . the
> disciples of the Qu'ran began those fearsome invasions
> which, for so long, menaced Europe itself. . . .
> The Christians of North Africa were their first vic-
> tims. . . . Wholesale massacres, the exile of entire
> populations transported by the victors to Arabia, and
> the effort of several centuries finally extinguished
> all resistance. The blood ceased to flow; cries of
> anguish or of vengeance were no longer heard; and
> there was nothing left in deserted cities to protect
> against the sacrilegious violence done to an entire
> people, except the ashes of saints in the depths of
> their desecrated tombs.[56]

Kenneth Cragg provides a fairer verdict: "The idea of a sword at
the throat of every Christian compelling him to Islamize is a
crude and overdrawn picture. . . . If Christianity did not persist
in more robust quality the fault was not wholly with Islam."[57]

Lavigerie did not see this. He was fired with the idea of restoring Christianity in North Africa. Elsewhere on the continent he believed that Islam and Christianity were engaged in a race to win souls.

> Checked and almost dying in Europe, Islam ceaselessly makes redoubtable advances among the African populations. It imposes itself on them by violence. It creates provinces and kingdoms, and one counts that in a hundred years it has bent under its yoke of iron no less than fifty million souls. . . . [In equatorial Africa] the peoples gained for Islam will be lost to us for centuries. The Muslim religion is truly the masterpiece of the spirit of evil. It gives to the most profound needs of man's heart, to religious needs, a sort of satisfaction by the portion of truth which it conserves; and at the same time it opens all barriers to his passions, it legitimizes all disorders of the senses, it defies brute force. How can we wrest away souls from its empire? Islam cannot perish but of itself, by its excesses which are the consequences of its doctrines and by the death which it carries above all within itself. This is expressed energetically by the oriental proverb: "The shadow of a Turk sterilizes for a century the field which it traverses." That fatal shadow arrived in equatorial Africa at the very moment when our missions were established there. Our Fathers have found it at Tanganyika and at Nyanza in the person of Arab slavers.[58]

Two recurring themes in Lavigerie's writings were the historical viciousness of Islam and the personal vices of its adherents. He

pointed to the institution of slavery as the most atrocious expression of Muslim society.[59] He had condemned Napoleon III's
"Arab Kingdom" for reinforcing a culture which he considered
inherently evil. Lavigerie believed that Muslims differed from
other non-Christians in their fanatical pride in Islam and its
direct lineage from the prophet Muhammad. In Lavigerie's vocabu-
lary Muslim fanatic became one word. He knew that a direct effort
to convert the North Africans to Christianity would promptly
offend their religious sensibilities and could easily provoke an
insurrection. A frontal challenge to Islam would raise barriers
to the gradual transformation and ultimate conversion which
Lavigerie envisioned.[60] Having visited the Middle East, he did
not need MacMahon to tell him that.

The first stage of Africa's transformation offered a great
opportunity and responsiblity to France. Her soldiers were partners with Catholic missionaries in a splendid task which neither
could accomplish alone. In this ecclesiology patriotism and
missionary zeal were inseparable. Long after MacMahon, anticlericals accused Lavigerie and his priests of provoking Muslim
fanaticism by proselytizing. He responded publicly to one of
these unjust attacks:

> Certainly, one need not be a priest, but only a man
> to wish the transformation of the poor, fallen races
> of North Africa. . . . But ordinary preaching, per-
> sonal proselytizing is powerless before the blind
> prejudices and implacable passions engaged in this
> resistance of barbarity. On the contrary, it is detri-
> mental until Providence itself has made the prepara-
> tion.
>
> The only true and effective preaching, in this
> moment, is the action of events which change the po-
> litical situation of these regions. Without knowing

it, without willing it, <u>our governors and our soldiers</u>
<u>are thus the agents of this new mission</u>. <u>They are the</u>
<u>force, and force, for the Muslims, is God Himself</u>.
. . . While they strip the natives of their power,
of their arms, of their secular traditions, we priests
seek to calm and reclaim their embittered hearts by
the exercise of devotion and charity. . . . No doubt
what we thus obtain is not hasty and imprudent conversions, which would only be preparations for apostasy; it is a more durable work, a certain preparation,
without jolts and dangers, for the transformation of
the African world.

Thus the seed is sown. The work of centuries will
make it ripen.

For us, who will not see the fruit, our reward is
in the witness that we thus serve the cause of humanity, of France, and of God.[61]

Many anticlericals in the Third Republic appreciated this
contribution to French expansion overseas. Jules Ferry and Léon
Gambetta, in particular, gave Lavigerie's efforts in Tunisia
their full support. They knew the lesson, if not the anecdote,
of the French general who met the Turkish plenipotentiary in
Syria after the Druse massacres. "I do not fear the forty thousand bayonets you have at Damascus - what I dread are those forty
robes," said the pasha, referring to the missionaries who hailed
the French expeditionary corps. "Why? Because those forty robes
make France sprout in my country."[62]

The potential influence of the Church in Asia Minor and Africa
was already formidable. Lavigerie's talent as an administrator,
politician, and fund-raiser equipped him to develop this influence
to the fullest in Tunisia. Lavigerie believed that the mission
objectives of the Church and the imperialist goals of the Third

Republic ought to be in harmony. By his personal efforts in Tunisia he promoted this harmony and advanced the programs of both Catholicism and the Third Republic, in spite of the bitter conflict between church and state in France.

Church–State Relations: Clericalism the Enemy—and an Article for Export

Lavigerie emerged in the leadership of the French hierarchy on the eve of a crisis which threatened to destroy the Church's Napoleonic Concordat and to end the cooperation overseas which greatly benefitted the Holy See and France. During much of the nineteenth century the French contributed the majority of personnel and funds assigned to Catholic overseas missions. Two events occured in 1870 which fundamentally affected the context of this mission program. In France a republican regime replaced the Second Empire, and nine years later the men who assumed its leadership undertook a systematic purge of clerical influence in government and education. Ironically, an equally bitter anticlerical struggle also developed in Italy following the Savoy Monarchy's invasion of Rome. The Holy See therefore remained dependent on French diplomatic support, and continued the traditional Franco-Vatican partnership overseas. Since his voyage to the Levant in 1860, Lavigerie had an important role in this partnership. As a bishop he aided French government support for the Eastern Catholic clergy against Italian efforts to Latinize them. The Catholic contribution to French influence overseas made republican leaders like Jules Ferry and Léon Gambetta hesitate to press the Church too hard at home. Lavigerie's part in the Tunisian venture bound him closer to republican leaders during the 1880s, and this increased his effectiveness as a mediator between them and churchmen in France and in the Curia. Lavigerie prevented a collapse of church-state relations in France and the

dangers to his program in Africa which would have resulted from
such a disaster.

The decade in which the Third Republic began building a new
colonial empire coincided with its attack on the Church. These
two programs were related in the career of Lavigerie; a study of
his activity in Tunisia must refer to the background and details
of church-state relations in France. Soon after driving MacMahon
from the presidency in early 1879, the anticlericals launched
their program of "republican defense" against the Catholic grip
on major institutions of the state: the army, the bureaucracy,
the courts, and, most of all, the schools.[1] Yet despite the bitterness of this attack within France, the Holy See moderated its
policy toward the government because of the support and protection which France still gave to missionaries and indigenous
Catholics overseas. The Vatican had traditionally supported French
influence in the Mediterranean, and Lavigerie strengthened the overseas link between church and state at the same time as anticlericals systematically severed the ties at home. While the Church's
position deteriorated in the métropole, Lavigerie consolidated it
in North Africa. The patriotic support which Lavigerie's priests
gave to their lawful government contrasted sharply with the behavior of many clergy at home, and it built a foundation for
Lavigerie's later attempt to promote a Catholic ralliement to the
republic.

Two historic institutions defined the relationship between
Catholicism and the government during this period. The Concordat
of 1801 prescribed the status of the Church within France until
its abolition in 1905. Lavigerie deserves much of the credit for
the fact that the Concordat survived the nineteenth century.
Overseas, the French Religious Protectorate of Catholicism in
the Ottoman Empire gave France a privileged position in the Turkish provinces where she competed against other countries for

influence. Lavigerie personified this overseas connection, and
his priests supported it: "We follow the flag of France, without
even concerning ourselves whose hands hold it."[2]

But Lavigerie himself was very judicious about whose hands
held it. The Archbishop of Algiers was, successively, a Bonapart-
ist, a legitimist, and a republican. To some of his critics these
timely shifts of loyalty seemed self-serving and opportunistic.
A fairer explanation would be his readiness to adapt to contemporary realities in the way which best served the Church. During
the Second Empire Lavigerie instinctively cultivated people in
power from the emperor on down. But he also declined the opportunity to be Cardinal-Archbishop of Lyons, and he openly battled
with the governor general of Algeria when the Church's rights
were at stake. After the empire's collapse in September 1870
Lavigerie got the Pope's permission for French bishops to run
for the National Assembly in order to defend the interests of
the Church. He himself lost in both of the elections of 1871.[3]

Lavigerie was a monarchist for the next four years. The
Communards of Paris, who had murdered his friend, Archbishop
Darboy, impressed Lavigerie with the dangers of republicanism,
if not with the social discontents which had partly caused the
Commune. In 1874 he wrote a letter to the Comte de Chambord, the
Bourbon pretender, urging him to take the throne by force if
necessary. Diehard monarchists published it in 1890 in revenge
for Lavigerie's Toast of Algiers. His biographer Baunard apolo-
gizes for the letter on the grounds that in 1874 Chambord had a
widely recognized claim to the crown and that the legal status
of the republican regime was still provisional.[4] But French conservatives were unable to negotiate "Henry V's" restoration, and
by default the Third Republic ceased to be provisional. Lavigerie
accepted this fact sooner than most French clerics, and he realized the necessity of making peace with the established regime.

He agreed with Mgr. Guilbert that "it is our duty to ensure that
the altar does not go down with the throne."[5]

Lavigerie's personal enemy, MacMahon, became President of the
Republic, which offered the Church momentary security. But during
the later seventies the president's conservative supporters encountered increasing opposition from moderates in the Chamber of
Deputies and in the Senate. These "opportunists" in the center
faced competition for republican votes from radicals on the left.
Some of the opportunists felt obliged to exaggerate their genuine
opposition to the Church's position of influence in French society and privilege within the state.

The legal position of the Church was defined by the Napoleonic
Concordat of 1801, which was both an instrument of governmental
control over the clergy and their guarantee of certain rights.
In the early Third Republic the Concordat system still offered
advantages to both parties, notwithstanding the ferocious attacks
upon it which some politicians made in public. It provided for
annual appropriations in the budget of the Ministry of Cults; in
small villages the central government paid a salary to its only
civil servant, the priest. Paris had the right to name bishops,
subject to preliminary agreement with the Holy See, and the
Concordat included strict prohibitions against episcopal councils
and group declarations. Jules Roche and others of the extreme
left urged its abolition in 1882; but the suggestion was, for
this period, a bluff or weapon in reserve rather than an immediate likelihood.[6]

Foreign Ministry officials at the Quai d'Orsay realized pro-
foundly the damage which the proposed rupture between church and
state would inflict upon their policy in the Mediterranean. One
casualty of such an act of war on the Church would be the Eastern
Religious Protectorate. Throughout the anticlerical struggle of
the 1880s French diplomats, and politicians who favored overseas

expansion, felt a patriotic interest in keeping the domestic conflict within bounds. Other European powers resented the claims
of the French Religious Protectorate, and the newly united Kingdom
of Italy wanted to take it over. Lavigerie and his assistants
worked loyally at Rome defending the special privileges of France.

The Religious Protectorate gave France a monopoly on Western
claims to offer diplomatic protection to European Christians in
Ottoman lands and to patronize indigenous Christians in the
Turkish orbit. The Porte's Roman Catholic subjects had a special
status under French tutelage. Eastern Rite Christians in communion
with Rome (Uniate Catholics) rounded out this "clientèle catholique" - Gambetta's phrase - on which France based her influence
within Turkish territories. The Eastern Protectorate originated
in treaties of 1535, 1569, 1604, and 1740, negotiated with
Constantinople for the purpose of securing French trading rights.
The religious clauses of these treaties had been included to provide an additional "instrument of moral power."[7] Their function
changed by the nineteenth century. The Druse massacres of Maronite
Christians in Syria and Lebanon occasioned the dispatch of a
French army to the area, with the endorsement of the other Christian powers.[8] But after 1870 Britain, Russia, and Germany developed
areas of influence in the Levant where they challenged the French
role as protector of indigenous Christians. European nationals
tended increasingly to depend on their own governments, and the
Eastern Protectorate functioned more narrowly. The Quai d'Orsay
still claimed the right to defend Christian juridical persons
(congregations) against Turkish law, and it offered protection
to Vatican diplomats who were not French.

In turn, Rome's support was indispensable to France for the
Religious Protectorate to be effective, even though it did not
derive from any treaty with the Holy See. The Concordat made no
mention of the Religious Protectorate, and Paris maintained that

no unilateral act of the Vatican nor rupture between church and
state could affect "the rights of the French government in
Turkey."[9] Despite increasing skepticism on the part of other
countries, Foreign Minister William-Henry Waddington obtained a
diplomatic ratification on these pretensions at the Congress of
Berlin in 1878. Article 62 of the Treaty of Berlin stated: "The
acquired rights of France are expressly reserved." The Porte
thereafter confirmed them with a treaty of capitulations. These
"acquired rights" were, nonetheless, rather ill defined; and they
lent themselves to clarification by means of pressure on the Holy
See.[10]

Rome's cooperation was inspired partly by the thousands of
personnel and millions of francs which France sent to Catholic
missions during the nineteenth century. France had replaced Spain
and Portugal in the leadership of the Catholic apostolate, and by
the end of the century an estimated two-thirds of the priests and
four-fifths of the brothers and nuns overseas were French. The
Oeuvre de la Propagation de la Foi, founded by Pauline Jaricot
in 1820, channeled contributions from many countries through its
headquarters in Lyons. This gave the Third Republic's ambassador
to the Holy See considerable stature on his visits to the palace
of the Sacred Congregation of the Progaganda Fide on the Piazza
di Spagna.[11] Lavigerie enjoyed similar prestige at the Propaganda
for the funds he had raised since first joining the Oeuvre des
Ecoles d'Orient.

French agencies like the Ecoles were an important means of
exploiting the Religious Protectorate in the Eastern Mediterranean.
The Vatican's cautious policy regarding the territories of the
Sublime Porte had traditionally been to refrain from proselytizing
for fear of giving Muslim authorities any pretext for molesting
or restricting the Christians already there. But this began to
change in 1879, when Leo XIII urged the sultan to let his Muslim

subjects take advantage of Catholic charity and instruction.[12]
France continued to subsidize such programs and to protect the
indigenous Christian minorities in the Ottoman Empire even after
French troops abandoned Rome to the Italian army in 1870.

Taking advantage of the Franco-Prussian War, Italy gave the
French Religious Protectorate a new lease on life by seizing what
remained of papal territory. This usurpation made the Roman Question a significant factor in European politics for several decades.
The Popes' refusal to accept the loss of the temporal power, as
well as Bismarck's victory over France, inclined the Holy See and
the French Republic to work together. The Vatican could find no
real support in the Roman Question from Catholic Austria, and
France was even more isolated diplomatically than the Pope. Within
France many Catholics felt a crusader's commitment to defend papal
claims, even to the point of compromising French national interests. This became a factor in church-state relations, for conservative Catholics who gave equal support to the cause of Chambord
and to the temporal power of the Church doubled the outrage of
republican anticlericals. By the time of Pio Nono's death in
February 1878 the chances of restoring either looked slim. But
Leo XIII continued the pose of an Italian "prisoner in the Vatican."
To borrow James E. Ward's phrase, the Roman Question was the pivot
as well as the Achilles' heel of Leo's diplomacy.[13] It perpetu-
ated his diplomatic dependence on France, even during the anticlerical eighties. It also poisoned church-state relations in
Italy well into the twentieth century; devout Italian Catholics
who favored monarchy as a form of government felt a conflict of
loyalty which weakened the Kingdom of Italy internally.[14] And the
Savoy government's seizure of the papal city severely limited its
natural opportunity of exploiting the influence which patriotic
Italian prelates exercised in the Mediterranean as representatives
of the Holy See.

Direct Italian efforts to challenge the French Religious
Protectorate were failures. The first attempt was a suggestion
offered after 1871 that the Eastern Protectorate of Catholics be
made an international enterprise. This proposal was based on the
certain expectation that such cooperative effort would fail,
leaving Italy to recover the Religious Protectorate for herself.[15]
The Roman government tried again in the late seventies to obtain
its advantages by offering military exemptions to Italian missionaries if they would operate under an Italian umbrella rather than
that of the French. Under pressure the Vatican sustained French
"rights" and rejected this second bid. Even after the Third
Republic began its open attack on the Church within France,
Cardinal Nina at the Secretariat of State assured Ambassador
Desprez in May 1880 that the Holy See desired to continue the
French protectorate overseas.[16] Nina's successor, Lodovico
Jacobini, as well as the new cardinal-prefect of the Propaganda,
Giovanni Simeoni, held firmly to this official policy of support
for France.

Lavigerie always feared that resolution of the Roman Question
or the election of a weak pope would enable Italy to curtail the
Holy See's independence, with possible consequences of schism or
Kulturkampf in other countries. He stressed this in a memoir of
1875 to Paris concerning internationalization of the College of
Cardinals.[17] After the conclave of February 1878 Lavigerie worried
about the health of the frail new Pope almost as much as his own.
But, in fact, Leo XIII's steady hand guided the Church during a
quarter-century of anticlerical trouble in Italy and France. The
Italian situation deteriorated so much in the summer of 1882 that
Leo talked of exile in Austria. Lavigerie confided to Paul Cambon
how the Austrians dreamt of such an opportunity: "They would push
the Pope to Constantinople or Jerusalem, and they would replace
our influence at Syria."[18] But such nightmares never constituted

an immediate threat to the favored position of France. By 1888,
after a brief flirtation with Germany, Leo saw clearly that
Bismarck's blood and iron would never lead him back across the
Tiber.[19] The Vatican could not follow through a German, Italian,
or Austrian alternative to her reliance on the "Eldest Daughter
of the Church."

A rift in the diplomatic partnership between the republic and
the Holy See would have brought disastrous consequences to the
Church within France. Papal policy steadfastly supported the
Religious Protectorate in the Mediterranean despite occasional
concessions to Italian demands, or measured responses to anticlerical attacks within the métropole. The Curia bureaucracy included some prelates who favored Italian national interests for
reasons of family ties or simple patriotism, and these monsignori
sometimes made trouble. But basically Paris secured Vatican cooperation to make the Religious Protectorate effective. French
difficulties primarily concerned Italian activity on the local
level.

One such example directly concerned France's and Lavigerie's
interests in Syria, an area which then included Lebanon and
Palestine as well. The Apostolic Delegate to Syria, Mgr. Lodovico
Piavi, worked closely with Italian diplomats at Beyrouth, particularly the consul Licurgo Maccio. Piavi, a Franciscan, used his
influence in the Levant to promote Italian language instruction
in religious schools and the establishment of new houses by
Italian congregations, in much the same fashion later employed
by Lavigerie in Tunisia. Prime Minister Minghetti began to subsidize Catholic schools in the Levant during the early seventies;
but the French consul, Théodore Roustan, persuaded most of them
to resist Italian attempts to purchase their loyalty.[20] After
Roustan left for Tunis in 1874, French efforts at Beyrouth to
fight Piavi's meddling continued for another fifteen years.

Reports from Roustan's successor, Consul General Salvatore
Patrimonio, refer to the pro-Italian activities during the early
1880s of the "Triumvirate of Lebanon," Piavi, Maccio, and the
Turkish governor, Rustem Pasha. Besides opposing French influence,
the apostolic delegate sided with Rustem's efforts to destroy
the influence of the Maronite high clergy. Piavi's policy was
hardly calculated to promote the oriental bishops' affection for
the Roman Pontiff, which gave Lavigerie a second reason for concern. Despite a French protest to the Vatican and Piavi's recall
to Rome for a reprimand, the apostolic delegate circumspectly
continued his policy.[21]

On a visit to Beyrouth in the service of the Ecoles d'Orient
one of Lavigerie's priests, Félix Charmetant, reported to him on
the situation as it remained in 1887. Orthodox Christians of the
area increasingly faced missionary efforts of British Protestants
and the Russians. They leaned more towards Rome than Moscow, which
offered a great opportunity for enlarging France's clientèle
catholique. But the apostolic delegate undermined this by propa-
gating the Roman liturgy. Instead of supporting Eastern Rite bishops already in union with the Holy See and helping them throw
their nets in the sea of schismatics around them, Italians like
Piavi competed with the Uniate clergy for flocks already Catholic.
Eastern Catholic bishops could not find voices for their choirs
after he and his associates finished Latinizing them. Charmetant
wrote to Lavigerie that at Jerusalem the Franciscans refused to
let Eastern Rite bishops and priests say Mass in their own language at Christ's tomb. This policy violated the Pope's expressed
views, and the Uniates sought French support. They looked in particular to Lavigerie for moral support as well as for the assignment of White Fathers to teach in their seminaries. The apostolic
delegate's welcome to Charmetant acknowledged the formidable
prelate who had sought during the 1880s to end Piavi's career in

the Levant: "After the Apostles who founded the Church, I do not
know anyone who has rendered Catholicism more services than the
Eminent Cardinal Lavigerie."[22]

Throughout the 1880s the Quai d'Orsay depended on Lavigerie
to help counter Piavi's influence and, it was hoped, to have him
removed. The White Fathers had overcome the Italian Franciscans'
monopoly of Catholic influence in the Holy Land by establishing
the Scholasticate of St. Anne of Jerusalem for Greek-Melchite
seminarians. As Lavigerie explained to the minister of cults in
October 1880, this was part of his larger program of attaching
(rattacher) Eastern Rite bishops to the French Religious Protectorate. Lavigerie expressed to the minister his ultimate goal:
"We can hope even to see the Patriarch of Jerusalem, one day,
chosen from among its [the Society of Missionaries of Algiers]
priests."[23] He had not abandoned his aim of controlling that important jurisdiction since his own unsuccessful bid for it in
1872.

The Quai d'Orsay wanted Lavigerie to go to the Levant in 1883
in order to collect enough first-hand information on the apostolic
delegate's activities to persuade the Pope to replace him. Consul
General Patrimonio noted to the foreign minister, Paul-Armand
Challemel-Lacour, that for Piavi's replacement there were several
outstanding candidates in Lavigerie's entourage who knew Arabic.
French diplomats had high hopes also for enlarging the clientèle
catholique, as one of them explained to the ambassador to the
Holy See: "If I am well informed, [Lavigerie's] presence can even
exercise a happy influence on certain dissident Christian communities who await only the occasion to return to the Catholic faith
and thus augment the number of our protégés."[24] But Lavigerie
traveled only as far as Rome. He was well received there, and his
recent elevation to cardinal's rank enabled him to get the
Scholasticate of St. Anne removed from Piavi's jurisdiction.

Lavigerie's appointment as apostolic delegate for St. Anne's
gave him the right to visit there "as often as I like, as delegate of the Holy See."[25] The departure from Beyrouth of Governor
Rustem Pasha in 1883 also benefitted France. By late 1884
Patrimonio reported to Prime Minister Ferry that there had been
a marked improvement in the situation. Italy's missions in Syria
consisted of only "a few ignorant monks" with no influence on the
population.[26]

In 1885 Lavigerie again planned a trip to the Levant. His
itinerary included visits to St. Anne's and to establishments of
the Oeuvre des Ecoles. The visit would provide considerable support for the Religious Protectorate, and Lavigerie eagerly
anticipated being the first cardinal to visit the Holy Land since
the crusades. But he called it off. The public explanation was
quarantine restrictions. Italians at Beyrouth said that Mgr. Piavi
had succeeded in killing the project because of his close ties
with the Propaganda. But, in fact, the foreign minister, Charles
de Freycinet, could not make good his promise to provide a French
navy vessel. During the tense election campaign of summer 1885
Freycinet presented the proposal to Henri Brisson's cabinet,
which refused it. Twenty-five years earlier the French navy had
given the Abbé Lavigerie a ship to go there, and Lavigerie considered it a humiliation not to have one as cardinal.[27] This episode directly touched Lavigerie's personal dignity and prestige,
and it defined the only limit to his patriotism. Otherwise he did
everything in his power to support France in the Near East.

At the Vatican no other European power seemed qualified to
carry out the responsibilities of the Eastern Protectorate. Republican and papal ministers did not permit church-state tensions
to go beyond certain limits. All-out hostilities could destroy
the usefulness of French clerics overseas, and a break in diplomatic relations followed by abolition of the Concordat would

leave the domestic clergy without funds. Several of the men who
directed the anticlerical program within France, including Jules
Ferry and Léon Gambetta, were also ardent imperialists. They
knew the price which a blind assault on the Church would inflict
on their policy overseas. Republican attacks on the Church within
France during the period of 1879 to 1889 were, with difficulty,
confined to a limited struggle rather than total war.

This round of church-state conflict began early in 1879 following the election of Jules Grévy to replace President MacMahon.
Grévy's election seemed reassuring at first to Lavigerie, who
admired his moderate spirit and high intelligence.[28] But attacks
on the Concordat - or proposals to turn it against the Church by
strict application of its provisions - had been in the air for a
decade.[29] Putting the Church in her place was an idea whose time
had come; most republicans considered her place to be one of
obedience to the state in temporal matters.[30] They stridently
threatened the Church in the Chamber of Deputies, whose president,
Léon Gambetta, repeated the battle-cry: "Clericalism, there is the
enemy!"[31]

Yet as head of the Budget Commission, Gambetta supported appropriations for Catholic schools overseas, particularly Lavigerie's.
Later, as prime minister, Gambetta told him: "Anticlericalism is
for France, Monsignor, it is not an article for export."[32] Paul
Cambon's Correspondance recorded Lavigerie's feelings in April
1882, soon after the fall of Gambetta's brief ministry: "He has
a great taste for Gambetta and hopes to see his return to affairs."[33] Until Gambetta's death on 31 December of that year,
Lavigerie hoped for his election as President of the Republic.
Gambetta was one of the leaders of the anticlerical campaign
begun in 1879. But Lavigerie had realized early that, in contrast
to the radicals on the extreme left, Gambetta's anticlericalism
was more calculated than visceral. He was president of the

Republican Union, and in order to keep the republican majority
united against the royalists, his group on the left and their
opportunist colleagues in the center had to compensate the radicals for the republic's failure to deliver promised social legislation. The hungry should "eat a priest" - this time, in Emile
Keller's words, "the dried up bones of some Jesuit."[34] Although
the majority of anticlericals were not officially opposed to the
clergy's work of saving souls, at home or abroad, they had decided to strip the Church of her influence in domestic politics.

Priests, brothers, and nuns supervised the education of more
than half of the republic's future citizens. President Grévy's
first cabinet, headed by William-Henry Waddington, began therefore
with an attack on Catholic schools. The director of the laic program was Jules Ferry, minister of public instruction. Ferry held
that post in most of the cabinets over the next five years. It was
Ferry who became the foremost advocate of colonial expansion. As
prime minister from September 1880 to November 1881, he planned
and directed the French occupation of Tunisia. Lavigerie was Ferry's
close partner in that project. Here was the real irony of
Lavigerie's career, for his support of French power overseas en-
deared him to many of the Church's enemies at home. While anticlericals sniped in the Chamber at the "Algerian Great Elector,"
their leaders in the cabinet worked with him as personal friends.[35]
On their first face-to-face encounter at Algiers Lavigerie and
Ferry fell into each other's arms, and this rapport carried over
into discussions of the domestic conflict. They were colleagues
during much of the time that Ferry supervised the purge of Catholic schools and congregations.[36]

Ferry presented his proposals in March 1879. They restricted
Catholic influence in higher education and limited the rights of
Catholic universities. Article Seven of one of these measures,
aimed particularly at the Jesuits and dropped from the law passed

one year later, forbade all teaching by members of religious orders not authorized by the government.[37]

The Vatican representative in Paris during this period was Mgr. Wladimir Czacki, apostolic nuncio to the French government from 1879 to 1882. Leo XIII's instructions for this difficult assignment were to cultivate the moderates in power and to work to avoid a rupture between church and state. Czacki found it easier to persuade dinner guests like Gambetta that maintenance of the Concordat was desirable, than to make monarchists stop polarizing the struggle. These conservatives hated Czacki for his efforts, and their activity was one of the reasons why his frail health broke in 1882. They tried to push things to a rupture in the hope that the resulting political upheaval would lead to restoration of the monarchy. Lavigerie wrote to the Pope that "the triumph of the royalist party in France in the near future is as probable as the fall of the stars."[38] But many Catholic leaders supported the royalists, thereby compromising the Church and jeopardizing her spiritual ministry. Leo, Lavigerie, and Czacki realized that reorienting Catholic political activity to a program of constitutional action was necessary in order to deal with the anticlericals.[39]

Charles de Freycinet followed Waddington as premier-foreign minister in December 1879, and he had to keep Ferry in his cabinet despite the mildness of his own views. The Chamber of Deputies passed Ferry's law for the "freedom of higher education" in mid-March 1880, although the Senate had struck its Article Seven. In response to an interpellation from the left in the Chamber, Freycinet nonetheless promised to enforce existing laws against the congregations. Despite the misgivings of President Grévy, but with pressure from Gambetta, Freycinet's government issued the two decrees of 29 March 1880. The first ordered the Society of Jesus to dissolve and to vacate its premises within three

months. The second decree required the other congregations to
apply for authorization from the government or also face dissolu-
tion. The Society of Missionaries of Algiers was one of the few
congregations already recognized by the government as institutes
of public utility. Most of the others were inclined to suffer
with the Jesuits rather than submit to the second decree's humiliation.[40] Conservatives now had the desired cause for holy war.

The crisis threatened at the worst to result in rupture of
diplomatic relations between France and the Holy See, abolition
of the Concordat, and an end to the annual cults budget of 50
million francs. Lavigerie delivered lengthy oral reports and wrote
others to the Pope during the following months. He saw two possible results of this grave struggle: catastrophic destruction of
the ecclesiastical organism or the successful defense of the
Church's terrain step by step. The bishops and the congregations
in France had phrased their protests against the March Decrees in
terms which seemed in the public eye to deny the legitimate rights
of the state. But Lavigerie saw the possibility for a realistic
compromise, provided the superiors general of the congregations
could agree to pledge loyalty to the republic.

Despite the menacing rhetoric of the anticlericals, Prime
Minister Freycinet wanted to spare the congregations, except for
the Jesuits. Vatican pressure through the nuncio persuaded the
heads of the other orders to accept a compromise. Police expelled
the Jesuits from their houses on 30 June, appeasing the radicals
momentarily. But the government was willing to stall on applying
the second decree long enough to obtain legislation permitting
freedom for the remaining orders.

Great secrecy covered Lavigerie and Czacki's negotiations with
the government for an honorable compromise, so as to avoid charges
of betrayal against both sides by monarchists and radicals.

Lavigerie had provided the first draft of the text sent to all
the heads of congregations, in which they were to pledge loyalty
to the republic and renounce explicitly any political activity.
The files of the Ministry of Cults already contained copies of a
letter, also composed by Lavigerie, advising them to continue
their charitable works.[41] But a conservative newspaper, La Guyenne
of Bordeaux, maliciously leaked the story on 30 August, and the
left cried treason. The Freycinet ministry repudiated the whole
affair, but did not last long enough to proceed with applying the
decrees. Two members of Gambetta's Republican Union left the cabinet and it fell in September. Ferry headed the new one which expelled the priests and brothers from their houses in October,
November, and December. The nuns were spared.[42]

During the months right after the decrees Lavigerie had tremendous difficulty protecting the unauthorized congregations in
the ecclesiastical province of Algiers. Prime Minister Freycinet
originally saw no means of evading the application of the March
Decrees to the North African departments of France. Governor
General Albert Grévy, the president's brother, recommended to
Paris that the Trappists be dispersed along with Spanish and
Brazilian missionaries. But Lavigerie submitted to Freycinet a
short memoir in April 1880 detailing the reasons why the decrees
could not be applied. First, they did not specifically mention
Algeria, as was legally required. Secondly, in political terms
it was impossible to apply the decrees to Catholic orders without
including Muslim congregations and foundations as well. Thirdly,
Lavigerie pointed out the absurdity of their logical result:
France could hardly invoke the Eastern Religious Protectorate on
behalf of houses opened in Tripoli or Tunis to shelter refugees
driven from Algiers. President Jules Grévy's brother might have
been more receptive to the government's moderate view on the

issue, but the governor general's associates in Algiers pressed
him to expel the congregations. His reports to Paris conveyed
their sentiments.[43]

As the original deadline of 30 June approached, excited telegrams passed between Paris and Algiers. Lavigerie wired his vicar
general on 17 June that the government had renewed its assurances
to him that the March Decrees were "not applicable" in Algeria.
On the same day the minister of interior and cults wired Albert
Grévy that for very exceptional reasons, regardless of the legal
applicability of the decrees, the government had decided to suspend provisionally their execution. Albert Grévy hotly replied
that application was "indispensable."[44] The government's decision
was reported a day later in the Algiers press, and radical journals accused the governor general of wanting to protect the congregations. But despite his own protests, Paris maintained its
ambiguous position that, although the decrees were executory
(exécutoires), their application should be suspended. Freycinet
gave Lavigerie new assurances. Governor General Grévy later
visited the Ministry of Cults at Paris, and the director general,
Léopold-Emile Flourens, persuaded him to accept the government's
decision to maintain the status quo.[45]

Although the government could spare most of the Algerian congregations, even after applying the second decree in France during
autumn 1880, the Jesuits were a separate case. In this problem
Lavigerie showed his willingness to compromise. He initially
reached an agreement with the authorities whereby the Jesuits
dissolved their community at the Collège Saint-François Xavier,
leaving two priests to care for the property while five others
took separate pastoral assignments in the Archdiocese of Algiers.
Lavigerie assured Flourens in August that "all seven are under my
absolute jurisdiction." It was therefore unnecessary to apply the

first decree in a situation where the Jesuits' community no
longer existed.[46]

Radical officials in Algiers continued to insist on formal
expulsion, and Lavigerie desperately urged Paris to resist this
pressure. A frontal assault would force these priests into direct
opposition, and after their reliance on repeated assurances they
would accuse the government of breaking faith. Lavigerie's suffragan bishops at Oran and Constantine, kept in line by their
strong-willed metropolitan, had heretofore refrained from cooper-
ating with the resistance of bishops in France. They would now
be labeled dupes or accomplices and forced to come out against
the government. Lavigerie suggested to the minister of cults a
declaration that the decrees were not appropriate in a situation
where the Jesuits had already dissolved their community: though
this would not satisfy the ultra-radicals, it should at least
quiet them.[47] The effect of this declaration proved temporary.

In September the Prefecture of Algiers outraged Catholic opinion, and violated the agreement between Lavigerie and the Ministry
of Cults, by sealing the deserted Jesuit college. Lavigerie protested and the Ministry of Cults wired an order to remove the
seals. The Jesuits accused Lavigerie of being part of this suppression, and a French mob further inflamed the issue by hurling
stones and insults at their empty chapel. Another angry crowd
of foreign Catholics (Maltese, Neapolitan sailors, and other
Italians) appeared at Lavigerie's house. They said that if it
happened again they would go down and stamp out the sacrilegious
gang. The archbishop replied that they would do so over his dead
body, but he promised an end to such outrages and followed up
with a calming circular. Lavigerie complained to Flourens of the
prefecture's stupidity in adding insult to injury and pushing
these Catholics to the point of riot.[48]

Flourens attempted to resolve the problem of the Algerian
congregations by asking Lavigerie in early October to persuade
them to request authorization from the government. After so much
previous effort in good faith to reach an accord, this was impossible. The government finally shelved the issue and settled
for the status quo.[49]

Jules Tournier blames the monarchists and the Jesuits for the
La Guyenne disclosure which destroyed efforts to reach a compromise regarding the second decree. The monarchists realized that
their only hope depended on the Church's remaining alongside
them, doing battle with the republic. The collapse of the
Freycinet negotiations temporarily stalled Lavigerie's efforts
to dissolve this alliance, which itself strengthened that between
moderate republicans and the radicals.[50]

But the extremists' success in maintaining political polariza-
tion in this crisis did not plunge the antagonists into all-out
war. Right after the announcement of the March Decrees, Freycinet
had instructed Ambassador Félix-Hippolyte Desprez in Rome to
assure Cardinal Simeoni that the measures taken against the
Jesuits would not affect policy outside France. The Quai d'Orsay
promised to continue to exercise the Religious Protectorate in
the Near and Far East without regard to Jesuit membership.[51]
Baron Alphonse de Courcel, former ambassador to the Holy See and
now political director of the Foreign Ministry, reiterated this
in a lengthy circular sent in mid-April to all diplomatic posts
abroad: "The motives which have dictated the Decrees of 29 March
are exclusively of an internal order. . . . But our solicitude
for religious interests and our respect for individual rights are
not at all weakened. Thus, the measures taken have no effect on
the conditions of our protection in regard to missions overseas."[52] The Vatican appeared to concur with the government in
wanting to keep the two areas of policy separate. Leo XIII knew

that the immediate obstacle to resolving the crisis was the attitude of French bishops and superiors general. During the
summer Mgr. Czacki and Lavigerie were negotiating with them. But
the La Guyenne disclosure of 30 August produced a period of extreme tension.

Several letters from Lavigerie define the range of church-
state relations during 1880. He wrote the first to the prime
minister just before the Freycinet negotiations collapsed.
Lavigerie optimistically reported that the attitudes of the Pope
and the Propaganda Fide were excellent toward French mission
activities in the Mediterranean. Lavigerie pledged to fulfill
his own responsibilities in this connection, which required extensive traveling - to Tunis and the Holy Land as missionary bishop,
and to Paris and Rome as fund-raiser and ecclesiastical statesman. His absences from his home base of Algiers required the appointment of a coadjutor to run the archdiocese. He already had
the Pope's unofficial approval, and he therefore requested leave
of the government to proceed with the details at the Ministry of
Cults.[53]

Then the Freycinet government fell, and by late November the
situation boded a break between church and state. Lavigerie reported to Flourens on 30 November that the Pope was "obsessed
with our [French bishops'] intransigeance," which was further
antagonizing the government. He expressed his own feelings of
helplessness at his inability to change things by himself, and
he remarked that any step on his part would be dismissed as a
bid for a cardinal's hat.[54]

The clearest statement of Lavigerie's relationship with the
government is a letter dated 15 October 1880. He wrote to the
minister of cults in response to radical press attacks on his
absences from Algiers. Lavigerie pointed out to Ernest Constans
that he was the troubleshooter who toured the lands of the

Mediterranean attaching (rattacher) bishops there to French
policy and influence. It was particularly important for him to
spend several more weeks every year at Rome countering the pressure of Italians at the Vatican. He referred to North Africa as
"one of the extremities of a vast field of charity and of the
apostolate."[55] France alone among the powers of western Europe
was neglecting Africa. Britain, Belgium, Italy, and Germany were
planting their nationals in different parts of the interior,
where France had no official representatives. Yet her missionaries
accomplished the most impressive penetration of all! Of the 43
White Fathers already sent to the interior by way of Zanzibar, 32
had survived and 15 more were on their way. Lavigerie had spent
600,000 francs on this apostolate, and the Pope had just divided
the continent into four mission vicariates.

> Four of our Missionaries of Algiers will be placed at
> the head of these vicariates, with an episcopal title
> in partibus, in such a way that, from the frontiers of
> Algeria to those of the British and Dutch colonies of
> the Cape of Good Hope, all the interior territory of
> Africa is henceforth placed, from the religous point
> of view, under a French authority. This is a result
> which, for the day when France believes she also must
> intervene actively in African questions, will have
> happy and fruitful consequences.[56]

Lavigerie could not say such things publicly, but there were many
French politicians who did not have to be told of his contributions to the republic. His closing remark noted that in political
matters, of course, the clergy of Algiers received strict instructions to refrain from all excesses of zeal.[57]

This rapport with the ministers was no guarantee, however,
against official harassment of his order of missionaries. In May

1880, on his way from Tunisia to Italy, Lavigerie had stopped at
Malta and purchased an old monastery just in case the White
Fathers should need to move. He comforted himself with the knowledge that they could take refuge with confreres at the Ecole
Apostolique of Malta, the Scholasticate of St. Anne at Jerusalem,
or the community of Saint-Louis de Carthage.[58] But it never came
to that. The two years following the March Decrees gave the
government some perspective. The consul at Beyrouth and the ambassador at Constantinople promptly complained about the effect
of the decrees on the recruitment of French Jesuit and Capuchin
missionaries overseas. Two years later Patrimonio assured the
government "that at this distance the causes of our internal
divisions disappear and that, in sum, our missionaries and our
sisters in Syria are patriotic and tolerant."[59]

While the republicans harassed the Church in France, consuls
and clergy worked together abroad. In North Africa Lavigerie and
Roustan cooperated to impose their control, respectively, on the
Vicariate and the Regency of Tunis. Even after the collapse of
the Freycinet negotiations of 1880, Lavigerie's close consultations with the Paris government concerning Tunisia kept open a
vital channel with Rome for negotiating the whole range of ecclesiastical problems. The crisis of the decrees passed without
becoming an open war between church and state very much because
of this link. The Ferry government turned from the laic program
to overseas expansion in early 1881. The invasion of Tunisia
required more time, troops, and money than anticipated; and
criticism of Ferry's leadership brought down his government in
November. Léon Gambetta's "Grand Ministry" governed France until
the end of January 1882.

Gambetta's government seemed more ferociously anticlerical
than it actually was. This "Ministry of All the Talents" included
Paul Bert at the Ministry of Cults, a choice which initially

impressed many observers as a "declaration of war against the
Church."[60] The Gambetta government had reassuringly promised
strict observance of the Concordat. But Bert soon initiated the
nouvelles Organiques, such restrictive measures against Catholicism that Director General Flourens temporarily resigned. Gambetta
limited some of these excesses, and Lavigerie trusted the prime
minister's restraint. Lavigerie recognized Gambetta's reluctance
to create new problems in addition to the divisions he already
had within his own party. But for that reason Gambetta also held
back from openly making peace with the Church. Conservatives
urged the Vatican to retaliate, and Lavigerie's candidacy for a
cardinal's hat became tangled in this struggle.[61]

The church-state conflict continued into 1882 as a limited
conflict on both sides. Although radical attacks on the Concordat
and fears for the safe passage of the cults budget were not to be
taken seriously, after the republican electoral gains of August
1881 there seemed to be a real danger of further laicization of
schools, attacks on Church property, and conscription of seminarians.[62] But once the anticlericals had imposed their basic program of restrictions on the Church, many of them began to sense
that the greater peril to the republic came from the extreme left.
Jules Ferry saw this clearly when he became prime minister again
in 1883.[63] Lavigerie's letters to Cardinal Jacobini during that
year reported the anticlericals' real feelings. The republicans
feared attacks from both monarchists and "anarchists." "The party
which takes action will be wiped out, and the party which waits
will win."[64] By late 1883 the death of Chambord made restoration
of the monarchy even more unlikely than before; it could come
only in the aftermath of a social upheaval like the Commune.[65]
"The Army will wipe it out to reestablish the Monarchist regime."[66]
Lavigerie urged Jacobini to play on the opportunist government's
fear of this, if he could do so without being provocative. Even

many radicals hoped to avoid the practical problems which separation would cause, despite the menacing public statements which
they made in keeping with election promises and secret society
oaths.

Of course, tension continued during the 1880s. It was caused
partly by anti-French cardinals at Rome, who urged the Pope to
take a hard line toward the republic and to seek a tie with the
Triple Alliance. Timid Cardinal Simeoni sometimes wavered in the
face of government and press criticism at Rome that the Holy See
compromised Italian national interests in the Mediterranean.
Lavigerie tried his best at the Vatican to counter these influ-
ences. At home he worked for the rest of his life to break the
alliance between Catholic leaders and monarchists.

Some bishops within France still used very bellicose language
in reference to the republic, even though the government was inclined to be reasonable.[67] Catholic journals like L'Univers
sullenly resisted any conciliation.[68] Such sentiment grieved
Lavigerie. For he believed that, in looking back toward the
monarchy, Catholics distracted their energies from a colonial
program which required everyone's patriotic support.

Lavigerie was able to moderate the anticlericals' program in
France because of the confidence he enjoyed in the French government and at the Vatican. His personal clout at Paris protected
most of the Algerian congregations from expulsion in 1880. But
he could not speak for all the bishops and superiors general of
France nor make them all loyal republicans. He had to adapt as
best he could to a climate of continuing tension. The Holy See
still needed France's support in the world and therefore decided
to maintain the traditional partnership, for which Lavigerie
became the broker. In ecclesiastical policy he promoted union of
Eastern Christians with the Roman Pontiff while pragmatically
supporting the use of their old liturgies. The language in which

Eastern Christians said Mass was not an essential of Church unity. What mattered to Lavigerie was that France continue to play a constructive role in their affairs. While joining in this aspect of French imperialism, Lavigerie laid the foundation for his country's extension of political control over Tunisia and other parts of Africa.

III
Saint-Louis de Carthage:
The Preparatory Years 1875–1880

"Cardinal Lavigerie renders to French influence in the Mediterranean more services than an army corps." This observation of an
Italian newspaper in the spring of 1881 was often repeated by
French and Italian statesmen. Gambetta added the comment: "That
is true, and one must recognize that it costs less."[1] This was
literally true in Tunisia, where Lavigerie's efforts made the
most decisive contribution of any cleric since Fleury to the
consolidation of French prestige and power.[2]

French diplomats had considered taking Tunisia since 1870.[3]
Foreign Minister Waddington obtained England's grudging consent
and Bismarck's earnest support for this at the Congress of Berlin
in 1878. But until the Paris government resolved to exercise this
option in early 1881, the official program was pursued locally
by the French consul, Théodore Roustan. Lavigerie's project for
bringing Tunis into the French ecclesiastical orbit was a major
element of Roustan's design, for it was the key to consolidating
French influence in the European community. Until the eve of the
Treaty of Bardo, the French were a small minority of less than a
thousand, surrounded by 25,000 Italians and 7,000 Maltese subjects of the British crown.[4] During the period before the protectorate Lavigerie deferred completely to Roustan's leadership.
Lavigerie's participation at Paris and Tunis in the formation of
the French government's Tunisian policy did not begin until after
the conquest.

The small community of White Fathers who worked at Saint-Louis
de Carthage after 1875 did not know the ultimate goal for which
they built the foundation.[5] After the representatives of the
Christian powers gave their official approval for a French protectorate in Tunisia, Lavigerie's priests became more active.
Their work during the three years between Berlin and the Treaty
of Bardo made an important contribution to the smoothness with
which the protectorate was eventually imposed. The modest charitable ministry provided to natives around Carthage, and the excellent French schooling offered after October 1880 by the Collège
Saint-Louis, earned the respect of Arabs and Europeans alike.
Because of the prudent restraint with which the priests conducted
their work, they generally escaped direct involvement in the increasing attacks which partisans of the French and Italians
leveled against each other. In 1881 French military power opened
the way for the clergy's full participation in the French program.
Not only was Lavigerie worth an army corps for France, in Tunisia
he preceded one by six years.

The Regency of Tunis, bordering on Algeria, Tripoli, and the
Mediterranean, had a Muslim population estimated between 1 and
1.7 million. Tunis itself numbered around 85,000 inhabitants, not
counting the nearby port town of La Goulette.[6] Ottoman Turkey
had wrested Tunisia from the Hapsburgs in 1574. In 1705 Hussein
ben Ali established the beylical dynasty, which reigned until
1957. The beys were technically pashas, governing the regency in
the sultan's name, although they acquired the trappings of monarchy and conducted diplomatic relations with western countries.
The elite which surrounded the bey was Turkish in origin and
style. A native bureaucracy ran the despotic administration, in
which some Jews participated indirectly. Local officials governed
Tunisia's fairly cohesive population which engaged in agriculture,
herding, crafts, and trade. External pressure and the regency's

backward state of development led Ahmad Bey (1837-55) to undertake administrative and military reforms similar to those begun
by Muhammad Ali in Egypt. Ahmad's sucessor Muhammad Bey (1855-59)
did not press this program of imposing change on a "confused and
resistant society."[7]

Tunisia was vulnerable to pressure from the Mediterranean
powers. Turkey had reasserted control in Tripoli, which marred
the Tunisian elite's affection for the regency's nominal suzerain.
The political situation was fluid over a period of several decades, and Tunisia sought security in the rivalries of the powers.
French influence in North Africa after 1830 provided a counter
to the Turkish threat of reconquest. For the French this buffer
state was the key to Algeria's defense. After the risorgimento
Italy likewise viewed Tunisia as the key to her position in the
Mediterranean; the eighty-five mile strait between Cape Bon and
Sicily divides the Mediterranean in two. Among the countries with
an interest in the regency, Turkey threatened the British navy's
position least. Richard Wood, Her Majesty's Consul General,
therefore followed a policy of supporting Tunisia's link with the
Porte as a means of safeguarding the effective independence of
the weakling Muhammad es Sadok Pasha Bey, who assumed the throne
in 1859.

Lacking intelligence or ability, Sadok devoted most of his
attention to a harem of boys known in diplomatic circles as "the
little garden of the bey." His corrupt chief procurer, Mustapha
Khasnadar (prime minister, 1837-73), pursued a policy of equilib-
rium between France and England. Khasnadar's personal friendship
with Wood gave Britain an advantage to counter that of Sadok's
confidant, the French consul Léon Roches.[8]

The beylic's traditions of elaborate public works, arms purchases, and graft placed increasing stress on the government's
finances. Foreign consulates meddled in Tunisian affairs and

weakened the authority of the beylic insofar as their nationals
and native protégés were exempt from Tunisian courts.[9] Increased
taxes precipitated a major revolt in 1864, and four years later
the government's bankruptcy led to conversion of the European
debt. France recovered the upper hand among the Christian powers
through the International Financial Commission established in
1869 to manage payment of the debt. France, Britain, and Italy
thereby imposed on Tunisia a sort of protectorate à trois. The
Financial Commission's inspector, "the Bey Villet," provided
France with an influence which survived Sedan down to his retirement in 1874.

Wood nonetheless promoted Tunisian autonomy during these years.
The bey renewed his ties with the Porte as a defense against
French pressure, acknowledging vassalage in return for a guarantee of autonomy in 1871. Wood's attempts to promote British
economic influence in the regency were less effective, and the
fall of Khasnadar in 1873 removed his friend at court. Khasnadar's
successor and son-in-law, General Kheredine, provided four years
of constructive and relatively clean administration. Trusting in
Turkey's 1871 guarantee, Kheredine sought a balance among the
Christian powers: "Already the British have enough privileges
and concessions that we should give them to the French and the
Italians."[10]

Théodore Roustan became French consul general at Tunis in
December 1874,[11] and he soon obtained a rail concession for a
French company, the Bône-Guelma. Roustan was an old friend of
Lavigerie from Syria, and he enthusiastically welcomed the arrival of the White Fathers who placed themselves at his service
in June 1875. Roustan worked to increase French influence in
Tunisia at the expense of the English and Italians. He maintained
a good rapport with Kheredine, who gave a very cordial audience
to the new French chaplains. Kheredine later paid a call on the

White Fathers and received their condolences when he fell from power in July 1877.[12]

Mustapha ben Ismael, the new prime minister, had an advantage over Kheredine in the bey's personal affection. Aging and without sons, Muhammad es Sadok adopted Mustapha, who married one of Sadok's daughters. The old traditions of waste and graft resumed. Initially Mustapha ben Ismael's ascension favored French influence, and Roustan kept him happy with little favors. Bitter memories of Italian patrons who had abused him during his days as a tavern waiter also inclined Mustapha towards the French as the struggle among Europeans intensified.[13] In the British tradition of balance of power, Richard Wood's policy shifted to support for Italy in order to keep the French from getting control. The Italians enjoyed more success against the French than had the British in competing for business concessions.

In the later seventies Europeans in North Africa considered trade to be the key to political influence in the area. Previously the French had seen the regency's importance as the key to Algeria's military security. But in the 1870s Governor General Chanzy wanted also to control the trade route between North Africa and the interior which he expected to see developed in Tunisia. Chanzy envisioned a French port at Tunis as the emporium for all the products of the interior and as the port of entry for everything destined for this new market. He abandoned his initial project of a Tunisian inland lake, but thereafter the key to his plans was control of rail concessions. France and Italy were eager to dominate the immense trade expected after the opening of this hinterland.[14]

Although the French delegation at Tunis energetically promoted commercial expansion, leaders at home were reluctant to change a postwar foreign policy of caution. The first president of the Third Republic, Adolphe Thiers, had defined a program of recovery

(<u>recueillement</u>). The French still remembered their losses in
Algeria and the recent Napoleonic disaster in Mexico. Colonial
expansion, anticipated by diplomats and officers in North Africa,
had not yet eclipsed recovery of lost territories in France as
the most important question of national destiny.

The White Fathers' activity at Carthage until this time had
also been cautious. On Roustan's advice Lavigerie instructed
them to keep to themselves. The annual exception to this was the
Feast of St. Louis. On 25 August the diplomatic corps and representatives of the bey gathered at Carthage for an official Mass.
Mgr. Sutter always attended, and willingly, even though the
Capuchins around him were, in Roustan's opinion, "Italians before
being priests."[15] One of the White Fathers always said Mass on
French naval vessels in port, and briefly during a field trip
the French Geodesic Commission turned Saint-Louis into a barracks.
But occasional relief efforts during natural disasters and first
aid for those who came to their door were, for the moment, the
limit of the French apostolate to the natives.[16]

In a situation where the vicariate clergy resented the White
Fathers' presence, it was important for them to choose the least
provocative area of activity when they expanded the scope of
their work at Carthage. Lavigerie formulated plans for the development of Saint-Louis very early, proposing to Roustan the
establishment of a hospital and an orphanage for the European
community, attached to the chapel and staffed by French sisters.
His letter of June 1875 prophetically stated his reason for
covering the building costs himself. In order to guarantee his
independence this had to be the Church's work: "For, if we have
today in France an honest and Christian government, who can
assure us that in the future, alas, perhaps in the near future,
we will not have one all different?"" As for the benevolent work
of these shelters, "No one could object, and it would be the

best and gentlest way of making the Europeans of Tunis feel the superiority of France."[17]

Nonetheless, the consul general advised for the moment against enhancing the French presence, so as not to alarm non-Christians. Lavigerie strictly followed Roustan's advice to continue with caution in order to win the approval and support of the bey: "We dominate the palace of the Bey and the ministers' residences, and all these personages take a dim view of the French flag over their heads. Saint-Louis has too much the aspect of a citadel. Foreigners do not fail to arouse their distrust and vanities, but with time and gentleness we will arrive, seeing as how we have let pass the moment when we could arrive otherwise."[18] The bey's attitude remained uncertain, and the White Fathers confined their activity to work around the chapel. Lavigerie's letters to the several priests who were assigned at Carthage urged them to avoid contacts with Muslim authorities and criticized Bresson for seeing too much of Mgr. Sutter. The priests were noncommittal in reply to inquiries from outsiders regarding the suggestion of a secondary school connected with Saint-Louis.[19]

At the end of their first year in Tunisia, William-Henry Waddington, then minister of public instruction and fine arts, wrote to the fathers at Saint-Louis, thanking them for their services to the French community and offering some books for their library.[20] Two months later, in July 1876, the Propagation de la Foi sent Lavigerie 5,000 francs for his ministry in Tunisia. He forwarded this money to Mgr. Sutter, because discretion precluded its use in a French apostolate. Since he was a source of financial support for the charitable works of the Italians, Lavigerie remained on cordial terms with the apostolic vicar, who was basically a gentle and conscientious priest. But later, as Sutter slipped into senility, he fell under the influence of more nationalistic members of the Capuchin community.[21] It was

therefore not opportune to challenge the Capuchins' position in
Tunisia. Throughout 1876 the White Fathers involved themselves
very little with affairs outside their own house. Lavigerie located his small orphanage for young blacks at Carthage in October
1876. The White Fathers took care of these children whom confreres
had ransomed from slavers in central Africa, and they soon added
a few homeless Arabs.[22]

The ruins of Carthage provided an opportunity for favorable
publicity which Lavigerie developed to the fullest. To Christians
Carthage was "a sort of grand reliquary."[23] The soil of Tunisia
contains many souvenirs of the successive Phoenician, Roman,
Vandal, Byzantine, Arab, Spanish, and Turkish occupations. Baron
E. de Sainte-Marie at the consulate was an amateur archeologist
eager to work with the White Fathers in exploring these resources
at Carthage. The priests became his apprentices until he left
Tunis in late 1876.

Fr. Louis-Alfred Delattre showed a particular aptitude in
archeology during his first few years at Carthage, and Lavigerie
ordered him in holy obedience to pursue it. The "veritable
idiot's" early work fell short of professional standards, but
Lavigerie was determined to make him prominent. He disclosed
this plan during a visit in May 1880: "We are going to make of
you another Cochet, but that will not stop me from letting fly
(décocher) some stinging darts upon occasion."[24] The founder
attached a great importance to Delattre's potential for enhancing
the Society's prestige, and his directives were unsparing.
Delattre was to seek out and purchase pagan and Christian ceme-
teries and to buy any inscriptions brought to him by Arabs. The
trusting priest was not always discreet in concealing his dis-
coveries long enough to obtain credit for announcing them himself:
"You resemble chickens who can not lay an egg without letting
the whole neighborhood know about it."[25]

For this project Lavigerie enlisted the cooperation of Léon
Renier, Professor of Antiquities and Roman Epigraphy at the
Sorbonne.[26] Renier agreed to sponsor Delattre's reports for publication at Paris. His early material required considerable
editing on the part of Renier, who informed Lavigerie that "publication of it as it is would disgrace you [Delattre] forever in
the science."[27] Renier's patronage was sufficient, however, to
make the inscriptions Delattre forwarded to Paris salable to the
Bibliothèque Nationale; and the Ministry of Public Instruction
and Fine Arts granted small subsidies for his research. Nonetheless, the inexactness of Delattre's first reports drove Lavigerie
to remark: "You are the antipodes of science; and as M. Renier
said, you absolutely dishonor yourself."[28] Delattre's work improved under strict supervision, and he prepared more reports to
be cleared for publication. The founder insisted that all articles
be signed as "Missionary of Algiers of Saint-Louis de Carthage"
so that credit would not go by mistake to the Capuchins. Lavigerie
himself publicly appealed for financial support in a letter of
April 1881, De l'Utilité d'une Mission Archéologique Permanente
à Carthage.[29]

After the French protectorate was imposed, the Ministry of
Public Instruction established a museum at Bardo in 1883 and appointed Delattre to be director. Several prominent Tunisians
approached him in 1885 to offer the leadership of their new historical, geological, and archeological society. Lavigerie ordered
him to accept the position, even though Delattre felt utterly
unworthy: "I have never been so tempted to disobedience."[30]
Although their letters disclose a humorous element of promotion-
alism, this program was a complete success in producing the
world's finest museum of Punic antiquities at the Bardo. It
launched Delattre on a distinguished and eventually autonomous
career, despite a very awkward beginning.[31]

At the end of their first two years in Tunisia, Delattre and
the handful of other priests at Saint-Louis awaited a visit from
Lavigerie on 3 July 1877. He received a lavish welcome. Staying
at first with Roustan, he then rented a house at La Marsa a few
miles up the shore from La Goulette and Carthage.[32] He spent his
twelve days in Tunisia at formal calls on official personalities
and conferences with his priests regarding plans for the future.
He distributed alms and spent hours with Roustan. The bey received
him with royal honors. Sadok bestowed on him the Grand Cordon of
the Order of Nicham, and he indicated his approval of Lavigerie's
plans for a school, hospital, and other charitable works.[33]
Lavigerie's increased influence soon aroused the jealous attention
of the British and the Italian consulates. Proceeding cautiously
in this environment, Lavigerie instructed the White Fathers to
admit only that they planned an extension of the Chapelle Saint-
Louis. He left for Rome on 14 July to consult with the Holy
Father.[34]

Roustan still considered it inopportune for the priests to
expand their activities.[35] His correspondence with Lavigerie
clarified their plans. Roustan saw nothing but advantage to the
French in granting Sutter's request that the French priests substitute for Italians in some of the understaffed Capuchin posts,
and Lavigerie complied.[36] But the consul prevailed on Lavigerie
to modify his building plans. They decided to build first an infirmary and then the college at Saint-Louis. This gradual expansion of benevolent works built on adjacent land as attachments to
the French shrine seemed less provocative.[37] Roustan approved of
construction on the nearby plateau, but he criticized the archi-
tect's design on the grounds that the cross surmounting the central section was likely to give offense because of its proximity
to the bey.[38] Lavigerie placed himself absolutely at Roustan's
service: "I do not abandon my projects, in the meantime, by

subordinating them to circumstances and to the necessities which
they create. . . . Like yourself, I have, in fact, but a single
desire, that of establishing and enhancing in Tunisia our French
and Christian influence, and I hold myself back from doing anything which could oppose your views."[39]

The two men were on the closest terms, having been friends
since 1860 in the Levant. From 1875 until Roustan's reassignment
in 1882 they were collaborators.[40] Their respective programs led
naturally to an intimate partnership, and it is difficult to determine precisely when they made their league to establish French
control over Tunisia. Lavigerie's intentions appeared clear in
1875, judging by a letter which counseled the Foreign Ministry
to enter Tunisia "loyally, not as conquerors but as allies and as
friends. . . . The real end and not the means must be the protectorate.[41] The ministry did not appear to jump at the suggestion,
but the Archbishop of Algiers was of one mind with the consul
general at Tunis. He expressed his policy of buying the regency
away by charity in a remark to Roustan during his July 1877 visit:
"On each bit of earth where Italy puts a man, we will put a
crown."[42]

However difficult it is to determine the exact point at which
Lavigerie and Roustan united to establish the protectorate, the
European powers settled the question provisionally in July 1878.
At Bismarck's Congress of Berlin the foreign ministers awarded
to France a paper victory in the competition with Britain and
Italy which had been going on for more than two decades. From
1878 France's diplomatic policy merged with the efforts of
Lavigerie and Roustan because of international rivalries and the
weakness of the bey. Goyau dates Lavigerie's project of placing
Tunisia under his episcopal jurisdiction from 1879. Indeed, in
all of his correspondence with Roustan one senses a new tone of
resolution from that year. Bismarck was likewise eager for Paris

to exercise her Tunisian option, contenting himself with keeping
France friendless in Europe and distracted overseas. Only Germany's
continuous diplomatic support permitted France the luxury of three
years of hesitations and half-measures before dispatching troops.[43]

The assistance of Lavigerie and the White Fathers became increasingly important to Roustan as the Franco-Italian rivalry
intensified, while partisan divisions within France kept the
government from taking action. Conflict between a republican
Chamber and a monarchist Senate made the government indecisive,
and hostile republicans hardly supported an enterprise which might
give credit to the monarchist President MacMahon. Gambetta at
this time openly opposed intervention, and concern for Italy's
disfavor gave doubts to others. Foreign Minister Waddington enter-
tained hopes of persuading the bey to sign a convention without
force, despite Roustan's colder reports on the situation. Sadok
twice rejected the draft treaties he presented. Charles de
Freycinet replaced Waddington as premier-foreign minister in
December 1879.[44] Another year passed before Paris resolved to
take its opportunity, partly becasue of the intense anticlerical
struggle which preoccupied French politicians throughout 1880.

Because of his government's hesitation Roustan had to continue
a policy of indirection, despite circumstances which favored conquest. France already had Germany's support; Turkey remained
powerless to resist, and Britain was resigned to the takeover.
The Foreign Office recalled Consul General Wood in February 1879,
signifying publicly the change of British policy. Thomas Reade's
appointment to succeed him on April Fool's Day was aptly timed
after Wood's two decades of extremely skilled diplomacy.[45] Roustan
retained cordial personal relations with Reade as with the new
Italian consul, Licurgo Maccio. Roustan and Maccio had kept in
touch by mail during the interval when they were not neighbors at
Beyrouth. But Maccio soon became "excited by the Irredentists of

the [Italian] Colony."[46] Damiani declared to the Italian Chamber
of Deputies on 21 July 1879 that "Tunis is the last door open to
Italy."[47] This is why, during the crucial years 1878 to 1881, the
rivalry between France and Italy became a "War of Two Consuls."[48]

But Tunis remained an idle post for the diplomats of countries
who lacked constituents in the regency. The upper strata of the
European community occupied the season with diplomatic receptions
and relatively gala balls. Between them and the squalid masses of
Italian and Maltese poor was a seamy stratum of quacks, charlatans,
and crooked lawyers peddling their influence with the consular
tribunals. This existed alongside what survived of the business
class after the crisis of 1868. The Marseillais and Genoans had
gone bankrupt, leaving most of the regency's commerce in the hands
of the Jewish bourgeoisie. These Grana numbered about 5,000. They
were well-to-do in contrast with most of Tunisia's 35,000 native
Jews, who shared the poverty of the Muslim masses. The Grana were
also referred to as the Livournais after their resting place on
the way from Spain, and many of them sided with the other Italians
against the French.[49]

Nonetheless, the membership of the two consular parties did
not follow strictly national lines. One of Roustan's most important agents within the bey's government was Roustan's mistress's
indolent Greek husband. The only Catholic who held high office at
the Bardo Palace, Elias Mussalli had been sub-director of foreign
affairs from 1860 until 1871, when he was fired for embezzlement.
He recovered his post eight years later with the help of his wife's
lover. Roustan's link with the royal household was Dr. Francisco
Mascaro, the bey's premier physician, "who alone among Europeans
sees him tête-à-tête each day." Roustan later requested Lavigerie
to appoint Mascaro to the honor (without salary) of medical inspector of the Collège Saint-Louis, and the consul's letter thanking him for prompt compliance noted its quick result.[50]

The rank and file of hangers-on in the "War of Two Consuls"
conducted their social life in the salons of two sisters-in-law.
Maccio maintained a discreet liaison with the wife of Pietro
Traverso ("a simple imbecile," in Roustan's opinion); and
Traverso's sister, Luigia Mussalli, served in most respects as
Roustan's official mistress. The compliance of "Madame Elias" was
legendary, highlighted by a blatant affair with his predecessor
Léon Roches. After other affairs with French personnel, she finally fell in love with Roustan, acquiring for herself the nickname
of "Passage des Consuls." Her salon was the center of the French
party for several years.[51]

Lavigerie scarcely ever referred to Mme Elias in writing. Her
love affair did not change his opinion of the consul general's
character, which he based on Roustan's devotion to the interests
of France. To borrow a French phrase from the clergy, he was a
good "Catholic from the waist up."[52] Roustan did not bring
Mme Elias when he went to Mass or paid a call on the White Fathers.
Only the secular implementation of his policy remained centered
in the lady's salon. He and Lavigerie made their plans for imposing a "religious protectorate" on Tunisia in meetings at the
consulate, at Saint-Louis or at La Marsa.

Several incidents marked the implementation of this design
during the years immediately preceding the French invasion. One
of them concerned French claims of the Eastern Religious Protectorate, and occasioned a report to the Holy See of its violation.
In March 1879 a Capuchin had gone to Maccio with a complaint
against the English consul for protesting a noisy disturbance
created during the celebration of St. Joseph's Day. The Italian
pastor of Bizerta had carried his observance of this favorite
Italian feast to the point of discharging firearms in front of
his church, and he thereafter scorned English complaints in a
very offensive manner. Roustan stated to the foreign minister

that the Capuchin's attempt to carry to the Italian consulate an
issue of the protection of Church interests was an unacceptable
invasion of French jurisdiction. It would set a dangerous precedent. Roustan notified Sutter, who promised to investigate. He
urged the Quai d'Orsay that, if this tendency continued, it would
be necessary to prevail on the Holy See to replace some or all of
the Italians with French members of the Capuchin order. Paris forwarded a copy of Roustan's letter to the Propaganda by way of a
warning.[53] Roustan continued the defense of his government's
claims regarding the non-French clergy while Lavigerie proceeded
to expand the work of the White Fathers.

The field of education presented the most appropriate opportunity in Tunisia for increased French activity. Most Muslim
students received their education from Qur'anic schools in the
towns and from the university at the Zitouna Mosque in Tunis.
A couple of secondary schools offered Western languages and
science. Ahmad Bey had established the Bardo Military School in
1840; Kheredine Pasha, the reformer-prime minister, had organized
the Collège Sadiki in 1875. The Italian government had subsidized
primary schools for Europeans since 1871. In 1878 the Alliance
Israélite Universelle opened a large Franco-Arab school for boys,
to which Roustan extended French protection the following year.
This was the first of half-a-dozen schools in the Alliance
Israélite's program to rejuvenate and Gallicize Tunisian Jews.
Lavigerie saw a serious need for French Christian education. Even
the French girls' school run since 1840 by the Sisters of
St. Joseph of the Apparition depended upon Italian priests for
religious instruction. Lavigerie engaged architects to prepare
designs for a boys' secondary school at Saint-Louis and a hospital
nearby.[54]

Lavigerie visited Tunisia again in May 1879 to make a personal
inspection and to negotiate with the architects and contractors.

He wanted to conduct his inspection incognito, so he forbade the
priests even to tell Roustan of his visit and arrived dressed
simply in black. He insisted on reviewing every detail, both of
construction plans and of the priests' habitation. What he found
distressed him: "I do not think it is possible to see anything
more dreadfully disgusting than the kitchen and refectory of
Saint-Louis."[55] The poor returns on the sale of religious articles
at the shrine indicated "an inexplicable negligence," all the more
culpable because these profits were earmarked for medicines to
aid the Arabs.[56] It became obvious to Lavigerie that the opening
of the college must be postponed a year rather than open it in
a state of disorganization that could draw criticism. There was
nothing to fear from Sutter, inasmuch as the Holy Father had
explicitly authorized Lavigerie to build the school, but Lavigerie
insisted on allowing all the time necessary to insure a beginning
that was perfect, if not prompt.[57]

Although he received permission in June from the Foreign Ministry to locate the college on French national property next
to the shrine, he was bearing the full costs of construction. At
Paris in August he requested that the Quai d'Orsay provide 30,000
francs for its furnishings. The construction site at Carthage was
beginning to attract both Protestant and Italian busybodies, whose
rumors became newspaper reports that the French at Saint-Louis
were building "a great chapel, a college, a vast hospital, a pawn
shop, and a French bank!!!!" (Delattre's exclamation marks).[58]
Lavigerie's more modest project was, indeed, advancing well, and
he visited Saint-Louis again in November. He impressed Fr. Bresson
by his exceptionally good mood and remarkable patience with
Delattre's enthusiasm for his "great" archeological finds.[59]

Sutter tested this patience later in the month. The Capuchins
persuaded the vicar, now in his dotage, to lodge a protest with
Lavigerie that the monument of Saint-Louis could not be modified

without authorization of the Holy See. He characterized the project as vandalism and wrote complaints about it also to Rome and
to the Prince of Orleans.[60] Sutter's protest to Lavigerie was
included in a bittersweet letter noting the reduction in his subsidy from the Propagation de la Foi and the discontinuance of
extraordinary alms Lavigerie had given him in previous years.
Sitting in Algiers, Lavigerie prepared a letter setting him
straight about the "rights of France," and he enclosed it with
another addressed to Roustan about "the unjustifiable pretensions
of the [titular] Bishop of Rosalia. . . . All this is evidently
just a manifestation of the Italians' resentment in the face of
the increase of French influence which is due to your skillful
and constant efforts."[61] He asked Roustan to forward the enclosure
to the vicariate or to take his own action, whichever he preferred. Lavigerie then turned to a more substantive matter.

Sutter's days as apostolic vicar were numbered. Lavigerie had
ordered the compilation of a complete exposé of the Capuchins'
inadequacy to serve the Catholics of Tunisia. He wrote Roustan
that in recent decades they had added only seven parishes to the
two already there.[62] Fr. Deguerry, the superior of Saint-Louis,
was gathering the particulars on "all the lacunae of the Capuchin
Mission," and on their unworthiness to continue serving a Catholic
community constantly growing in size. Anything Roustan could contribute would help. This collection, submitted in its final form
to the Propaganda in April 1881, alleged specifically that one of
the Capuchins ran a bank out of the vicar's house with a capital
of 800,000 francs. The Catholic cemetery was a particular scandal.
But the exposé's basic theme was the inability of the Capuchin
community of twenty priests to minister effectively to a territory
one-third the size of Italy. This document made the doubtful allegation that in some areas Christians worshipped in mosques or
even participated in Muslim services.[63]

Implicitly, with French government support and his own ability
to tap funds, Lavigerie's manpower offered the ideal remedy. But
the terms had to be satisfactory. Lavigerie described an unacceptable compromise proposal in his letter of 23 November. "The Prefect of the Congregation of the Propaganda, shocked by the sad
news which ceaselessly arrives from that Mission, and by the
series of scandals given by the avarice of some and the immorality
of others, has proposed to me to divide the Apostolic Vicariate
of Tunisia into two, and to give to me with the cooperation of
the Missionaries of Saint-Louis the spiritual jurisdiction of one
of the Vicariates, with the title of Apostolic Delegate." But
Lavigerie rejected control of half the vicariate as useless and
ineffective. He could wait until Mgr. Sutter's retirement or
death made it timely to submit Deguerry's dossier to Rome.

> I am convinced that if I make known to the Pope that I
> will accept the charge of [all of] the religious ser-
> vice of Tunisia with my missionaries, the question
> will be favorably resolved. You will thus obtain with-
> out embarrassment a result which will be a new triumph
> for your policy, to annex Tunisia to French Algeria
> officially, from the religious point of view, and to
> be able thereby to create all the establishments
> (schools, hospitals, etc.) which will prepare for the
> definitive union.[64]

Roustan's efforts to increase French influence in the regency
intensified during 1880. Lavigerie himself could sense the level
of hostility in the spring during his five-week visit to supervise the preparation of the Collège Saint-Louis. He arrived on
4 April aboard a French navy dispatch boat. He consulted at length
with priests and architects regarding arrangements for the opening
of the college, which camouflaged his series of conferences with

Roustan. His public relations were successful in terms of giving
a good impression and tactfully avoiding demonstrations or incidents. But the Capuchins sent Mgr. Sutter to call upon the
archbishop near Carthage at his recently acquired residence in
La Marsa, where he made what the White Fathers interpreted as "a
sort of declaration of war against us."[65]

Sutter complained to their superior that his priests lacked
religious spirit, that their frequent visits to the nuns gave
rise to talk, and that they traveled around too much. Lavigerie
investigated the charges before replying to the octogenarian,
"who these last days has made a semblance of attack against our
Fathers of Saint-Louis. But a vigorous sortie on my part has put
the enemy in full flight, and I leave him to reflect."[66] He instructed the priests to keep to themselves and avoid travel.
Before leaving he equipped Roustan to silence any further accusations: when Sutter appeared at the French consulate and renewed
his criticism of the fathers, Roustan pulled out the 4,000 francs
Lavigerie had left with him for the Capuchin missions, the key
tactical gesture for the moment. Thoroughly humiliated, Sutter
begged him not to mention his behavior to the donor.[67]

Roustan's reports to Freycinet of the good impression made by
Lavigerie's visit drew the prime minister's expression of satisfaction "to see him furnish for the development of French influence in Tunisia the cooperation of his personal authority."[68]
With this encouragement, Lavigerie sent another request to the
Foreign Ministry for a subsidy of 40,000 francs under the chapter
of funds for religious establishments. He emphasized that he himself had borne the capital cost of 200,000 francs for an institution which strongly enhanced French influence in the regency.
The most important personages of Tunis, despite their opposition
to the republic, were asking him to accept their sons, for example,
Thomas Reade and General Muhammad Baccouche, the bey's director

of foreign affairs. Taib Bey, Sadok's younger brother, asked
Lavigerie to take his two grandsons. The Quai d'Orsay replied on
3 August with a commitment of 20,000 francs for the first year,
and it passed on to Jules Ferry Lavigerie's other request for
some paintings and statues from the Ministry of Public Instruction and Fine Arts.[69]

As the October opening date approached, Lavigerie's letters
to Carthage contained many detailed instructions on furnishings
for the college and the shipping arrangements for supplies which
he was sending the priests from Paris. Regarding this cherished
and long-awaited project, no detail was too trivial for his review. "My dear friend, . . . I have received the prospectuses in
Italian and Arabic. What has gotten into you that you have the
stupidity to make my signature in Italian Charles arcivescovo?
Can you not translate the name, which is a baptismal name as
Carolo? You doubtless think it is necessary to furnish arms to my
enemies."[70] The infirmary linen finally arrived in December, much
to the satisfaction of the nannies. The Muslim employees who had
been stealing wine in the refectory were summarily shut off, ending a source of scandal to the ministers of the bey's other
brother, Sidi Ali.[71] The college opened on schedule, with four
students, and Lavigerie arrived in late October 1880 for a visit
of three and a half months. By the end of the year there were
more than fifty boarders from elite families, ten of whom were
Arab. The priests scrupulously respected the religious and ethnic
sensibilities of their Muslim, Jewish, Italian, and Maltese students.[72]

Roustan praised the school's value in promoting the French
language and undercutting fanaticism in a letter of late November
requesting the Quai d'Orsay to fund twenty scholarships to be administered by the consulate. Lavigerie had agreed to reduce the
1,000-franc tuition to 700 francs, and Roustan was eager to

increase the patronage at his disposal. An Italian Jew of the
French coterie had already sought Roustan's help in financing the
education of his children. Amedeo Volterra's letter rather heavy-
handedly stressed his "constant and absolute" support for French
interests, and Roustan endorsed it before forwarding it to
Lavigerie.[73]

Roustan ceaselessly recommended the college to the Quai d'Orsay,
but he was likewise concerned for primary education. He strongly
supported the Alliance Israélite's school, which eventually en-
rolled a thousand boys. Until Lavigerie's appointment as apostolic
administrator and the French occupation combined to facilitate
more extensive patronage, the teaching brothers and nuns in
Tunisia were hard pressed for support in caring for their own six
hundred students. Roustan emphasized the Catholic schools' importance to the Foreign Ministry, which appropriated 15,000 francs
for him to distribute among them on the condition that they favor
French language instruction and that they confide catechism lessons to French masters. Nine thousand went to the Sisters of
St. Joseph and the rest to the Brothers of the Christian Schools.
Their superiors gratefully promised "to make the French name
loved."[74]

During 1880 Roustan needed all the help he could get. He was
more harassed than ever with the Italians' constant intrigues.
"It is a perpetual combat."[75] The "unofficial organ of the Italian
consulate" circulated the rumor in May that the Archbishop of
Algiers's recent visit had been part of a French government attempt to extend the borders of the Diocese of Constantine so as
to include the Vicariate of Tunis within Lavigerie's metropolitan
jurisdiction. Moreover, "L'Avvenire di Sardegna [printed at
Cagliari], not knowing more than to invent against me, accuses
me of having made a banquet on Good Friday with the Jews! That
came at the wrong moment because, although I am a Catholic more

by conviction than by practice, for all my life I did not eat anything that day except boiled eels and vegetables in oil."[76] These charges were taken up by another paper hostile to the French, the recently established Arabic journal L'Indépendent, whose initial costs had been borne, among others, by Sadok's brother, Sidi Ali Bey, and a sheik who stole type from the National Printing Office. Under attack for blasphemy, Roustan bared his troubles to Lavigerie: "Of what will they not accuse me now? La Gazette du Midi, which has become [the Italians'] mouthpiece at Marseille, meanwhile begins to harbor some doubts about my 'Good Friday banquet.' It states that perhaps I did not eat ham that day officially, but only in private [emphasis Roustan's]."[77] This attack was too ridiculous to take seriously, but in the middle of 1880 both sides were fighting to the finish.

A prominent Italian, Raffaele Rubattino, outbid the French rail company of Bône-Guelma to take over the Tunis-Goulette-Marsa line in July. But the T.G.M.'s expensive acquisition brought no real advantage, for the Bône-Guelma received another concession to build a port at the capital linked by rail with the interior. Meanwhile, the bey's personal dissipation continued, and the bey-lic's finances were in hardly better shape.[78] General Elias Mussalli had advised Roustan in the spring that, with patience, a few modifications in the draft treaty of protectorate would per-suade the bey to sign within a while. Dr. Mascaro, on the other hand, suggested that after the failure of so many attempts, Roustan would succeed in getting Sadok's signature only by force. He should strike quickly so as to save the bey and his country not only from the Italians but from themselves. As for Roustan, "It is the advice of M. Mascaro which I share."[79]

Roustan's advantage depended on the sympathy of the prime minister, who still resented the Italians from his tavern days. Mustapha ben Ismael's support facilitated concessions for French

business interests, and Roustan continued to bind him and his
favorites to the French party with trinkets and decorations.
Mustapha's ascendancy over the bey was absolute, but he lamented
to Roustan in April that he was beset on all sides for his policy.
He could count on no support but that of the French and the bey.
The higher officials of the Bardo Palace blamed all their troubles
on his policy, and they worked for the Italians to counter it.[80]

Britain's guarded support of the French ended with the May
victory of the liberals, who attempted to reverse the Disraeli-
Salisbury policy. But Queen Victoria favored French interests,
and the foreign secretary, George Granville, instructed Thomas
Reade at Tunis to conform to the official policy of strict neu-
trality. This did not prevent Reade, in an advisory capacity,
from passing on to the Italian government his analysis of the
strained relationship between Maccio and the bey. Reade's efforts
to bring Maccio back into grace with the Tunisian government
failed because of the Italian consul's tactless refusal to recognize the bey's predicament. Sadok could only apologize to
Maccio for yielding telegraph and rail concessions to the French
in the face of irresistible pressure. Yet the Italian consul
persisted in his policy of "studied nonrecognition of the prime
minister," and this slight to his adopted son embarrassed the
bey in the eyes of his own subjects. Reade had admonished Maccio
to relent in his mortifying demands, for they only increased
Sadok's dependence on Roustan.

> The inevitable result of this policy will be to compel
> the Bey, who is now honestly and manfully struggling
> to preserve his independence, to succumb unwillingly
> to the often-proffered shelter of a French protec-
> torate, and this time more certainly because M. Roustan
> is apparently profiting by the action of M. Maccio to
> put forward a series of demands of concessions which

are eminently calculated not only to destroy the integrity of the Tunisian government, but to provoke
a serious conflict between Italian and French interests.[81]

Observers in Tunis noted that "the French, not being able to
conquer the country, want to buy it."[82] At the end of the summer
Roustan felt he was near his goal. This optimism was shattered
in the fall, when Mustapha ben Ismael broke with him and joined
the Italians. He thereafter harassed French concessionaires and
slowed down or halted their constructions. It was evident to an
observer like Bismarck that "the good cards have changed hands;
Italy holds them now."[83]

The overall situation was becoming more and more intolerable.
Roustan wrote to the foreign minister in early 1881 summarizing
it under several headings. With regard to the question of fron-
tiers, the border violations frequently committed (or at least
invented) in eastern Algeria on the part of nomads from Tunisia's
Khroumiria offered France an excuse for military intervention.
Concerning questions of property, Mustapha's government forbade
Tunisians to sell to the French, "putting us gradually outside
the common law."[84]

While French entrepreneurs struggled against this harassment,
Lavigerie coped with Capuchin efforts to undermine the French
position. Coincidentally, the expulsion of religious congregations
in France which took place in autumn 1880, enabled the Capuchins
in Tunisia to exploit would-be exiles from the Trappist community
in Algeria. Ominous remarks by Governor General Grévy regarding
application of the March Decrees in North Africa led the Trappists
of Staouéli to believe that their expulsion was imminent. Their
abbot, Augustin, sent the procurator, Alexandre, to Tunisia
along with another monk to purchase a house. After arriving on
20 November they blundered under the wing of the Capuchins, who

welcomed these potential refugees into their house. Alexandre
had the bad grace even to bring one of the Italians along when
he appeared at Roustan's. This was all the more remarkable because the Archbishop of Algiers was in Tunisia at the time.[85]

Lavigerie prevailed upon this "crack-brain" to move with his
confrere to Saint-Louis de Carthage. For several uncomfortable
weeks Lavigerie worked in consultation with Roustan to obtain
government assurances that these naive monks would not be expelled from Algiers and placed under the jurisdiction of Italians
so eager to exploit them against France. Roustan wired the Quai
d'Orsay that, in the event the government did not intend to close
the Trappe in Algiers, it would be wisest to have the two monks
recalled by their superior, Augustin. Roustan also humored them
in the meantime so as not to drive them back to the Italians
from whom they had just been pried away. He recommended to them
a French realtor who had instructions to lead them on a wild
goose chase in seeking new property.[86]

At the end of November Alexandre realized the uselessness of
remaining and packed for home. But before leaving he enlisted the
help of another agent in negotiating the purchase of some property.
This Dr. Juving bore a grudge against Lavigerie in connection with
his brief tenure in the medical service of the recently opened
Collège Saint-Louis. As Lavigerie explained to Roustan, "He claims
he was ousted because he was not Communard enough, they are his
words. The accusation is rich, especially about an archbishop."[87]

Lavigerie emphasized to Roustan, who conveyed this argument to
the Foreign Ministry, that the monks' reaction of jumping into
the Italians' arms should impress the government with the necessity of leaving them unmolested in Algeria. There should be no
question of this, especially with regard to Trappists, who were
"very inoffensive folk, since they never talk."[88] The incident
moved Foreign Minister Barthélemy to intercede with Constans at

the Ministry of Cults for a clarification regarding their position. By then the French cabinet was well aware of the imprudence
of driving the Trappists out of Staouéli. The Ministry of Cults
represented this view to Governor General Grévy in Algiers, and
Flourens informed Lavigerie in early January 1881 that the
Trappists definitely would not be disturbed.[89]

Paris provided this guarantee after a month of activity on
the part of Lavigerie, who kept after Roustan for clarification
of the Trappists' position at the same time as he urged their
abbot to assure the government of their devotion to France. Although Augustin never went so far as to disavow his clumsy procurator, Alexandre, he promised Roustan on 20 December that any
house in Tunis would be strictly a dependent branch of the
Staouéli mother house. Lavigerie gave Roustan his own guarantee
on 29 December that they would always conserve their canonical
rights to remain "distinct and independent" of the Italian mission. Finally, after the Cults Ministry's guarantee of January,
Lavigerie got the Trappists to forswear the idea of any establishment in Tunisia. His assistance throughout the two months of this
affair was praised fully in Roustan's reports to Paris, and the
ministry asked him to thank Lavigerie for his good offices.[90]

Roustan had scarcely disposed of the Trappist problem when he
discovered that the Italian government was planning to have
Italian nuns open a school at La Goulette. Ambassador Desprez
promptly spoke to Cardinal Simeoni, who assured him on 5 January
1881 that there was never a question at the Propaganda of sending
Italian sisters to Tunisia. In their regular conversations Desprez
and Simeoni frequently talked of Tunisia and of the Eastern
Religious Protectorate. Simeoni kept to his position that the
republic's domestic policies did not affect Vatican support regarding overseas questions. Ten days later Desprez reiterated his
own conviction that Roustan's report was mistaken. The Italian

government was attempting forcibly to convert the endowments of
the Propaganda into state bonds. It was hardly the time for Italy
to ask a favor, and Simeoni assured Desprez again that such would
be refused.[91]

Then in late March 1881, the cardinal-prefect informed Desprez
that he had just learned from the superior general of the Sisters
of St. Joseph, who ran a French school for girls in the regency,
that Salesian nuns from Italy proposed to move to La Goulette,
where they had obtained a house. Roustan exploded: "How can the
sisters come here without an authorization from the Holy See?
Under what protection will they be placed? If it is under that of
the Italian consulate, that will be an innovation in the East,
for even in Cairo we protect the Italian sisters."[92] Desprez felt
that this must have had the connivance of Sutter, and the Propaganda asked for an explanation. Sutter said that the Italian
consul had suggested it to him a year earlier. He had replied at
the time that Tunisia already had a Catholic school for girls,
and that the proposal required the Propaganda's approval anyway,
not his. According to Sutter, Maccio took that for granted and
had gone ahead with purchasing a house. Roustan remarked to the
Quai d'Orsay about the dubious role of Simeoni, who claimed to
have been very ill informed. The prefect nonetheless continued
to tell Desprez that he fully appreciated France's objections
and that the nuns could not move to the mission vicariate without
his preliminary agreement.[93] The proposal to staff the school
with Italian nuns simply died. Both the Trappist proposal to take
refuge in the Capuchin vicariate and the Italian project of a
convent school were blocked, although they consumed a great deal
of Lavigerie's and Roustan's time.

Putting out brushfires and consolidating the French position
at Carthage were the limit of Lavigerie's open activities in
Tunisia until 1881. The White Fathers accepted the Italian hegemony

in Mgr. Sutter's vicariate and refrained from any attempt to
rival the Capuchins' ministry. They served as chaplains to the
small French community, and they taught the children of some of
the other most important families. The priests spent the rest of
their time ministering to the poor and sick in their vicinity,
and they bargained for good real estate on which to build the
churches and charitable works of the future Archdiocese of
Carthage. But that ambition was a secret. Before a Frenchman
could get control of the clergy of Tunisia, the Third Republic
had to take over the country.

IV
Imposition of the Two Protectorates: 1881

The imposition of the French protectorate in May 1881 is a classic in diplomatic history. Formal takeover, however, can easily differ from actual control, and here Lavigerie's role in Tunisia was crucial. The resident minister of the republic consolidated his absolute authority over the beylical administration, and the French army gradually subdued the rebellious tribes of the interior. Gallicization of the natives was not an immediate objective of the French program; indeed, fifty years of native passive resistance to the "mission civilisatrice" in Algeria made many French doubt that they would see it achieved in a lifetime.[1] But Tunisia's European colony presented Lavigerie with an immediate task. His own "religious protectorate," more than any other factor, enabled the French to pacify these dissidents. The Capuchin mission, run by Italian patriots under a senile figurehead, was potentially the rallying point of opposition to the new regime. By obtaining from the Vatican his own appointment as apostolic administrator Lavigerie preempted control of the Tunisian clergy from Italy and prepared to expand its ranks with loyal servants of the Third Republic.

The timing of his appointment to succeed Sutter just after France imposed the Treaty of Bardo was partially coincidental. Yet one consideration in the Vatican's decision was the need to bring ecclesiastical governance in line with political realities. The military expedition into the regency held the attention of the French press in the spring of 1881. With little public notice

however, the other Tunisian question of ecclesiastical jurisdiction was determined in the offices of the Vatican and the Propaganda Fide. The Pope's ministers delayed, consulted, and gauged
European diplomatic opinion for several months before making
Lavigerie apostolic administrator. Further French pressure for
his nomination as cardinal, unsuccessful until the following
year, came from an official desire to enhance the prestige,
hence the effectiveness, of Roustan's most important instrument
for assimilating Catholics to French rule. Lavigerie's efforts
during 1881 to obtain episcopal jurisdiction and to compel the
Capuchins' obedience were the beginning of this expanded role.

Lavigerie spent most of the year in Algiers and Tunis, yet
from that distance he pulled the strings which worked the levers
of power at Paris and Rome. His confidential agent at Paris was
Fr. Jacques-Joseph-Félix Charmetant, a North African who enjoyed
his complete trust. An original member of the White Fathers,
Charmetant had been superior of the Society's first Algiers seminary at Maison-Carrée, and he organized the first caravan from
Zanzibar into equatorial Africa. With his health weakened but his
superior intelligence undaunted, Lavigerie assigned him to
Europe.

Charmetant served his master as Fr. Joseph served Richelieu.
At the Vatican in 1878 he negotiated approval of the Society's
rules, assignment of new mission vicariates in Africa, and other
matters which required a proxy at Rome. After enlisting the confidential service of Mgr. Zitelli, a <u>minutante</u> (specialist) inside the Propaganda, Charmetant moved to Paris as Lavigerie's
special procurator. He left the Society in 1879, supposedly because of a clash of temperament with the founder, but he remained
Lavigerie's procurator at Paris. Charmetant became active in the
<u>Oeuvre des Ecoles d'Orient,</u> which provided a cover for his secret
liaison with French officials. His release from Lavigerie's

authority was only for appearances: "But you will remain always, at least until my death, a priest of the Diocese of Algiers."[2] The government recognized Charmetant's efforts with the Legion of Honor in June 1882. Against his better judgment, Lavigerie permitted the council of the Ecoles to name him acting director in 1883, and Charmetant strained his health further in this dual service until 1886.[3]

This assignment required extreme caution. Many of Lavigerie's letters were to be shown only to people at the Quai d'Orsay. Some of Charmetant's reports to him were sent in an outer envelope addressed to a third party in the North African clergy. They used "Noël" or "G." in reference to Léon Gambetta, and one of their codes was keyed to a dictionary of which each had a copy. Lavigerie sensed from press leaks or other indications that some of their wires and letters passed through the "black chambers" of French politicians.[4] The abundant Charmetant letters, of which the archivists of the White Fathers have typed copies, are the richest source of information concerning Lavigerie's relations with the French government during and after the invasion of Tunisia.

Charmetant's messages from Lavigerie contributed to the French ministers' deliberations on the Tunisian question. Despite the fact that the Christian powers of Europe had approved a French takeover in 1878, French leaders did not make the decision to act until early 1881. Prime Minister Ferry, preoccupied with domestic problems, was naturally hesitant in an election year; Foreign Minister Barthélemy-Saint-Hilaire was rather timid. Chamber President Gambetta and Jules Grévy, President of the Republic, opposed antagonizing Italy. As late as January 1881 Gambetta seriously hoped to reach an understanding with Italy providing for the transfer of Roustan and Maccio and a treaty guaranteeing Tunisian independence. Although Ferry later became

the most energetic advocate of overseas expansion after the decision to begin with Tunisia, the most effective advocate in
government circles until 1881 was the political director of the
Foreign Ministry, Baron Alphonse de Courcel. He enlisted the
help of other diplomats in persuading Barthélemy that the government must choose between the alternatives of regaining for France
her rightful place among nations or "relegating us to the rank
of Spain."[5]

Gambetta held out until March and then gave his full support
to the goal of military occupation. Biographer Jules Tournier
attributes this about-face to a letter from Lavigerie delivered
by Charmetant. Radical and monarchist journals, in their later
attacks on the whole Tunisian venture, pointed to Gambetta's sud-
den change of heart as evidence of corruption. But Gambetta's
decision is primarily attributable to the persuasiveness of
Courcel and others in the diplomatic corps.[6]

Quick preparation followed. Barthélemy had laid the groundwork
in February with a statement that France could not tolerate much
more harassment from the nomadic Khroumirs. German support was
still steadfast, the British position ambiguous, and Italy and
Turkey were powerless. Another incursion into Algeria on 30 March
furnished the required excuse. After a week of front-page publicity in Paris, Prime Minister Ferry obtained on 7 April a
5 million-franc credit to send an expedition to chastise the
frontier tribes. Roustan notified the bey that soon French soldiers would march as allies to deal with their common pest.
Thirty thousand troops advanced in two columns from Algeria at
the end of April, and the French navy landed another eight thousand at Bizerta.[7]

One of the first steps in the imposition of French power before
the military occupation even began, and the key to Lavigerie's
own plans for the protectorate, was the acquisition of episcopal

control in Tunisia. An initiative by the Capuchins to replace
Mgr. Sutter with one of their own caught Roustan by surprise.
The superior of the Sisters of St. Joseph informed him in early
October 1880 that she had heard from Rome of the impending
appointment of Fr. Emilio da Strevi. Emilio had long been the
most provocative opponent of France in the Capuchin community;
in Roustan's words, he was "very active, very intriguing, and the
declared enemy of all that is French."[8] Roustan urged the Foreign
Ministry to prevent this nomination, and he likewise asked
Lavigerie to use his influence at Rome against this threat to
their program: "I do not want to watch the undoing of the edifice
so laboriously raised."[9] This was immediately after the collapse
of the Freycinet negotiations concerning the March Decrees, and
the new Ferry government was expelling the congregations.
Lavigerie was therefore pessimistic in his reply to Roustan concerning a French appeal to the Vatican about Sutter's replacement.[10]

Taking advantage of French hesitation to impose a protectorate
on the beylic, Italy was attempting to strengthen her own religious protectorate in Tunisia. But as the Quai d'Orsay's plans for
the invasion became more definite, Lavigerie and the French ambassador to the Vatican increased their pressure on the Propaganda
against appointing a new Italian Vicar of Tunis. Deprez discussed
the question delicately with the minutante for Africa in early
January 1881. Mgr. Masotti promised that such a proposal could
not be sprung by surprise, and Desprez reported to Paris the
assurance "that Sutter had not made any step until now to obtain
a coadjutor." Masotti's ignorance or mental reservation is not
completely clear, but, in fact, the archives of the Propaganda
Fide contain biographical summaries for three candidates nominated
on 19 June 1880. Emilio was actually listed last in order of preference after Frs. Liborio and Vitale. A letter from the procurator general of the Capuchins at Rome supported Liborio as

Sutter's first choice. Later in January the Quai d'Orsay instructed Desprez to treat this important question directly with
Simeoni, regardless of less authoritative denials.[11]

The issue had arisen simultaneously with the Italian proposal
to send nuns to La Goulette. Emilio was pastor in that town, and
he was obviously involved with Licurgo Maccio's intrigues. Everything led the French to believe he was the leading candidate.
Roustan emphasized to Courcel the primary importance of preventing the nomination of this "enragé francophobe" if their program
of Gallicization were to succeed. Roustan further stated that
their second step must be to obtain a red hat for Lavigerie so
as to enhance his influence at Rome and facilitate the transfer
of Tunisia to his jurisdiction. Precisely for that reason certain
cardinals at the Vatican opposed any increase in his influence
and were delaying his nomination.

Pope Leo had unofficially invited the French government to
recommend Lavigerie for the Sacred College soon after his election
in 1878, but under the presidency of MacMahon the bid drew no response. The director general of cults had recommended him again
to Prime Minister Freycinet in August 1880, stressing "his sin-
cere adhesion to our republican institutions."[12] Desprez worked
at Rome from October to prepare his elevation, and the Foreign
Ministry stressed again in January its many advantages for French
interests in North Africa. But the strained relations between
church and state resulting from the recent anticlerical campaign
gave Lavigerie's enemies at Rome the leverage they needed to
stall his appointment throughout 1881. Furthermore, the government gave a higher priority to his obtaining Sutter's mantle.
Until the following winter Lavigerie had to badger the Quai
d'Orsay to press for his elevation to the cardinalate, although
they worked in tandem on the Tunisian succession.[13]

Success required speed lest the Italians arrange Emilio's appointment and confront them with an accomplished fact. Lavigerie wrote to Roustan on 15 January 1881 to recommend "a resolute step at the Court of Rome and to indicate the cord which it is necessary to touch, according to my knowledge of men." Even though the cabinet debate regarding the Tunisian invasion was not yet resolved, Lavigerie recommended that Desprez promptly submit to the Propaganda an unofficial but "emphatic political veto" to the nomination of an Italian. "But in order to be sure of succeeding one must go as far as to say that in case the matter should be decided otherwise, France reserved the right to impose on the government of the Bey such measures that the Apostolic Vicariate would be put in no condition to bother us, and for the future. . . . It is not necessary to specify anything; this is the best means of succeeding."[14] Three weeks later Lavigerie heard from Rome that the Propaganda had been effectively frightened and was ready to temporize. This gave Lavigerie the time he needed to arrange his own takeover.

In February Simeoni issued another denial to Desprez that there was any question of appointing a coadjutor, but by March he admitted the necessity in view of Sutter's great age. He still refused to admit Emilio had ever been a candidate, and Desprez thought he seemed inclined to prefer Liborio. Simeoni promised to stall as long as possible. On 6 March Desprez reported that the prefect of Propaganda was more responsive to the candidacy of Lavigerie. Simeoni did not respond to Desprez's remark that making Lavigerie a cardinal would simplify things, but neither did he dispute the point that the interests of the Church in Africa would benefit by extending east the jurisdiction of the Archbishop of Algiers. Simeoni asked Desprez what would justify that step and what arrangements would be appropriate. At the

Quai d'Orsay Courcel let Charmetant copy a passage from Desprez's
report of this interview, and he asked Lavigerie's procurator
for confidential advice on the subject so that he could help
Desprez build Simeoni's case.

At the beginning of April Simeoni told the ambassador he was
prepared to choose a Francophile Capuchin for the vicariate, and
he did not shut the door on naming Lavigerie. Desprez asked the
Quai d'Orsay for advice on how best to continue pressure.[15] On
10 April Lavigerie sent a suggestion from Algiers through his
man at Paris: "It is necessary only to remember that Cardinal
Simeoni is essentially a scrupulous and timid man, that it is
necessary consequently to tell him above all that which will
alarm his conscience and make him fear alternatives even more
grave, in order to bring him to the combination which is proposed
to him."[16] Lavigerie recommended an approach of reducing their
requests as much as possible, and of making the Vatican fear the
consequences of refusing France even more than those of rejecting
an Italian nomination.

Through the spring Charmetant continued to keep Courcel informed on Lavigerie's reflections. The archbishop suggested in
June that Desprez could end the Vatican's delays with one word:
that if they continued to hamper legitimate French interests in
Tunisia, the government would simply have the beylic withdraw
the Capuchins' authorization to remain there. Lavigerie wrote to
Charmetant that this fear had already been voiced at Rome, and
that if the government were to give it apparent substance, with
the existence of the mission itself at stake, the Capuchins and
the Propaganda would instantly be more cooperative.[17]

In the meantime Lavigerie had been suggesting the same interpretation more gently to Simeoni. Three days after the Chambers
voted in April to fund the expedition against the Khroumirs, he
confidentially informed His Eminent Lordship of what was soon to

pass, "in order that the Holy See and the Propaganda may thereby profit." Four months earlier Lavigerie had alerted him of French plans that now were no longer tentative. Although the French were prepared to drive the bey out if necessary, they preferred to reduce him to a nominal sovereign. Aware of the fact that the Vatican was inclined to ascertain the opinions of other countries before acting, Lavigerie attempted to convince Simeoni that the powers were in accord: England had Cyprus, Italy would later take Tripoli, and Germany was to appropriate Crete. Their public statements and gestures were "a veritable comedy intended to mask the game vis-à-vis Turkey." He confided these secrets to Simeoni's discretion as fact, not hypothesis. Once the French were masters in Tunisia, they would not tolerate the continued opposition of the Capuchins. "If necessary they will go even to the most violent acts in order to expel them rather than leave them in their present situation, because they intend to Gallicize the land and to prepare annexation to Algeria."[18]

Lavigerie proceeded to tell Simeoni that the government had asked him to succeed Mgr. Sutter, and that soon Desprez would approach the Holy See directly. He stated that with the assistance of his coadjutor, it would be possible for him to accept the Apostolic Delegation to Tunisia while remaining Archbishop of Algiers. He was, of course, totally at the disposal of the Propaganda, and on one point he recommended a hard line: "As regards the Capuchins, the first condition which I would impose on the government, as I have already declared, would be to respect all their acquired rights and not to touch anyone among them."[19] By April the question of Sutter's successor was known in political circles, and the Vatican faced Italian pressure against the suggestion of replacing him with a Frenchman. Desprez urged the Holy See to cooperate on the grounds that extension of French control in North Africa would best serve the cause of religion

there, and that this should outweigh Italian national considerations.[20]

Two objections soon raised against Lavigerie in the Curia
were the ecclesiastical usage against giving two dioceses to one
bishop and the necessity of awaiting the incumbent's death.
Lavigerie counseled Charmetant that both objections were specious.
The rule against holding a second diocese was often waived, especially in mission lands. Sutter's incapacity to carry on, demonstrated by his request for a coadjutor, had become a subject
of public notoriety. The vicar had lost his memory and fallen
into a "veritable state of infancy."[21] In actual circumstances
which required a bishop of intelligence and energy, it was suitable for the Holy See to demand his resignation and to confide
the administration of the vicariate to a neighboring prelate,
provided Sutter were left with his titles.

Lavigerie again emphasized the importance of speed, lest the
Capuchins use these delays to create more problems and render the
new administrator's task more difficult. "Thus it suffices merely
for the Holy See to grant it, and in order for the Holy See to
grant it it suffices merely for France to demand it in the name
of her interests."[22] This was the strategy for placing in the
hands of France an instrument for amalgamating the Italians and
Maltese under French control. "Evidently what France must plan
here under the cover of a protectorate is the progressive
Gallicization of a type such that the question of complete annexation must ripen and finally, with time, be settled, as it were,
by itself."[23]

French troops were in Tunis by 12 May. Roustan and General
Bréart informed the bey that the time had come to clarify the
relationship between their two countries. They presented Muhammad
es Sadok with the Treaty of Kassar Said. This agreement, more
commonly named after the Bardo Palace, left Sadok with nominal

sovereignty, but it preempted Tunisia from international politics
and entrusted its foreign relations to the supervision of France.
Within two weeks the bey expressed to Dr. Mascaro his sense of
relief that the contest was over: "Until now I was like a piece
of meat torn by four dogs."[24] The fathers of Saint-Louis likewise
welcomed the civilizing presence of the French army: "We learn
with joy that in the camp of Manouba it is strictly forbidden to
swear."[25] The invasion kept them busy tending the wounded and
moribund among French forces around Tunis as well as guarding the
children entrusted to them at the college.[26] Lavigerie was busy
trying to get control of the vicariate.

But by then the Capuchins at Rome were working strenuously
against his scheme. They attempted to buy time with the argument
that some provision must be made for Sutter's retirement. On
Lavigerie's endorsement the government gave the Vatican a blank
check for Sutter's pension. Actually officials at the Vatican
were also stalling. They wanted to gauge the reaction of European
powers to the Treaty of Bardo, and they were anxious not to offend Turkey, for at that moment they awaited the Porte's ratification of the Holy See's choice for Patriarch of Armenia.[27]

Both Italy and France knew that the defeat of Emilio's candidacy would be a death blow to Italian influence in Tunisia, and
struggle within the Curia intensified. Despite the fundamental
conflict between the Holy See and the Italian government over
the Roman Question, even in the families of some cardinals there
were members of both the Curia and the royal government. Influence was brought to bear upon one in behalf of the other. "The
Capuchins and the Macciotins have united their interests, and
they throw at the timid Cardinal Simeoni assaults which stop him
at every turn."[28] Attacks upon France appeared in the Catholic
paper L'Aurora until the ambassador protested to the Secretariat
of State.

Desprez reported in late May that, although Jacobini was
playing things close to his chest, the prefect of the Propaganda
was noncommittal but encouraging. Simeoni spoke in terms of
giving Sutter's successor the title of apostolic administrator
rather than delegate, leaving the Capuchin community inviolate
under an apostolic prefect. Lavigerie objected to the dangerous
and ambiguous dualism of authority in such an arrangement. He
complained of Desprez's lack of persistence and initiative in
obtaining the decision France required. Charmetant stressed to
the Quai d'Orsay that this question of divided authority was a
much more important issue than the 6,000 francs demanded for
Sutter's pension. But for the moment it was necessary to accept
these terms, leaving revision until later. At the end of May
Lavigerie advised that such a scheme was acceptable if implemented right away, provided Emilio were not appointed prefect of
the Capuchin enclave.[29]

The tide had turned in Lavigerie's favor. Leo XIII decided
not to submit the arrangement to the plodding consideration of
the regular Congregation of the Propaganda. A special ad hoc
congregation treated it in the first week of June, and the Holy
Father approved the cardinals' propositions. Simeoni wrote to
Sutter requesting his resignation. Desprez told Barthélemy that
the decision was the best one they could have hoped for; it had
the support of both Jacobini and Simeoni. The apostolic prefect
was to have jurisdiction within the Capuchin community only in
questions of internal discipline, and he would be directly subject to the Propaganda. The Pope wished to defer public announcement of this decision for a while, lest the appearance of haste
inspire a political interpretation. The secretary of state requested an official note from the French government generously
phrasing the terms to which France submitted, in order to provide a "pièce justificative" for their agreement.[30]

The necessity of awaiting Sutter's resignation delayed until 28 June the actual signing of the brief appointing Lavigerie. Jacobini wrote to the French government reviewing the terms. One of Desprez's strongest arguments had been the incomparable financial support which a French administration could give the Church of Tunisia. Jacobini summarized the key condition for this ad nutum (provisional) appointment: that France

> will not neglect to procure for the Apostolic Administrator, whether by the budgets of cults or by the resources of the Tunisian administration itself, the means necessary to erect the episcopal palace and the seminary, adding to them other schools and parishes in proportion to the needs of the new situation, and giving to these missions an impulsion such that, while they develop better the religious interests, they will also assure the progress of civilization in Africa as much as the consolidation and extension of French influence.[31]

At that point the structure of French political control was provisional as well. The brief Treaty of Bardo did not even use the word protectorate, and in May Jules Ferry had only an imprecise idea of the design by which Tunisia was to develop under Resident Minister Roustan's direction. Barthélemy circulated a white paper dated 20 June publicly renouncing any idea of annexation or conquest. The foreign minister noted the imprudence of joining 2 million [sic] Tunisians to the larger Muslim population only recently pacified in Algeria. The sole desire of the French in Tunisia was to maintain peace.[32]

According to the representations made by Charmetant to the ministers, Lavigerie's effectiveness in helping them depended on his elevation to the cardinalate.[33] But the tension between

church and state in France at the beginning of 1881 enabled
Lavigerie's enemies in the Sacred College to keep him out. His
candidacy was part of the whole range of disputes between the
French government and the Vatican. Although generally both parties were careful not to let domestic differences affect their
cooperation overseas, this restraint was wearing thin. Leo XIII
responded to the radicals' outrages by freezing the number of
French cardinals. When two of them died, the government was not
able to fill France's quota. Throughout the year Rome made no
objections to Lavigerie's nomination, but after a while the refusal to give any commitment in its favor made the "perpetual
candidate" fear his elevation would come on the "Greek calends."[34]
Lavigerie stayed at Algiers through the spring of 1881, refusing
to go to Paris lest he seem to be promoting himself.

Lavigerie waited things out in Algiers also to prod the government into working harder for his red hat. During the Tunisian expedition Ferry and Courcel wanted Lavigerie's advice in person.
Charmetant expressed to Courcel in early May Lavigerie's humiliation at having to endure such a long delay, and he unofficially
threatened that Lavigerie would take himself out of consideration
for cardinal if the government could not end this "false situation." This bluff seemed to inspire a "genuine terror" in Courcel,
who told Charmetant, "That would be a real moral disaster in view
of the services which he is called to render in the Mediterranean
basin."[35]

By early June Charmetant realized that the Vatican would not
elevate a Frenchman without some appeasement by Paris. As part
of the annual custom of pruning the budget of cults, the Chamber
had recently stricken the salary supplement for cardinals and
withheld their installation fees. This infuriated the Vatican
because Ferry's government had let it happen without objection.
As much as French diplomats regretted this measure, Barthélemy
would not push the issue for fear of triggering more abuse in

the Chamber. While awaiting the results of the August French elections, Leo XIII decided to postpone the distribution of all new hats. Desprez, as well as Lavigerie's sources at Rome (doubtless including Mgr. Zitelli), gathered only praise for the candidate from the Pontiff's lips. The apostolic administrator's appointment was moving to conclusion, but by June it was clear that the question of new cardinals was shelved until the final cults vote.

Lavigerie's frustration at this waiting game was doubled by his difficulties in Tunisia.[36] He might have obtained the apostolic administrator's appointment more easily by appealing to Simeoni and Jacobini as one eminence to another. Even after French pressure and papal friendship secured the Tunisian succession, there remained several practical obstacles to his actual control of the Capuchin mission. He faced the task of getting rid of Maccio's old allies without the additional leverage which a cardinal's prestige would have conferred. When he arrived in Tunisia in late June, people remembered him as the man who had prevented the Trappists from moving there. The land was in great disorder from tribal resistance to French rule, but during their conferences Lavigerie and the resident minister found perfect accord. On the evening of 7 July Mgr. Sutter brought Lavigerie the pastoral stole he had received decades earlier from Queen Marie-Amélie. Lavigerie knelt and asked him to place the vicar's symbol of authority on his shoulders. The old man's gentleness and warmth genuinely touched him.[37]

Sutter's younger confreres were less cooperative. French intervention had prevented Emilio's nomination as prefect of the Capuchins,[38] but he continued his intrigues with friends in the Italian consulate. Fr. Liborio, the provisional prefect, was hardly more inclined to accept the new order. A "Short Exposé" penned by Lavigerie provides a lively narrative of their program of resistance and the apostolic administrator's reaction.

Lavigerie's first step was to assure Mgr. Sutter's financial independence of the Capuchin community by going to the monastery
to pledge personally the payment of his 6,000-franc pension.
Lavigerie also wanted to assure the other priests of his good
will and to renew their ecclesiastical faculties to continue
their parish ministry.

The day after his first visit to Sutter he returned to greet
them personally. The house appeared empty, and Sutter told him
that all the other monks were out tending their flocks. When
Lavigerie insisted on seeing them to renew their powers, Sutter
observed that this was needless, for the Capuchins' spiritual
delegation came from the Propaganda. True as that was for the
community's internal affairs, public ministry was another matter.
Lavigerie insisted that they receive their diocesan faculties
from him - and make the submission which that implied.

> "I beg you to tell them that before my departure [in
> several days for Rome] they will have to present them-
> selves to me, so that their powers relative to the
> care of the faithful and the administration of sacra-
> ments may be renewed for them. Without that their
> powers will be suspended."
>
> At these words Mgr. Sutter seemed to be moved and
> he said: "But perhaps I am mistaken. A few of our
> Fathers might be about the house." So he checked,
> and actually there were six.
>
> As soon as they came before the Apostolic Adminis-
> trator he said to them in substance: "I renew [your
> powers] and I beg you to tell your confreres that I
> renew all the powers that they hold of the Apostolic
> Vicar. I wish above all to tell you that, in the
> difficult circumstances in which we find ourselves,

I will be your father and protector, as was Mgr.
Sutter."

The Fathers did not respond. They left, and one of
them, about to repeat what the Archbishop had come to
tell them, added: "We don't believe a single word of
it, and we have no need of him."[39]

The Capuchins' second act of defiance related to the temporal-
ities of the vicariate, which were worth about 24,000 francs.
Lavigerie insisted on distinguishing the properties of their
community from those which by nature were diocesan assets. The
Capuchins claimed that everything belonged to them. They contested
Lavigerie's right to an accounting by Sutter, who had agreed to
provide one and to submit this question to the judgment of the
Propaganda. Rather than contest this in court at Tunis and cause
a scandal before the Muslims, Lavigerie awaited a decision from
Rome. He settled at Carthage rather than take over the cathedral
church at Tunis or move into Sutter's old apartment at the monastery.

Before leaving for Rome to plead his case, he issued a bishop's
letter taking possession of the vicariate, which he directed to
be read from the pulpits the following Sunday. The monks refused
on the grounds that, like the monastery, their parish churches
were exempt from the usual canonical jurisdiction of a bishop:
their powers, granted to them through the Propaganda, were perpetual; they were in no canonical need to be renewed, nor was
their renewal worth telling the people at Mass. While failing
to make this public gesture of submission, they informed Rome
that the bishop's letter had been read, for, indeed, it had - in
the dining room of their monastery at Mgr. Sutter's direction.

Sutter himself had asked to be left with the powers of Curé of
Tunis. This parish included more than half the Catholics in
Tunisia, and Lavigerie discovered that without his authority

Liborio had taken it over. Marriages conducted by this usurper
were null; truly this was a case for censure! The revolt spread
from the clergy to the faithful, who according to newspaper accounts were preparing a public protest against Rome's decision
to replace Sutter. "Finally topping off their errors, the chiefs
of their party prepare a public opposition to the Holy See and
a type of schism."[40] The French repeated this theme again and
again at the Vatican. Lavigerie appointed Fr. Deguerry to run the
vicariate as procurator, and he left Tunis on 11 July for three
months of business at Malta, Rome, Paris, and Algiers.

He arrived at Rome on 22 July for an audience with the Pope
and a week and a half of other conferences devoted to protecting
the prize he had just obtained. "The Capuchins are moving heaven
and earth here in order to seize the possessions of the
Vicariate."[41] A conference of cardinals was scheduled for 29 July
at the Propaganda to settle the dispute. Lavigerie sent a coded
wire to Roustan including the text of a declaration to be obtained
from the Tunisian government regarding beylical property given to
Mgr. Sutter in previous decades. This document specified that the
use of such property had been entrusted to Sutter as chief of the
Catholic community in Tunisia, not as head of the Capuchins. The
bey's minister promptly provided this statement, and in accordance
with Lavigerie's request the French residence immediately wired it
back to Rome uncoded so that it could be given to the cardinals
at the conference. A similar declaration was obtained from the
Propagation de la Foi at Lyons.[42]

During the week preceding the conference Lavigerie persuaded
the Propaganda that, since he resided at Saint-Louis it would be
useful for purposes of raising money in France to attach the
memorable name of Carthage to the title of his jurisdiction. He
urged Jacobini to recall Emilio and to send several French
Capuchins to Tunisia as army hospital chaplains. Five of them

arrived on 15 August and went to their separate assignments.
Meanwhile, a formal letter to Leo XIII repeated his complaints
of the assault on papal authority.[43]

Both Lavigerie and Sutter attended the conference of 29 July
at the Piazza di Spagna. Sutter corroborated the uncoded telegrams,
and the conference ordered that the goods of the mission were to be
settled along the lines set in the twelve-year-old constitution
Romanos Pontifices, which distinguished between diocesan and
conventual property in a mission jurisdiction. Liborio was to
promulgate the pastoral letter immediately. The conference sustained Lavigerie on the question of parochial faculties. It obliged
the Capuchins to present their parish books to the apostolic administrator, although he could not examine those of their community. The Pope approved this ruling on 31 July, and Lavigerie
left for Paris.[44]

Upon his arrival on 4 August he read Paris newspaper reports
of the Tunisian Italians' request for his revocation. The leader
of this movement was apparently the consulate translator, Sig.
Pestalozza, whom Roustan called Maccio's tool (l'âme damnée).
Pestalozza's mother and sister headed a group of women who peti-
tioned Rome for the recall of Lavigerie and the return of Sutter.
Emilio, whom they supported for his successor, was always at La
Goulette intriguing with them, and nothing but Sutter's own insistence had prevented them from organizing a demonstration at
his departure for Rome.[45]

In the meantime, Fr. Liborio was directing his requests for
permission to grant marriage dispensations directly to the Propaganda rather than to Procurator Deguerry. Nonetheless, once
the conference decrees were laid upon them, the Capuchins made
"a beginning of submission." They finally promulgated Lavigerie's
pastoral letter, and French diplomatic pressure on the Holy See
intensified for the recall of Fr. Emilio. Through the rest of

August the chargé d'affaires, Baron Pierre-Henri de Bâcourt,
stressed the necessity of speed in the strongest terms. Bâcourt
got a Vatican pledge every time: Emilio was being recalled by
his Capuchin superiors rather than by means of a direct order
from the Propaganda; it was important he give the appearance of
responding to Capuchin letters of obedience rather than political
pressure from the Secretariat of State, and this took time.

France's toubles did not depart with Emilio in early September.
He went to Rome, and in concert with the Italians he continued
to promote trouble in Tunisia.[46] Later in the month Liborio again
attempted to despoil the vicariate by firing Sig. Fondati, whom
Lavigerie had retained after twenty-nine years of service as man-
ager of the mission's properties. Liborio notified the tenants to
pay their rents to himself. The French had no doubt that these
revenues would be used to finance this Italian enclave's activities against them. This "new and incredible enterprise" defied
the Propaganda and threatened a scandal, for Fondati planned a
lawsuit. Lavigerie wrote to Charmetant from Algiers that the
situation was becoming absolutely intolerable. The Quai d'Orsay
sent more cables to the chargé d'affaires at Rome.[47]

Although Lavigerie and Ambassador Desprez had obtained a Roman
promise that the regular nomination of an apostolic prefect at
Tunis would be delayed indefinitely, Bâcourt worked "in a sense
all contrary, doubtless to please the Capuchins at Rome. Impossible to see more weakness or more ineptness."[48] He hastened the
regular appointment of Fr. Salvatore da Napoli to replace Provisional Prefect Liborio. The Propaganda ordered Salvatore to
take the next boat to Tunis, even though his credentials were
not ready. He arrived in early October with explicit instructions
to steer clear of the Franco-Italian rivalry and to avoid any
demonstration of political sympathy. Lavigerie also returned at
that time. Roustan commented to Barthélemy that, with his usual

strong hand, he expected Lavigerie to put the vicariate in order
quickly. On his first day in Tunis, 10 October, the Capuchins
welcomed Lavigerie "very humbly." Even Liborio "surrendered,"
and he left Tunisia a few weeks later. Lavigerie wrote to Simeoni
on 19 October that relations with the Capuchins were now harmonious because the new prefect, Salvatore, realized that mutual
support was in the Church's interest. At last the Italian clergy
of Tunisia submitted formally to French authority.[49]

As of October 1881 the Apostolic Administrator of Carthage and
Tunis moved his ordinary residence from Algeria to Tunisia so
that, once rid of internal opposition, he might commence building
another French diocese overseas.[50] Lavigerie's blueprint for this
had been provided to French authorities in a memoir of July 1881
entitled "L'Oeuvre de Françisation." It expressed their mutual
concern lest "the Italian clergy preserve the present situation
and remain masters of all the parishes, that is to say, masters
of the moral and religious direction of the whole European population of the Regency." Lavigerie intended to neutralize them by
"restricting their action and their influence by dividing them."
He intended to establish immediately at Tunis a second parish
with borders which included the greater part of the European community, limiting the Capuchin parish merely to the older walled
section (Medina) of the city. In other parts of Tunisia French
priests were to head new parishes gerrymandered away from Capuchin
jurisdictions, and they would preempt all the towns where the
Capuchins were not yet established. Lavigerie urged that the army
maintain French priests as chaplains there on the pretext of
serving medical stations. He suggested the possibility of getting
an order from the Pope directing the admission of French Capuchins
to the community in Tunisia. He stressed the importance of ending
the vicariate's dependence on foreign priests by establishing a
diocesan seminary to train recruits from Algeria and France.[51]

Fr. Salvatore de Napoli complained to his superior general at
Rome in January 1882 about Lavigerie's measures and the chauvinism
to which he attributed them. The apostolic administrator had
taken away the vicariate goods and the cemetery, and the prefect
lamented the inadequacy of the stipends which Lavigerie provided
to maintain the Capuchins in their parishes. Although the community of fifteen retained title to many of their properties, this
financial dependence on Lavigerie enabled him to strengthen his
control. Salvatore stated that his prefecture had no genuine
authority and that, if things did not change, their mission would
whither away. The Capuchins had ceased to be agents of the Italian
consulate, and, indeed, they claimed to be struggling for surviv-
al.[52] Lavigerie considered these complaints to be essentially a
bid for independence, and he responded by refusing to fix the
Capuchins' stipends in the vicariate budget without examining
their conventual books. He pointed out to Cardinal Simeoni the
advisability of their coming to terms, for the support they received from his own purse would die with him. They agreed to submit the dispute to the Propaganda, and the cardinals' conference
of 30 June 1882 assessed the vicariate 7,000 francs as the
Capuchins' annual subsidy. By the end of 1882 Lavigerie reported
to Simeoni their excellent relations.

After Lavigerie's return in October 1881 to take personal control of the vicariate, he began to turn the clergy of Tunisia into
an ally of the French administration. The enemies of the republic
had to seek inspiration from their consulates or the press, with
the exception of one priest whom Lavigerie sent packing within
forty-eight hours for preaching a sermon against France.[53] The
Tunisian "religious protectorate" of 1881, obtained through
Lavigerie's special relationship with the Vatican, completed the
limited advantage which France already enjoyed there by means of
the Eastern Protectorate. Although his elevation to cardinal was

delayed until spring 1882, the coordinated efforts of Lavigerie
and the government obtained the Tunisian appointment by means of
pulling "the cord which it is necessary to touch according to my
knowledge of men."[54] Faced with the implied threat of expelling
the Capuchin congregation and encouraged by the advantages which
Lavigerie's exceptional abilities as a fund-raiser could offer a
mission province, the Curia yielded. Charmetant was the liaison
who worked with Paris officials, and most of the direct pressure
in this well-coordinated program was applied by the French
embassy at Rome. The orchestration was Lavigerie's.

French government officials took great satisfaction in the
establishment of this "religious protectorate." Lavigerie's influence over the European population of Tunisia made their other
tasks easier. It also made him one of the colonial authorities.
The esteem for Lavigerie's patriotism felt by French officials at
Paris and at Tunis, and their respect for his judgment in African
affairs, led them to depend on him more than ever for advice. He
thus acquired an influence in Tunisian policy which went beyond
questions concerning religion and the European population whose
clergy he now headed.

V
Consolidation of the French Regime

April 1881 marked the beginning of Lavigerie's full involvement
with the government of North Africa. His participation in the
establishment of the Tunisian protectorate was crucial during
the following twelve months. Numerous primary and secondary sources
acknowledge in general terms Lavigerie's importance in the formation of Tunisian policy. Government leaders praised his efforts,
critics condemned his preponderance in Tunisia, and local residents sensed his importance in the power structure even if his
decisive role was not apparent nor altogether clear to them. His
greatest contribution was to support the protectorate, for after
Bardo the country needed protection, more than anything else,
from direct rule by French officers and civil servants.

After Jules Ferry sent troops to secure "the key to our Algerian
house,"[1] Lavigerie's presence in Tunisia became vitally important
to the ministers making decisions in Paris. Lavigerie already had
a good rapport with Ferry, Gambetta, and Freycinet, the three men
who served as premiers during the protectorate's first year.
Lavigerie continued to prod them as well as Church officials to
expedite his elevation to cardinal, an aspect of French influence
in the Mediterranean which enjoyed less priority in government
circles than he felt it deserved. Paris officials were groping
for guidelines toward a policy in Tunisia, and Lavigerie supplied
them with detailed memoirs. Most of the decisions reached by
French leaders followed these recommendations. The most important
question of policy was the form of French control. From the beginning of the protectorate Lavigerie argued against annexing the

regency to Algeria. He deserves much of the credit for preserving
the beylical regime against pressure for annexation.

This question of annexation provided some of the ammunition
used by enemies of Jules Ferry. His ministry came under bitter
attack in autumn 1881 for the unforeseen costs and casualties of
the invasion. In the famous "séance tunisienne" of 9 November
Ferry vigorously defended the government's conduct, but he lost
the vote of confidence.[2] Although the succeeding "Ministry of All
the Talents" under Gambetta brought an increase of church-state
tension for two and a half months, Tunisian policy remained the
same. Charmetant had been secretly briefing Gambetta ever since
the spring. The new premier-foreign minister trusted and welcomed
Charmetant even more than had Ferry.[3] When Gambetta's "Grand
Ministry" fell in late January 1882, Lavigerie's old admirer
Freycinet took his second turn as premier and foreign minister.
This change improved French relations with the Vatican, which
gave Lavigerie his red hat in March.

There was a turnover of French diplomatic personnel during
this same period. In February 1882 Baron Alphonse de Courcel left
the political direction of the Foreign Ministry for the embassy
to Berlin.[4] At the same time Théodore Roustan finally quit Tunis
for Washington, in the aftermath of press attacks on his integrity.
Until the arrival in April 1882 of Roustan's successor, a protégé
of Ferry named Paul Cambon,[5] Lavigerie helped the staff of the
French residence at Tunis keep the European community under control.

During the first year of the protectorate Lavigerie provided
a steady French influence within the regency, and a continuity
in the formation of Tunisian policy at Paris. But his position
remained delicate in light of conservative and radical opposition
to the protectorate. Lavigerie fully realized that public disclosure of his role would have a terrible effect on his works all

over the Mediterranean. The men who sought his advice would be
forced to turn against him for fear of being called proclerical.[6]
After the uproar in 1880 following the La Guyenne disclosure the
ministers were too cautious to leave much documentation for such
a relationship. The most important source for this segment of
the protectorate's history therefore consists of the letters between Lavigerie and Charmetant, who reported from Paris faith-
fully on his interviews with Courcel, "the minister," "G[ambetta].,"
and others. The archives of the Ministry of War at Vincennes contain information on the military situation in North Africa which
Lavigerie provided to the Army Intelligence Service for the half-
year while the Tunisian interior underwent military pacification.

Lavigerie deserves considerable credit for the success of the
initial invasion. The Ministry of War benefitted greatly in 1881
from the information supplied by its "secret delegate," the
Archbishop of Algiers. Several years earlier Lavigerie had given
in writing to all his missionaries in North Africa a secret order
"in the name of religion and of patriotism" to make known to the
ministry all that they learned of military conditions and activities against France. This information net, stretching from
Morocco to Tripoli, was to send through him details on German-
supported military preparations in Morocco, French administrative
measures taken in Algeria, agitation among the Berber tribesmen
of Kabylia, and any interesting rumors picked up in Arab markets.[7]

The Army Intelligence Service needed such assistance. The
Italian consul at Tunis, Licurgo Maccio, was working to stir up
the Khroumirs.[8] German agents, posing as archeologists or geographers, kept in touch with the tribes in Morocco, Algeria, and
Tunisia. Bismarck intended to inflame them as a means of neutralizing French troops in the event of another war in Europe. The
French General Staff knew that Tripoli, administered by Turkey,
was a "veritable foyer of revolts in Algeria." Algerians who hoped

to expel the conquerors smuggled weapons and ammunition across
southern Tunisia on a regular basis. In their religious perspective this was not a simple political or cultural conflict between
Arabs and French, but rather a struggle of Muslims against Christians. Only the tribes' "blind and distrustful hatred" of all
Europeans limited the German potential to embarrass France in
North Africa.[9]

On 5 March 1881 the French General Staff assigned Captain
Jean-Conrad Sandherr of the Intelligence Service to determine the
conditions of the tribes in Tunisia and the activities of Italian,
German, or British agents there. In the greatest secrecy Sandherr
asked a mutual friend, the deputy Emile Keller, to take him to
Charmetant in order to enlist the help of North African priests.
Charmetant told Sandherr that none would help him without
Lavigerie's instructions; therefore his first step should be go
to the archbishop at Algiers. Charmetant also recommended he pose
as an archeologist when travelling around the tribes. Lavigerie
told Sandherr that he was "happy to contribute to the success of
[such] a mission" on condition that the missionaries' participation in it never be revealed. Sandherr emphasized this in one of
his reports: "It would be very grievous if their patriotism worked
against them."[10]

During the spring Sandherr travelled around North Africa setting up an intelligence net among merchants, courtiers of the bey,
Italian spies willing to be double agents, and the clergy. At
Kairouan he recruited an old French Trappist. "Furthermore, for
Kabylia, Carthage, Tripoli, Goulette, etc., the Missionaries of
Africa."[11] He stopped at Saint-Louis de Carthage in April to re-
ceive information first hand. Lavigerie later scolded Fr. Bresson
for making a very inadequate report, and he became more conscien-
tious. In June Bresson reported to Sandherr that the mood of the
Tunisian population in the north was good toward the French, and

that the source of agitation in the south was in Tripoli.
Fr. Deguerry reported information concerning the mood of tribes
through which he had passed, a particular matter of concern to
the French.[12]

Lavigerie continued to supply advice directly to Paris. On
the eve of the French invasion he sent letters through Charmetant
to the officials immediately concerned. He summarized the facts
for the government in a "Note on the Situation of Native Morale
in North Africa." Many Algerians, particularly the Kabyles, did
not believe that the French had lost patience with the bey's inability to maintain order on the Tunisian border. Much of the
inspiration for native sabotage in Algeria came by way of Morocco.
Italy had little part in this, but Germany financed it with
Spanish cooperation; the German consul general at Algiers worked
secretly through Arabs who had been squeezed out of their jobs
by the civil administration. One half million warlike men in
Kabylia made the French position extremely vulnerable in the event
of military complications in Tunisia. Lavigerie made specific
remarks concerning personnel changes in the military administration of Kabylia.[13] Changes were necessary, for the Kabyles were
"superexcited." Colons had taken their best land, and they feared
losing the rest of it.[14] Military and civil administrators placed
in charge of them lacked prestige. On 1 May Lavigerie advised
that the Algerians' insolence would continue until the taking of
Tunis and the surrender of the bey. Thereafter the cinders of resentment would burn under a calm surface.[15] These precise and
detailed reports made a strong impression on Courcel, who told
Charmetant, "We need men like Mgr. Lavigerie for ambassadors.
What firmness and what ability in that man!"[16]

Lavigerie's advice drew an even warmer response from the prime
minister. "There are truly two persons in that man," said Ferry
in reference to the archbishop.[17] Charmetant communicated secretly

with Gambetta, whose influence in the government was equal to a
minister's even without the title. Gambetta told Charmetant in
late March that "no one was as competent as [Lavigerie] in what
concerns French interests in the Mediterranean basin."[18] A month
later Courcel at the Foreign Ministry expressed again his admiration of Lavigerie's knowledge of North Africa. He asked Charmetant
to lend him the archbishop's recent letter of 24 April to show
to the minister. The Quai d'Orsay made a copy of this detailed
report on conditions in Tunisia.[19]

The French leaders were particularly struck by Lavigerie's
estimate of the threat posed by Kheredine,[20] the Circassian-born
former prime minister (1873-77). When he was in power, enemies
who felt threatened by him told Muhammad es Sadok that Kheredine's
aim was to take over the regency. After Kheredine's fall from
power and return to Constantinople, many Tunisians still admired
his honesty and idealism.[21] Throughout 1881 Lavigerie warned of
the danger which Kheredine still posed to French power in North
Africa. Yet Lavigerie counselled the Quai d'Orsay during the April
invasion that Kheredine's ambition could serve French interests
to the extent that it terrified the bey, his brothers, and
nephews.[22] Exploiting Sadok's fear of being replaced by Kheredine
or by another member of the dynasty was the means of making the
beylical regime an instrument of French power. This was an argument Lavigerie used in addressing the most important issue of
Tunisian policy, which concerned the form of French control.

For several years after Bardo French officers, civil servants,
and politicians argued over the alternatives of direct annexation
of Tunisia as opposed to indirect rule through a protectorate
regime. The original concept of the protectorate is attributed
by various sources to the ancient Greeks and Romans, to the
British policy in India, and to the Toul-Metz-Verdun provisions
of the 1559 Treaty of Cateau-Cambrésis.[23] Lavigerie became one

of the protectorate's strongest advocates. Yet the treaty drafted
for Sadok's signature in 1881 did not specifically use the word.
During the year immediately following the bey's surrender the form
of the regency's administration had to be devised. Lavigerie's
suggestions to Paris regarding a French regime for Tunisia had
not been consistent during the 1870s; but the Third Republic's
anticlerical program brought the issue into clearer focus in the
1880s, as he explained to Charmetant: "From the Catholic point
of view, we have no little interest in preventing annexation to
France in the present circumstances. Annexation would be, in
fact, the forcible application to the Church in Tunisia of the
laws and rule of France, and consequently, persecution. The present state [in 1885] is absolute liberty for all our works, such
as it exists in all the Muslim states of the Mediterranean
basin."[24]

Lavigerie used other arguments for maintaining a protectorate
in the letter of 24 April 1881 which Charmetant showed at the
Quai d'Orsay. In order to soften the effect of French power on
the Arab population it should be concealed behind a beylical
figurehead. The bey and his two brothers feared one another as
well as the former prime minister, Kheredine. Lavigerie was con-
fident that Sadok, a man "enervated by every debauchery," could
be intimidated to accept whatever Roustan imposed. Ali Bey and
Taib Bey "are both equally incapable, equally ignorant, thinking
only of guarding their goods and their life, perpetually menaced
even by their brother."[25] Fear of one another would make the
three of them pliable instruments of French control.

For the rest of his life Lavigerie opposed annexation of Tunisia
until such time as the population had been assimilated under the
protectorate.[26] In recommending this to the government Lavigerie
emphasized his expectation - not merely the possibility - that

the European situation would soon be liquidated by a war.
Imposition of a Christian regime on fanatical Muslims would provoke a holy war at the first moment of an attack on France.
Holding down the expanse of territory between Morocco and Tripoli
would require 250,000 troops. Lavigerie considered it folly to
annex a territory only at the risk of losing it in the next war,
probably along with Algeria. With promises of munitions from
France's enemies, the tribesmen of Algeria were waiting for the
opportunity to "throw us into the sea. . . . They say that
M. Bismarck does not oppose our taking Tunisia completely. Knowing what I know and in his place I would certainly do as he is
doing. In the case of a second war he could not prepare for us
a more disastrous diversion and embarrassment."[27] France's vul-
nerability in North Africa terrified Lavigerie at times, although
he exploited it in order to maintain the sanctuary which the
Tunisian protectorate provided for Catholic congregations.

Lavigerie also suggested administrative and economic reasons
for keeping the protectorate. Annexation would put Tunisia under
the Ministry of War, the regime least conducive to liberty. "It
is, in fact, liberty alone which can make a fecund and prosperous
colony. It is only in calling upon private initiative and in
letting that initiative develop freely that one can arrive at
satisfying results in practice."[28] The regency must be populated
with industrious Frenchmen eager to till the soil and enrich the
land, not with starvelings, ambitious officers, and cadres of
civil servants, as in Algeria. Lavigerie realized that outright
annexation would result in the same type of military excesses
and exploitation of the natives which he had opposed in Algeria.
From the start of the 1881 invasion he argued for maintaining the
beylical government closely controlled by French officials. He
reiterated this conviction in 1882 when Sadok Bey lay dying, and

in the mid-eighties when General Georges Boulanger led an annexa-
tionist movement on the part of careerist officers and civil
servants in Tunisia.

Paris officials required more than a year after Bardo to settle the many administrative details of French control, and the
army in Tunisia spent a half year defeating armed resistance to
it. Lavigerie expressed to Charmetant his estimate of the military
leadership displayed during the spring: "The campaign of Tunisia
is very badly conducted. - It is a real muddle from the military
point of view. - Let us hope that the policy will be better. The
symptoms of the next insurrection in Algeria increase each day.
It is important to finish this quickly and wisely."[29] By mid-June
1881 Fr. Deguerry reported to Sandherr that in Algeria "the missionaries of Kabylia no longer have apprehension of the eventual-
ity of a Kabylian insurrection."[30] But in late June the Tunisians
revolted at Sfax and other points on the southeast coast. The
bey's surrender to the invaders had provided a pretext for rebellion also on the part of nomadic tribes in the south, where his
authority was scarcely recognized. Lavigerie informed Captain
Sandherr in early July that "Kheredine is the spirit of the insurrection movement of the South Coast, where he has numerous
creatures."[31]

Nine days later Lavigerie again warned Sandherr:

> We find ourselves in the presence of a double conspir-
> acy, Turkish and Italian. General Kheredine's influ-
> ence gains more ground every day. Kheredine's dream,
> as I have wired you, would be the reestablishment,
> to his profit, of the Califate of North Africa and
> Arabia [sic], while awaiting the fall of the Ottomans.
> Although a freethinker basically, Kheredine arouses
> Muslim fanaticism, as seen even by his book on Islam
> and its role. He wants to pass for the most fanatical

of all the Muslim princes, and thus arrive at his ends.
His plan is to have the Sultan cede him the Pashalicate
of Tripoli for money. From there, he will give a hand
to the insurrectional government of the Southeast
Coast of Tunisia, and begin by chasing us from Tunisia.
By his instigation the Sultan would send Turkish troops
to Tripoli.[32]

But French diplomatic pressure during July and August blocked
Turkish military measures in Tripoli.[33] The French National
Assembly was in session during these events, and the Chambers
did not protest the Ferry government's decision to send reinforce-
ments. Before the end of the year a total of 50,000 troops from
France and Algeria were needed to impose the bey's authority on
the insurgents. The French navy bombarded Sfax into submission
on 10 July, and within a few days Gabès and the island of Djerba
gave up.[34]

The real problem was in the interior and in the south.
Kairouan, one of the holiest cities in Islam, was the key to
breaking this resistance in the interior. Commandant Breton explained the French army's task to a fellow officer in a letter of
11 October: the attack on Kairouan must spare its Muslim shrines.
For if the French outraged the religious sensibilities of the
people, they risked provoking a campaign of assassinations at
Tunis, and a holy war throughout the country which would tie down
French troops forever. The immediate task was to appease the
country and maintain the bey under French protection.[35]

Lavigerie sent to Paris his own lengthy assessment of the situation on the same day as Breton's, just after returning to
Tunisia.

I persist in thinking that everything which has gone
wrong in this country is the fault of the military

authority. The chiefs lack capacity, vigor, and initiative; the soldiers have no morale. As a result, everything gets snarled, measures are not taken in time,
generals lose their heads, and irreparable harm
follows. . . .

No one seems to me to understand fully the essential
difference which exists between the two indigenous
populations which people Tunisia. For there are here,
as in Algeria, two quite distinct populations: the
Moors, who are fixed to the soil by commerce in the
cities and by agriculture in the countryside, and the
nomads or Bedouins. The Moors are peaceable, in general
scarcely fanatic; and they all desire peace, because
they can only lose by a war. The nomads, or Bedouins,
are fanatic, plundering, and cruel; consequently they
all desire war, especially civil war, because they
have everything to gain by it. That is the secret of
the strange anomalies . . . of the Tunisian situation.
Our generals here do not seem to me to understand it.

Their objective is Kairouan, and they are right
from one point of view, that of terrifying Muslim believers who imagine that our cannons will be rendered
powerless against the walls of the holy city by the
very hand of Muhammad. But they are wrong in making
it their single objective. The inhabitants of Kairouan,
like those of Tunis, do not want war, they are under
the yoke of nomads or Bedouins who terrorize them and
dominate them under the pretext of religion. Thus,
when Kairouan is taken, which will happen the same
day we appear before its walls, the population of the
city, which is inoffensive, will remain there, and
the nomads will leave to rally the tribes of the

north and south and to pillage a little everywhere
they can.

If I were general-in-chief, I would make only a
token demonstration on Kairouan, and as soon as the
city was taken I would quickly direct the attack columns on the points where the nomads plan to carry out
insurrection. What is necessary, in fact, is to find
one's obvious enemy, surround him, overwhelm him, and
to finish it up with terror.

For that, one must have, starting from today, an
internal espionage service capable of fully informing
our military chiefs of the insurgents' intentions.

But that does not exist, and for me, an old African
who has thoroughly studied our wars in Algeria, particularly those of [Marshal] Bugeaud, everything I see
grieves me.[36]

But the tribal resistance soon collapsed. Kairouan surrendered
in late October, a victory for which Lavigerie celebrated a solemn
Te Deum at Carthage. Only a few towns remained to be conquered in
November, although brigands still roamed the countryside. By December Sandherr reported to the General Staff that there remained
only "questions of submission, contributions, personnel, convoys,
etc."[37]

At that point the more serious threat to French mastery over
Tunisia came from radical and conservative journals in France.
After the opportunists' election gains of August, Ferry and
Gambetta between them temporarily controlled the new Chamber
better than their critics in the press. The opposition denounced
the Tunisian seizure for alienating other countries in Europe,
disorganzing the army, and duplicating the Mexican fiasco of the
1860s. Ferry's stealth came under attack in the Chamber. In late
October, after two weeks spent pacifying the Tunisian clergy,

Lavigerie told Roustan of the deplorable effect produced by recent controversy in France. Just when he had obtained the
Capuchins' complete submission, the mistaken hope of French dis-
engagement stirred them up again. "They [critics in the Chamber]
have done more against us in eight days than the Arabs in six
months."[38] Many Catholic conservatives rivaled the radicals in
denouncing the Tunisian venture. The former opposed imperial expansion as undercutting the cause of recovering Alsace-Lorraine.[39]

On the other hand, some Catholic journals supported the Tunisian
venture, and Lavigerie had much to do with reinforcing Catholic
support for the government's policy. Le Français and L'Univers
welcomed the news of Bardo, noting the enhancement of French prestige. C. Alfred Perkins's very thorough study, "French Catholic
Opinion and Imperial Expansion, 1880-1886," indicates that although nationalistic considerations and a vague sense of economic
advantage ranked ahead of missionary concerns among Catholic lay-
men, "the work of Lavigerie reinforced a favorable attitude in
those who were already tending to accept expansion." The Archbishop of Algiers confronted pious monarchists with the basic
dilemma of weighing the Church's missionary commitment against
their conception of French Catholicism's domestic interests. Many
conservatives maintained strong feelings against the government's
policy, but they were not influential on the mass of French
Catholics. Perkins's examination of the Semaines religieuses
yields no evidence of opposition on the diocesan or parish level.
To a great extent Lavigerie turned Catholic opinion around by
identifying the government's policy with the earlier Tunisian expedition of St. Louis.[40]

But nothing could mollify the radicals. Their attacks upon the
opportunist majority did particular damage to the authority of
Roustan. The radical press harped on financial scandal and narrow

motives of interest. In the 27 September edition of <u>L'Intransigeant</u>,
Henri de Rochefort accused Gambetta and Roustan of making a 100
million-franc profit on the exchange. Many lesser opportunists
and hangers-on, indeed, had become rich in the affair. Shortly
thereafter the Algerian press accused Lavigerie himself of "cor-
nering Tunisian land by clericalism." But all of these accusations
against higher officials were libelous; the Ferry government insisted on vindicating Roustan's name - and its own policy - by
bringing a suit against Rochefort. The sensational three-day
trial in December was the scene of much disorder and noise which
quite obscured the truth. Camille Pelletan charged: "There has
been a payoff, Your Honor!" Newsboys hawked the edition reporting
Rochefort's acquittal with cries of "Roustan's condemnation!"
The verdict had a demoralizing effect within Tunisia, again encouraging Britain and Italy to renew their resistance to the
French.[41]

This compounded the task of consolidating military control
over the country. Even after the surrender of Kairouan, the French
faced many problems; and Lavigerie accepted Courcel's invitation
to offer confidential advice directly. A letter of 5 November
discussed the problem of the desert nomads, "a population absolutely abandoned to its instincts of savage war and pillage."[42]
Lavigerie forthrightly stated that only the collaboration of
people in the bey's entourage or the consular corps could explain
the shrewdness and efficient coordination of their guerilla campaign. Tunis was in chaos. Lavigerie advocated a tough policy and
recommended that the insurrection would not subside until after
"two or three terrible lessons." French authorities should not
think merely of capturing hit-and-run insurgents, but rather the
army must attack in force the depots of their wealth. Otherwise
French troops were striking in a void like "Don Quixotes running

after windmills." Lavigerie considered the indemnity suggested
for the rebels of Sfax to be ridiculously low, and he recommended
20 million francs in two annuities.

> What I say of Sfax, I say in the same proportion of
> Kairouan. There too, since one can not give an armed
> lesson because of our adversaries' ruses, it is neces-
> sary to give one <u>merciless on the rebels' property</u>,
> or on that of all who are joined with them. . . . Such
> rigor is, in my eyes, a political necessity of the
> first order for the Government of the French Republic.
> If it does not employ it, this will contribute con-
> sciously to prolonging the war and sacrifices of every
> type, those of blood and of soldiers especially. If
> on the contrary, it is severe in its justice, [the
> enemy] will fear it, will hesitate, and will stop.[43]

Lavigerie suggested that confiscating the properties of Sfax
and Kairouan by a beylical decree and then forcing their residents
to ransom them for one-quarter of their value would have a sober-
ing effect on the desert insurgents who drew upon this wealth.
At the same time it would yield more than the 1.5 million francs
needed by the Financial Commission to pay the January coupon on
the bey's debt. France could also double the civil list of
Muhammad es Sadok, who was concerned principally with continuing
his "material life." This would "link his fortune to ours." The
levy of contributions of war offered the means of saving the
beylic from a default which British and Italian bondholders would
otherwise blame on France.[44]

Four days after the date of this letter the Ferry cabinet fell.
Léon Gambetta took the portfolio of foreign affairs on 14 November
in his own "Grand Ministry." He sent a dispatch to Roustan four
days later expressing displeasure that the Sfax indemnity was not

yet paid, especially in view of the fact that the assessment was much lower than that suggested by others. His emphasis on the importance of the Sfax and Kairouan contributions in saving the regency from bankruptcy indicates that he had just read Lavigerie's memoir.[45] Roustan replied the following day, proposing to collect an immediate indemnity of 6 million francs from the Sfaxians on account, leaving the ultimate figure to be set later.[46] The government fixed the first day of February 1882 as the deadline for the Sfaxians to pay this amount.[47] All of their efforts to obtain it through mortgaging their property failed, and the government was unable to induce the cooperation of French banks for fear of more charges of cabinet corruption. The severe terms offered by Maltese banks would have resulted in the acquisition of many properties by foreigners.[48] The Sfaxians turned to Lavigerie as a mediator.

The authorities were vitally concerned about the Sfaxians' difficulty in arranging a loan with French bankers, for a Maltese or British mortgage would undoubtedly result in some defaults and foreclosures. In order to prevent further economic penetration of Tunisia by British interests, the French were determined to block such a loan. But Lavigerie informed Roustan on good authority in mid-February that if the bey forbade a pending deal with the Egyptian Bank Company as being objectionable to the French, London would make it an "object of conflict." Her Majesty's Government had consented to the French siezure of Tunisia on the premise that no British interest would be injured, and the interest rate in question was twelve percent. Lavigerie noted that the only alternative was for one of the big French houses to match the proposal, and this took time. These difficulties had led French authorities in January to postpone the deadline for paying the 6 million francs, although shrewd timing of the announcement deceived the Sfaxians with regard to the precise reason.[49]

Delegations from the town had pleaded with Roustan to ease the
terms, and they turned desperately to Lavigerie during his January tour of the coast. When he landed at the dock, the Arabs
pressed around him begging his help for the family heads held
hostage for payment. Before he would speak, the archbishop insisted
they assemble in the church. Standing before the altar dressed
in his pontifical vestments, he told the Arabs that they must re-
pent and swear submission to France before he could obtain relief.
Accepting these terms, they cheered him as their deliverer and
celebrated through the night. The following day they unharnessed
the carriage which took him back to his naval vessel and pulled
it through the streets of Sfax. In Goyau's words: "A few minutes
in a church had been sufficient for him to establish the sovereignty of France in that corner of the earth."[50]

The term coexisting sovereignties is perhaps a more accurate
description of the nature of French authority in Tunisia.[51] During
Gambetta's ten weeks in power he depended greatly on Lavigerie's
advice for organizing it. Gambetta faced military pressure to
depose the bey; the generals pleaded to be relieved of guarding
Sadok's throne. At the end of seven months in Tunisia 2,000 French
soldiers were dead. But Lavigerie pointed out that after France
deposed the dey in Algeria, pacification had required eighteen
years and cost 150,000 lives. Notwithstanding criticism in the
Chamber and the grumbling of ambitious officers, Lavigerie maintained that the Muslim regime would serve France well, once it
was purged of all troublemakers.[52] Gambetta welcomed Lavigerie's
reports "On the Persons to Retain or to Discard in Tunisia,"
"On the Repayment of the Tunisian Debt," and on other questions.
Gambetta stated later, "I was never better informed on Algerian
and Tunisian affairs than by my conversations with Fr. Charmetant."[53]

The prime minister received Charmetant on 2 December and referred to his discourse of the previous day as evidence of his

increasing agreement with Lavigerie's views on Tunisia. He requested more confidential advice concerning North Africa, and he
praised the work of the White Fathers overseas.[54] Two weeks later
the prime minister informed Charmetant of a decision: "The
Tunisian organization, such as the Archbishop of Algiers under-
stands it, is admitted in principle. But that is a complete edifice which can only be raised a little later, for its execution
raises practical difficulties now which must be turned or ironed
out." The foundation had to be built first, and Gambetta had to
protect himself against public attack. But he considered the
Tunisian question urgent, and he asked Charmetant to get further
details from Lavigerie on implementing his suggestions. Since
Courcel, the political director of the Foreign Ministry, was
moving to Berlin, Gambetta asked Charmetant to report directly
to him in secret.[55]

On 24 December Lavigerie wrote Gambetta, "My Dear Friend," a
long letter detailing his proposals for the French regime. The
first suggestion was the establishment of a protectorate council
of those who represented the action or authority of France in
Tunisia. This group should report to the Budget Commission of the
Chamber. Lavigerie emphasized the importance of keeping the
meetings of both committees in confidence, rather than allowing
members to leak their remarks to the press. The personnel of the
beylical government was a particularly important topic for the
council's attention.[56]

Lavigerie stated his opinion that the French had made a mistake
by including Article Four in the Treaty of Bardo, which promised
to respect Tunisia's previous engagements with other countries.
This provision saddled the French with the International Financial
Commission and with the capitulations, treaties which exempted
foreigners in Tunisia from beylical justice. Britain and Italy
had a "fortress against us" in the Financial Commission, which

managed the bey's customs; and possession of Tunisian bonds by
foreigners was an obstacle to French mastery of the country. A
French guarantee of interest on the bey's debt was necessary in
order for him to redeem the bonds, as well as to get rid of the
Financial Commission. Only then could France put the protectorate's
finances in order. The capitulations gave European consuls at
Tunis "all the attributes of governmental power." The Italian and
British consulates claimed 40,000 and 25,000 protégés, respectively, including those naturalized. "Their subjects laugh at
everything, even military laws."[57] The jurisdiction claimed by
the consular tribunals had the potential to shackle the Tunisian
government. Lavigerie stated that the bey's government should
renounce the capitulations, which had lost their reason for being
since the protectorate. France should coordinate this step at a
moment when the European powers were embarrassed in some matter
where they needed French support.

Lavigerie recommended reducing the number of French troops
gradually and establishing Muslim troops alongside them, as in
Algeria, with mobile forces for use against revolts. With regard
to the distribution of land, Lavigerie recommended that laws be
decreed by the bey guaranteeing property security, in order to
induce French mortgage bankers to enter Tunisia. Other than confiscation, which had been a disaster in Algeria, this was the only
means of getting native land into European circulation quickly.
But the French must prevent any fraud! Concerning the bey's government itself, it was necessary to gather political power in
French hands while compensating the bey and his officials with
an honorary position. "Thus, in the measure that one retires them
from the reality of power, it is necessary to augment their revenues."[58] Lavigerie told Gambetta that financial reforms would
provide the money needed for that.

This letter of 24 December 1881 outlined the basic program
begun by Théodore Roustan and continued by his successor during
the next few years. Following Lavigerie's suggestion, the Council
of the Protectorate was soon established on a permanent basis to
formulate policy under the resident minister's coordination. But
Lavigerie was not able to obtain an appointment on the council
for himself. The decree establishing a similar council in Algeria
ten years earlier had given the archbishop a place at the governor
general's right, but in 1881 the monarchists no longer governed
France. Lavigerie's participation was limited, officially, to
sessions dealing with questions of public instruction. Officials
at Paris tried to soften the blow by expressing to Charmetant
their esteem for Lavigerie: other members would sit on the Protectorate Council ex officio, he because of his personal competence.
In other words, the apostolic administrator's welcome there would
not extend to his successor. Roustan was to be instructed to call
Lavigerie to the sessions. The French government preferred to
shape the protectorate regime by means of simple ministerial instructions, essentially subject to modification, rather than by
formal decrees. This allowed flexibility for gradual change in
the regime, and it protected the government somewhat against interpellation in the legislature and from attack by the press.
These explanations for Lavigerie's exclusion from the Protectorate
Council were calculated to ease his chagrin. Outwardly, Lavigerie
accepted this encounter with force majeure. He later publicly
expressed a preference to remain in the background, and his exclusion from the council was never an obstacle to his influence.[59]

Lavigerie had his private channel of communication with the
French government, and he used it to advise Gambetta on the ques-
tion of finding a new resident minister for Tunisia. Théodore
Roustan had been so much discredited by the calumnies repeated

during the libel suit against Rochefort that he decided at first
not to return to Tunis. A letter written the week before Christmas to "My Dear Friend" stated Lavigerie's assessment of that
problem: "There were weaknesses of private life, [but] there was
nothing of foundation in the attacks addressed to the public
man. . . . M. Roustan has been a useful and intrepid agent of
France, full of patriotism, and, if I may venture to say, of a
daring attitude which is always excellent abroad."[60] Permitting
Roustan to be baited into a "press trial" had been the "grave . . .
political . . . fault" of Ferry's foreign minister, Barthélemy.
"One should have known in advance that Mme Elias would figure in
it. With such a scandal we are truly delivered to beasts at Tunis.
. . . Our enemies triumph. The British, the Italians are naturally
without pity. General Japy and M. Lequeux, our provisional consul,
told me yesterday that they almost do not dare show themselves in
the street in the presence of the insulting manner which the foreign population shows in their face."[61]

Lavigerie urged the government to evidence its determination
by appointing a worthy successor to carry on Roustan's work. He
recommended a capable general familiar with Africa, or else a
prominent civilian whose appointment would not be interpreted as
a hesitation in policy. He must be married! "The milieu of Tunis
does not accommodate bachelors; it is very corrupt, absolutely
dishonest, and there is not a woman in the city who would not be
ready to play the role of Mme Elias the minute a Minister of
France let himself respond to her advances." The French directors
at Tunis needed a first lady to preside over their social life,
for they were all bachelors and had no place to gather but in the
salons of France's enemies. Lavigerie felt a successor must be
named quickly,[62] but Gambetta wanted Roustan to continue, at least
for a while. "I do not want nor need to sacrifice him."[63] Roustan
returned to Tunis until February. Gambetta told Charmetant he

intended to remove Roustan with a promotion, and that took time
to arrange.[64]

The mutual respect and confidence between Gambetta and Lavigerie
contributed greatly to the formation of French policy for the
protectorate. Gambetta valued Lavigerie's development of a French
clergy in Tunisia. The premier and foreign minister expressed to
Fr. Charmetant his feelings toward Catholicism overseas: "The more
I study the religious question, the more I assert that it does not
at all resemble in the West what it is in the East. . . . Everything which benefits Catholicism in those countries, benefits
directly the interests of France."[65] But despite this fundamental
harmony abroad, the continuing church-state tension within France
retarded Lavigerie's program in Tunisia to the extent that it delayed his elevation to the cardinalate. During 1881 the Vatican
had supported French interests in Tunisia as much as one could
ask. Indeed, the Holy See had borne some of the onus of responsibility for events there before the court of public opinion. But
while praising the merits of France's candidate for the Sacred
College, the Pope refused to set a date for the consistory.[66]

The inclusion of Paul Bert in Gambetta's cabinet stalled
Lavigerie's promotion to the Sacred College. Lavigerie continued
to apply pressure on personnel at the French embassy to the Holy
See, as well as on officials in Paris. In mobilizing support for
his cause, he used every argument he could contrive to prod the
government, which itself became irritated at this obstacle to the
career of its most useful bishop. Charmetant expressed to Courcel
in late November the fear that Rome would let the candidacy lapse.
He noted the political director's astonishment at the suggestion
of such "an act of gratuitous malevolence and almost aggression
against our side."[67] Charmetant showed Gambetta Lavigerie's letter
of 21 November, which mentioned the danger that an open break with
Paris would lead the Vatican to replace the provisional Apostolic

Administrator of Tunis with an Italian. The prime minister replied:
"The [religious] question will, indeed, become grave if the Holy
See takes from [Lavigerie] the administration of Tunisia at the
moment when, more than ever, we are decided to remain there. The
presence of Mgr. Lavigerie is necessary there especially now, and
I understand the necessity of getting for him a grander situation
as cardinal, if that is possible."[68]

The nuncio, Mgr. Czacki, had repeatedly assured Lavigerie of
his support, but in December Lavigerie learned from a source in
Rome that Czacki was using his candidacy as a lever against the
anticlerical regime of Gambetta and the cults minister, Paul Bert.
"The more he thinks the government wants it or needs it for
Tunisia, the more he insists that [Rome], without refusing, give
no official response. . . . I am a hostage."[69] The self-styled
"servant of a Master Whom they could never lock up in a tomb"[70]
was momentarily helpless, blocked by the hard line of the nuncio
to Paris despite the government's efforts on his behalf. This
ecclesiastical waiting game continued for the brief duration of
the Gambetta cabinet.

Gambetta neglected Lavigerie's promotion during the first half
of January 1882, immersing himself totally in preparations for
reforming the constitution. The French Chamber of Deputies balked
at the reforms proposed by the government, which fell at the end
of the month. After Gambetta's fall (and Paul Bert's departure
from the Ministry of Cults) the Vatican relented. The new premier
and foreign minister was Charles de Freycinet, whose first cabinet had proposed Lavigerie's elevation to the Sacred College a
year and a half earlier. Ambassador Desprez wired on 4 March no-
tifying the government that the Holy See awaited one French nomination for the Sacred College.[71]

Lavigerie's elevation had its greatest benefit in Tunisia.
Roustan had gone back to Paris in February for consultations

before assuming his new post as minister to Washington.[72] His
successor at Tunis, Paul Cambon, remained in France for personal
business and consultations until April. During that interval
Lavigerie was the steadiest supporter of the French regime among
the European population of the regency. Once Roustan was gone,
Thomas Reade, the Italian chargé Raibaudi-Massiglia, and their
Spanish colleague, de Rameau, provoked a "consular outburst"
regarding Lavigerie's proposal to remove the Catholic cemetery
from the center of Tunis. The Freemasons and the Italian chargé
opposed placing the new cemetery outside the city limits, and
L'Avvenire di Sardegna objected that its graves would be exposed
to desecration by Arab fanatics. Lavigerie wrote Roustan of what
had happened: "De Rameau topped it off by challenging my authority
to order or forbid prayers in the cemetery. The consuls have tried
to stir up the population. Raibaudi almost succeeded with the
Italians, but the Maltese stuck by me, almost too much. All is in
order."[73] Lavigerie weathered the storm without the backing of
the French resident, for Cambon did not land at Tunis until
2 April.

This support provided by the Maltese subjects of the British
crown was the key to obtaining the acquiescence of other Europeans
to the French regime. These devout people were the second largest
European group in Tunisia. Lavigerie's Maltese policy succeeded
in isolating the Italians and reducing their opposition to French
rule. At the start of the protectorate the Italians outnumbered
the French more than ten to one. In particular, the wealth and
cohesiveness of the Livournais made this Jewish bourgeoisie a
source of serious resistance at first. By their ties with the
Italian consulate they were capable of stirring up the hostile
Sicilian community. But the Livournais relented after it became
obvious that their businesses would benefit from the French establishment of order, commercial infrastructure, and public works.

The key to neutralizing Catholic Italians was Lavigerie's Maltese
policy. After suppressing the open opposition of the Capuchins,
Lavigerie won the Maltese by treating them with courteous consideration and by cultivating their personal respect. Much to
Roustan's surprise, Maltese support for their new religious leader
was smoothly transferred to the French regime which stood behind
him. Roustan commented to Gambetta on 7 January that their devotion was almost as great as their fanaticism. "One would have to
be familiar with the land to appreciate this result."[74]

The commander of the Naval Division of the Levant testified to
the success of the Maltese policy in his February report to the
minister of navy and colonies. Admiral Conrad stated that, inasmuch as the principal obstacle to French control resided more in
foreign elements than in the Tunisians themselves, the greatest
support the republic had was in the Catholic influence of a man
like Lavigerie. He possessed the power to erode gradually the resentment of the Italians by the confidence which he inspired in
the Maltese, "a community less rich and intelligent, but more
fanatical and more numerous." Although he believed that only the
continued maintenance of troops in the regency would convince
adversaries that the protectorate was permanent, Conrad emphasized
that the Catholic influence begun by Lavigerie must be extended
by means of French schools for all nationalities. He stressed
that an accord between the political and the religious power in
Tunisia was indispensable.[75]

The navy willingly gave Lavigerie the use of a vessel for his
episcopal tours of the eastern coast. The enthusiasm of the
Maltese always covered the coldness of the Italians. At Nabeul,
Sousse, Monastir, Mahdia, and Sfax, the ceremony was the same.
From the port the townspeople would follow Lavigerie to the local
church to receive a sermon in Italian, the announcement of a new
school, and alms for the poor - always including the Muslims.

His Capuchin companion, Fr. Felice, translated the sermon into
Maltese. Lavigerie's majestic bearing made a tremendous impression
on these people, and Admiral Conrad recommended that the best
agents for gaining their loyalty were priests and nuns. He expected that Lavigerie would recruit priests for Tunisia in Malta and
set up a seminary there to train them. He cited Fr. Felice for
having a particularly helpful effect all along the coast, where
many townspeople, Catholics in name only, had not seen a priest
in ages. Conrad was very optimistic regarding the prospect of
winning the Maltese over to the French as a counter to the Italians.[76]

Lavigerie's reorganization of the vicariate's clergy implemented this policy. He increased the number of Maltese in the
Capuchin community, and he balanced the three French members of
the new diocesan council of temporal administration with two
Maltese, two Italians, and one Belgian. After Queen Victoria
escaped an assassination attempt in March, Lavigerie had a Te Deum
sung on the first Sunday of April in thanks for her deliverance.
The Maltese crowded the provisional cathedral to hear his litany
of praises for the domestic virtues of their queen. His own popularity soared.

The formalities of Lavigerie's elevation to cardinal occasioned
more demonstrations at Tunis and Malta. After receiving official
notification of his appointment in March, Lavigerie awaited a
pontifical noble guard which was to bring the zucchetto to Saint-
Louis de Carthage on 16 April. He was apprehensive lest more high
ceremony provoke resentment among the Italians. After the presentation Lavigerie's entourage started for festivities at Tunis.
The driver, who had already celebrated too much, ran the carriage
into the mud, forcing the new cardinal and two of his bishops to
walk there in the rain. This did not dampen the Maltese waiting
at Tunis, who demonstrated such enthusiasm that the French

government resented their upstaging the presentation of the
biretta at Paris.[77] The government refused Lavigerie's request
to send the biretta to him, and since his pleas of ill health
went unheeded he left for France to receive it on 20 May from
the President of the Republic. After the presentation ceremony
at the Elysée, which La Justice ridiculed as a "fête burlesque,"
Lavigerie received the red hat at Rome in the consistory of
3 July.[78]

Lavigerie planned to go home by way of Malta, ostensibly for
the purpose of baptizing several of the black orphans who were
training to return to equatorial Africa as medical missionaries.
Recent attacks by Italian anticlericals had driven Leo XIII to
the point of considering another threat of departure. With the
thought of taking exile in Malta, Leo's parting words were, "Go
see how they will welcome a cardinal."[79]

Most of Malta's 150,000 residents greeted Lavigerie at the
harbor when he landed on 10 July. He had insisted there be no
incident or aspect of politics, although the French sympathies
of the crowd were obvious. This demonstration of his popularity
received wide press coverage in France, and the director of the
consulate reported to the premier and foreign minister the details
of this unofficial visit. Despite the festival's exclusively religious character, no British officials attended the reception,
and they abstained from the public subscription for decorations
and fireworks. The route from the dock to the episcopal palace
was decked with Maltese, French, and papal flags. The enthusiasm
of these Maltese exceeded all Lavigerie's expectations; obviously
it matched his popularity among their compatriots in Tunisia.
British agents continued their efforts to detach the latter from
France, but with little success.[80]

Two years later, when the Holy See regularized the status of
Carthage as an archdiocese, Lavigerie's choice for auxiliary

bishop was the Maltese Capuchin Antonio Buhagiar. For his consecration, precautions were taken against the Italians, but they
remained calm. Buhagiar's countrymen celebrated with fireworks.
Cambon considered the former pastor of Sfax to be "the most intelligent of men," whom he expected to contribute greatly to
French influence. "We must, however, conceal our contentment if
we want to conserve for our instrument an effective force."[81]
Lavigerie's Maltese policy was the indirect means of making the
European population of Tunisia yield to French authority. Its
quick results surpassed all expectations within a year of the
French takeover.

By the time of Paul Cambon's arrival in April 1882 the major
military, administrative, and clerical threats to French control
had been contained or overcome. Most people in Tunisia had only
a vague idea of how greatly Lavigerie contributed to this result,
for he realized the necessity of seeming to be outside of politics.
"I succeed here, by the grace of God; and the sympathies of the
Catholic population are greater each day. The Italian Capuchins
themselves are absolutely won and submitted. But it requires much
reserve and prudence to fill my mission here as I must."[82]

Lavigerie had eyes and ears all over North Africa, and particularly in Tunisia; as a result the authorities valued his advice
and warnings. When Sadok Bey's younger brother Taib was arrested
and scheduled to be transported to the Bardo Palace, Lavigerie
quickly urged Charmetant to have precautions taken for his safety,
lest Sadok and his favorite, Mustapha ben Ismael, poison him in
the custom of the beylical court.[83] Lavigerie depended on
Charmetant's judgment in timing his proposal for arranging for
the elderly bey's successor.[84] Later, when Ali Bey wished to send
his son and heir, Prince Muhammad, on a tour of France, he
broached the idea to Cambon through the cardinal.[85] From the
moment of Cambon's arrival, Lavigerie quickly cultivated with

the new resident general the same fundamental friendship he had
with Roustan. They worked together to complete the definitive
form of the French regime in Tunisia.

During the first year of French control Lavigerie was fortu-
nate that the officials who counted the most in Tunisian
policy - Ferry, Gambetta, Freycinet, Barthélemy, Courcel, Roustan,
and Cambon - all respected and liked him. Lavigerie was the steadiest French influence in Tunisia during the vacancy of the French
residence in February-March 1882. Government officials followed
Lavigerie's recommendations so closely during the year after
Bardo that they found it necessry to conceal this source of advice
during a period of continuing anticlericalism. Certainly he and
Roustan had discussed Tunisian problems in their many conferences,
and undoubtedly Lavigerie's proposals represented Roustan's in-
sight as well as his own. But recommendations from Tunisia were
doubly persuasive when "My Dear Friend" Gambetta and other Paris
officials received them through the archbishop.

VI

Lavigerie, Cambon, and Massicault:
A Preliminary to the *Ralliement*

Conditions overseas eased the partisan tensions which divided
Frenchmen at home. In North Africa French patriots joined together
enthusiastically to advance their influence on foreign and on non-
Christian populations. Lavigerie wanted to encourage within France
the same spirit of cooperation between Catholics and ardent republicans. During the first decade of the Tunisian protectorate he
built a foundation for the French ralliement of 1890.

Lavigerie's work with officials of the protectorate after
Roustan's departure was for the most part harmonious. Tunisia was
an early theater for the talents of two men who later had great
impact on French history. Paul Cambon, at the threshold of one of
the most distinguished careers in the diplomatic service of the
Third Republic, consolidated the work of Théodore Roustan. After
a rapid advancement in administrative posts in France,[1] Cambon
became resident minister at Tunis in 1882. He regularized the
structure of the protectorate administration and put the beylic's
finances in order. Cambon's policy later came under attack from
the commandant of the occupation corps, General Georges Boulanger.
This demagogue exploited the resentment of French officers and
civil servants against Cambon's authority, finally driving him
out of Tunisia in 1886. Although Lavigerie never opposed Boulanger
openly, he and Charmetant supported Cambon discreetly. The third
French resident at Tunis, Justin Massicault, was not Catholic like
Roustan and Cambon, but he cooperated cordially in Lavigerie's
continuing program of diocesan expansion. Despite Massicault's

radical tinge, he developed genuine respect for Lavigerie and
for his contribution to French influence in Tunisia.

Lavigerie stayed in the background of Tunisian politics, although he continued to send his suggestions to Paris, particularly
during Jules Ferry's second ministry (February 1883 to March 1885).
Lavigerie was an early collaborator with Paul Cambon in organizing
the Alliance Française, and he worked for another decade to restrain the Italian community in the protectorate. This drew him
inevitably into the Mediterranean rivalry between France and
Italy, whose relations deteriorated in the late 1880s. By then
Lavigerie had become an international figure, particularly because of his campaign against African slavery. In 1890 he staked
all of this prestige in the attempt to persuade French Catholics
to rally behind their lawful government. His dramatic Toast of
Algiers failed to resolve church-state tension in France, although
his earlier ralliement of the clergy in North Africa had been an
overwhelming success.

Lavigerie's partnership with Paul Cambon began in early 1882,
even before the new resident's arrival in Tunisia. During February
and March, while Cambon discussed his new assignment with officials in the government, Charmetant also worked in Paris to advocate Lavigerie's views. He reported that the new resident had
been touched by Lavigerie's letter of encouragement.[2] Cambon welcomed this moral support, for he realized the challenge ahead of
him. He faced it alone. In contrast to Gambetta, Prime Minister
Freycinet prescribed no definite guidelines. This was more a sign
of indecisiveness than flexibility, for the Freycinet cabinet had
no hard and fast Tunisian policy. Cambon's best guide at Paris
was the advice of his old piston Jules Ferry: "Go, look, propose."
The minister of war, Jean Billot, advised Cambon of the ominous
fact that "all the military are pessimistic because they are not
allowed to treat Tunisia like a conquered country." The

responsibility for organizing Tunisia was his. If he should fail, he would take the blame, for he received no written instructions.[3] Cambon later agreed with Lavigerie's observation that "Freycinet's policy consists of making promises and not keeping them."[4]

Early on 2 April Cambon arrived at La Goulette with two secretaries, Baron d'Estournelles de Constant and M. Bompard.[5] Cambon promptly paid his respects to the bey and then met with Lavigerie for a candid discussion. The cardinal was "affectionate and amusing, adoring Gambetta, speaking ill of Freycinet."[6] Henri Cambon's biography refers to Lavigerie as "an invaluable resource" for his father, and he describes them as close friends with minds running on the same track.[7]

Cambon devoted his first month in Tunisia to preparing recommendations for a report to the government. The major points of his program resembled those which Lavigerie had formulated for Gambetta in his letter of 24 December 1881. Although Cambon considered the beylical debt and finances to be important, he felt that the question of the capitulations was the most urgent. The jurisdiction of the consular tribunals gave other countries the means to paralyze the bey's government. They could refuse to enforce laws of which they did not approve. Cambon knew that in order to persuade Italy and England to abandon the capitulations, and in order to be rid of the International Financial Commission, France would have to guarantee the Tunisian debt. The French Chamber balked at this in 1882, but Cambon anticipated eventual success for his cautious, patient approach.[8]

The bey's failing health led personnel at the French residence to consider the choice of an heir. Lavigerie urged that uncertainty about the succession be avoided by careful planning before Sadok's death. The two obvious candidates were his brothers. Sidi Ali Bey had redeemed his initial hostility to France by leading a group of native troops on patrol with the French army in the interior,

but the younger Taib had only recently been rehabilitated after
internment in the Bardo for plotting against Sadok. Lavigerie
stressed to d'Estournelles the importance of insisting that the
heir accept French control before mounting the throne. Lavigerie
did not want to mix openly in this political question, but he
sent Charmetant a letter to read to Gambetta. He again argued
against the generals' suggestions of annexation: a military regime would require immense sums for administration, antagonize
Britain and Italy, provoke a holy war, and play right into the
hands of Bismarck. Lavigerie recommended maintaining the beylic
under Sidi Ali.[9] Jules Ferry, who among the ministers had the
clearest vision of colonial affairs, also argued against consolidating Tunisia with Algeria. Ali wanted the throne badly enough
to sign a secret treaty accepting the conditions already imposed
by the French on Sadok. The residence reported to Paris on 18
October the doctor's diagnosis of the seventy-year-old diabetic's
condition. Complications of dysentery and syphilis had resulted
in gangrene, and Sadok's end was near.[10]

When it came in late October, Tunisians received the news
with indifference. Paul Combon marked Ali Bey's ascension with a
sort of solemn investiture in the name of the President of the
Republic. Cambon advised Charles Duclerc (premier and foreign
minister, August 1882 to January 1883) of the need to appoint a
Tunisian prime minister with some look of authority in order to
give Ali the appearance of sovereignty. Cambon organized a cabinet
of Muslims to carry out the decrees of the bey proposed by himself. Ali Bey noted his satisfaction: "Without France I would be
a simple pasha at the mercy of the Sultan."[11]

The milestone in Cambon's administration was the La Marsa Convention, which cleared the way for the abolition of the capitulations. The complete failure of the British consul's efforts to
raise local opposition to this latter change was one result of

Lavigerie's influence on the Maltese. The La Marsa Convention
was drafted in Paris, signed by the bey on 8 June 1883, and ratified by the National Assembly ten months later. It defined and
normalized the relationship between France and Tunisia. In return
for financial and administrative reforms in the beylic, the French
government guaranteed the Tunisian debt. This facilitated negotiations with other countries begun in September for abolishing
the capitulations.[12] The British consul tried to rally Maltese
opposition, but Cambon intervened through the cardinal, who passed
the word down to the Maltese Capuchins that this should stop.
Cambon sent his closest assistant, d'Estournelles, to London to
negotiate with the Foreign Office. Over Reade's objections Britian
abandoned the consular jurisdiction as of 1 January 1884. Word of
this reached Tunis in late December, and the Maltese reaction was
indescribable. By 31 December, 300 signatures had been obtained
for an "address," and Lavigerie's priests were collecting more.
Fr. Felice led a crowd of Maltese on New Year's Day to the residence, where they listened to him give a speech and celebrated
the end of the capitulations by kissing Cambon's hands.[13] Cambon
worked during the subsequent year to implement the reforms facilitated by the La Marsa Convention and the abolition of the capitulations. By the end of 1884 the political and administrative
design of the protectorate was almost completed.[14]

Although education had been a less urgent concern, Cambon realized its importance. He asked Lavigerie's help in organizing
an Alliance pour la Propagation de la Langue Française. Its purpose was to Gallicize students beyond the reach of religious
schools. They modelled the Alliance Française after the Alliance
Israélite Universelle, which already conducted an impressive program in the Mediterranean. Gentiles received French instruction at
the Alliance Israélite's three schools in Tunisia, and the Quai
d'Orsay gave the organization small subsidies, but its confessional

character kept it from serving well as an agency for French cul-
ture among Muslims. Cambon decided to adapt its system of local
committees to a larger work, and Lavigerie encouraged his idea.
During his late 1883 trip to Paris, Cambon set up a central committee including, among others, the President of the Protestant
Synod, the Grand Rabbi of France, General Faidherbe, Admiral
Jauréguiberry, and the former ministers of public instruction
Victor Duruy and Paul Bert. Although Cambon and some of the
Alliance's other founders intended to give it a Catholic influence,
the Alliance Française began as a patriotic work for men of all
opinions and faiths. Lavigerie agreed to be one of its honorary
presidents.[15]

The French press applauded his participation. Le Temps expressed the wish that all bishops might be so conciliatory. La
Paix noted that it was possible to be a patriot and a good Catholic at the same time; its issue of 22 April 1884 published
Lavigerie's letter to the rector of the Cathedral of Tunis appointing him to the local council of the Alliance: "It is not in ab-
staining nor in holding back that [Catholics] can effectively do
good and prevent evil; it is in mixing in all the struggles and
knowing how to use their rights that they will triumph over their
adversaries."[16] Unfortunately, some Catholics in France considered
the Alliance to be the lay rival of the Oeuvre des Ecoles.
Lavigerie himself was distressed to read the prospectus of the
Alliance Française, which listed his name in the central committee
among "the choice flower of French atheism." But the composition
of the Tunis committee was quite acceptable, and Cambon gave him
assurances regarding the membership of the Paris committee.

Then, in the summer of 1884, the Semaine religieuse de Cambrai
stated that nineteen members of the fifty-man central committee
were Masons, and it denounced the supposedly Masonic aspects of
its program. The Archbishop of Cambrai had been one of the

strongest supporters of Lavigerie's efforts to raise funds for
Tunisia. His condemnation of the Alliance Française put Lavigerie
in an impossible position, despite Cambon's efforts to give the
organization a more moderate color.[17] Cambon was disgusted:
"Truly, the clergy are discouraging. One can not make them take
part. For them it is all or nothing."[18] Lavigerie was forced to
ask the active president, Victor Duruy, for a new slate of directors. Lavigerie wanted to "exclude mercilessly all those who
are openly anti-Christian."[19] The election failed to provide an
acceptable committee; Paul Bert remained by a margin of two votes.
The Catholic press followed these developments closely. On
25 February 1885 Lavigerie resigned his honorary leadership, outwardly "without noise and without hostile thought."

He sent Charmetant instructions from Algiers on withdrawing
the Catholic members from the Alliance and reconstituting an organization of these dissidents as an offshoot of the Oeuvre des
Ecoles. On 14 March 1885 the council of the Alliance considered
the bombshell of the Catholic resignations. A heated discussion
revealed that the council had never known nor ratified Cambon's
initial assurances concerning the prominence of the Catholics'
role. President Duruy could not mediate the problem. Charmetant
advised Lavigerie that the formation of a rival "league" was im-
practical. He protested being called a "pedestal of liberalism"
for his own unhappy role as intermediary in these events. The
Catholics left the central organization, and they diminished
their role in Tunisia, where the local committee ran language
classes, libraries, and canteens for students. Despite the embarrassment caused by the Archbishop of Cambrai, the Alliance
Française continued to aid congregationalist schools, and
Lavigerie remained on good terms with its moderate leaders.[20]

Lavigerie had an important role in another affair which was
much more serious as a potential scandal. While staying out of

public view, Lavigerie helped to mediate a conflict which threatened great embarrassment to the French regime. A dispute arose
between Ali Bey and his late brother's adopted son, Mustapha ben
Ismael. Prime Minister Mustapha had received or stolen real estate and jewelry from Sadok Bey, including restricted properties
of the crown. Soon after the invasion the French got rid of the
prime minister who had turned against them the year before, and
they replaced him with the corrupt old man of Tunisian politics,
Mustapha Khasnadar. In Lavigerie's opinion, Khasnadar's "nomination, the precipitous destitution of Mustapha, who was the man
above all to make and support, was a fault of the FERRY cabinet.
I did everything to prevent it, for I found myself at Paris,
but it was too late."[21] Khasnadar's entourage then renewed their
intrigues with England against French influence, and Sadok
greatly missed his adopted son, Mustapha Ben Ismael. After Sadok's
death, Ali Bey and other creditors sought to recover the millions
which they claimed from Mustapha as debts and restitution. Ali
himself claimed 3 million piasters (1.8 million francs) for
beylical property his brother had given Mustapha illegally, as
well as crown jewels which Ali itemized in lengthy inventories.[22]

Now in the spring of 1884 the tables were turned on this man
who once had terrorized all, even members of the beylical family,
with fear of the dagger or poison. His guilty conscience made
him fear reprisals. Mustapha went to Lavigerie, begging asylum
for himself and his family. Lavigerie told him that Ali Bey could
not murder him without risking his throne and that sheltering
those in danger was a bishop's job. He urged Mustapha to negotiate
a settlement with the bey. But Ali wanted to strip him, and he
asked Cambon not to let Mustapha out of the country. Cambon feared
the publicity of a trial and made Mustapha go to France, where
he tried to liquidate his goods and property. Lavigerie warned
Cambon against exposing these matters before a court. "It is

impossible to see more blunders combined."[23] The bey wanted to
reveal all the infamies of Mustapha's ministry, but Lavigerie
feared that the defendant would throw in Ali's face all of the
family's crimes, which Lavigerie believed had been many. Mustapha
could document bribery among prominent Frenchmen. Critics of
French policy in Tunisia would ask how the government could cover
such crimes. "To guard the protectorate it is necessary above
all not to dishonor it."[24]

Lavigerie himself refused to deal further in the affair, or
even to see Mustapha. But he wrote to Cambon, d'Estournelles,
Charmetant, and to Mustapha in a letter which Charmetant only
showed to the addressee, that the problem should be resolved in
a settlement out of court. Charmetant relayed this advice to
Prime Minister Ferry's staff. The Quai d'Orsay decided to try to
bring Mustapha and the bey together in an unofficial and administrative way so as not to let Mustapha know that the government
feared a trial. This litigation dragged on for several more years.
Some claims were settled out of court, others went to trial. But
a major scandal was avoided, in large measure because of
Lavigerie's good offices.[25]

The greatest challenge to the protectorate system came neither
from Tunisians nor from foreign consulates, but from the commandant of the French occupation corps, General Georges Boulanger.
This demagogue eventually drove Cambon from his post. After
Boulanger's appointment to replace General Logerot in February
1884, Cambon explained to him the subordinate role of the military authority in Tunisia. Boulanger outwardly accepted Cambon's
authority until the end of Jules Ferry's second ministry (February
1883 to March 1885), but Premier Henri Brisson (April 1885 to
January 1886) was not strong enough to restrain him. Boulanger
exploited the simmering resentment of ambitious officers and of
the Algerian judges of the French court system, who since their

arrival in 1883 resented having to follow Tunisian forms of
justice. Brisson's foreign minister, Freycinet, promised to back
Cambon; but General Edouard Campenon, minister of war, was uncertain in supporting the resident against one of his own officers. Brisson would not fight his own war minister, but President Grévy's steadfastness enabled Cambon to survive for a while.

Boulanger and Honoré Pontois, leader of the judges, accused
Cambon of corruption in Paris's La Lanterne. Cambon refused to
be baited into the same sort of press trial which had driven
Roustan from Tunis. Foreign Minister Freycinet appointed a commission under Flourens to investigate the charges. Its unpublished
report of 24 December 1885 praised Cambon's integrity, his policy,
and his achievements in Tunisia. In January 1886 Cambon received
the Legion of Honor - and the news that Boulanger was minister
of war in the new Freycinet cabinet (January-December 1886).
This made Cambon's position in Tunisia impossible. It took
Freycinet almost a year to arrange his transfer as ambassador to
Madrid.[26]

Lavigerie behaved very carefully during these events. He
criticized the judges and Boulanger privately, but he remained
cordial in his direct dealings with the general. Two letters to
Boulanger in 1885 thanked him for his many favors: his visit to
the Collège Saint-Charles had been an encouragement to the
priests' work. Boulanger intervened on behalf of a religious
brother who found himself by a misunderstanding accused of draft
evasion; Boulanger arranged for this man and another cleric to
serve their military obligation in Tunisia. In February 1886 the
new minister of war promised Charmetant to help all he could
with chaplains' positions for Lavigerie's clergy. "He told me
how he prided himself on the good relations he had always had
with Your Eminence at Tunis."[27] But during the same period
Lavigerie gave definite support to Cambon. In late 1884 he wrote

to Charmetant: "We have an interest of the first order here to maintain and fortify M. Cambon. God knows whom they will give us after him! Probably some radical whom they want to get rid of and who will bring us the Kulturkampf in Tunisia. So do your best."[28] At the same time he supported Cambon's bid for the Senate: "He is a wise, upright, and just man who comprehends the situation marvelously."[29] In 1884 Lavigerie also supported the successful candidacy of Cambon's uncle for bishop, even though acknowledging the Abbé Larue's mediocre qualifications for the little See of Langres.[30]

When Cambon came under open attack in 1885 Lavigerie wrote to Premier and Justice Minister Brisson, denouncing the jurists for wanting to "make the protectorate impossible and bring annexation." The French judiciary in Tunisia was not set up in response to "the necessities of this land." Lavigerie criticized the appointment of Protestants, Jews, and freethinkers to a tribunal which administered justice to Italian and Maltese Catholics, people who were deeply attached to the externals of their religion. "You should hear what they say about [the judiciary]. Perhaps its lack of prestige is also one of the causes of its incurable weakness. . . . In any case the necessary but very regrettable uproar made by General Boulanger no longer permits one to close his eyes." Lavigerie insisted that the Tunis Tribunal renounce its dream of immediate annexation and defend the real interests of France. Its personnel needed to be changed.[31]

A few months later Lavigerie wrote to Charmetant criticizing the ambition and jealousy of Boulanger. The general derived his support from an "auxiliary army [of] dead wood and job-seekers," as well as conservative journals in France. Lavigerie instructed Charmetant to make the rounds of the conservative editors and tell them that they played the game of France's and the Church's enemies. Cambon had doubled the Tunisian budget revenues in one

year. Annexation as favored by Boulanger would absorb all that
with a crowd of civil servants. Tunis had 3,000 French nationals,
whereas the nearby Algerian Department of Constantine had as many
functionaries.[32]

At the end of June 1886, while Cambon still looked for a grace-
ful way out of Tunisia, Lavigerie sent his new procurator at
Paris, Mgr. Carmel Brincat, an article to place in an important
secular journal under a pseudonym. Lavigerie wanted to undercut
any public support for annexation at the time of Cambon's departure. The military party, checked for the moment, still intended
to establish Arab Bureaus as in Algeria.[33] Cambon left in late
1886, having won the struggle over policy in Tunisia at the price
of destroying his own position there. His successor Justin
Massicault finally succeeded in reducing the size and influence
of the French army in Tunisia, except in the south, which stayed
under military control.[34]

The new resident minister was the former prefect of the Rhône.
Lavigerie assured Massicault in late 1886 of the clergy's support:
"The divisions which exist elsewhere have not until now risen
among us."[35] Their relationship was outwardly correct and cordial
despite Lavigerie's initial criticism. The cardinal wrote to the
Foreign Ministry protesting Massicault's clumsiness in dealing
with the Italians. He requested that the Quai d'Orsay reassign
him, lest his naiveté result in the loss of all that Cambon had
gained.[36] In fact, Lavigerie very much resented Massicault's
support for Freemasonry, which was mostly an Italian movement in
Tunisia. Lavigerie confided to Cardinal-Secretary of State Rampolla
that Massicault was "basically radical and anti-Christian." His
wife and sister were "openly atheist." In Lavigerie's opinion, he
leaned for support on his fellow Masons and became their captive.
Lavigerie especially resented Massicault for letting the Masons
build an Italian secondary school and a hospital which competed

with his own.[37] Despite this undercurrent of distrust, the two
managed to work together until Massicault's death in early November 1892, three weeks before Lavigerie's.

Lavigerie and Massicault had different estimates of the Italian
problem. This large community remained restless under French rule,
and the clergy made a good target for their resentment. Although
a restrictive press law kept written attacks to a minimum, Nicolo
Converti's "revolutionary journal" Operaio got away with denouncing "the priests, who constitute the black police of souls for
the profit of states."[38] Another journal that had slandered
Lavigerie's clergy more explicitly, ended up in court. A Capuchin
church burnt down in September 1884. La Sentinella of Tunis commented, "Some say that the finger of God shows itself in this
event, but ninety-nine percent say it shows the finger of the
cathedral." Lavigerie led the drive for contributions to rebuild
the church, and at the same time he sued the editors. They had
to beg his mercy, pleading that a sentence of jail or damages
would force the paper to shut down.[39] In 1887 Lavigerie reported
to Cardinal Rampolla the attacks of Masons in Tunis, whose slander
appeared in Roman newspapers. While he was raising money in France,
they reported that "His Eminence, Cardinal Lavigerie, having revolted against the Pope, has just been sentenced to exile in the
Sahara." On his return to Tunis they announced that he had finished
serving his sentence.[40]

In his discussions with Massicault during that year Lavigerie
often mentioned the continuing hatred of the Italians and the
Muslims for the French. The resident reported to Paris that,
"according to him, despite the present peace, we have much to
fear, and our [military] forces are very insufficient." Massicault
did not fully confirm Lavigerie's opinion, but he realized that
they could not completely end the vengefulness of the Italians.
The resident's policy was to be courteous, to avoid legitimate

cause for complaint, and to try to increase the French influence
He believed that most Tunisians had come over to the French party.
The Italian consul, Malmusi, had replied to Massicault's inquiry,
that there was no "Tunisian Question" for his government. Italy
accepted the French protectorate as an accomplished fact.[41]

Diplomats and politicians at Tunis and Rome often noted the
impact of Lavigerie's work on the Italians. Malmusi's predecessor
once complimented him on his program of churches, schools, and
charities in Tunisia: "Ah, Monsignor, how much good you do, but
what ill that does to us!"[42] After the floods of late 1882 in
northern Italy, and again after the Ischia earthquake of 1883,
Lavigerie organized diocesan appeals for contributions. Le Monde
of Paris printed a letter of thanks from the Italian chargé,
Raibaudi-Massiglia.[43] The German consul, Julius Eckardt, saw
clearly that "Lavigerie knew how to humor the weak side of the
Italians so skillfully that he seemed like their friend."[44]

Some of Lavigerie's Italian admirers had second thoughts, however, particularly after Francesco Crispi became prime minister
in August 1887. Crispi was the foremost exponent of grandezza,
and Franco-Italian relations deteriorated during his ministry.
Having lost Tunisia, Italy took an interest in Tripoli, and the
Porte had just signed a treaty with France moving its Tunisian
frontier twenty miles east. Italy, as well as Britain, was greatly
concerned lest the French add Tripoli to their North African empire. Furthermore, a September 1888 decree from the bey requiring
French-language instruction in all Italian schools, naval constructions at Bizerta, and the Franco-Italian tariff war of the late
eighties all combined to revive Italy's sense of grievance.[45]

In late 1888 Lavigerie drew a great deal of criticism from the
press at both Rome and Paris for his attempt to ease this tension.
Ali Bey seemed moribund, and Italy feared France was going to
annex Tunisia and perhaps Tripoli. Crispi remained apprehensive

despite French denials.[46] Lavigerie attempted to mollify Italian
public opinion in late 1888, telling Italian reporters how much
he regretted the misunderstanding between their two countries.
Il Popolo Romano and Il Tribuno attributed to him the suggestion
that Italy satisfy her ambitions in North Africa by taking Tripoli.
Italian leaders, who suspected a Vatican inspiration for this
suggestion, wanted to use it to frighten the Turks into joining
the Triple Alliance. The cardinal's indiscretion provoked a wave
of criticism in both the French and the Italian press. By the
time the Turkish ambassador arrived at the Quai d'Orsay to deliver
his government's protest, Lavigerie clarified his remarks: in a
strictly private capacity he had urged the Italians to join his
work against the African slave trade and to "carry to Tripoli
the succor of their zeal and of their charity."[47]

Cardinal Lavigerie had the distinction among French bishops
of being pilloried in a national assembly besides his own. Crispi
accused him in 1889 before the Italian Senate of expelling Mgr.
Sutter for political reasons, and he condemned the Italians who
contributed to Lavigerie money which would be better spent at
home. The cardinal's public reply noted that Sutter had required
a French pension because the Italian government had despoiled
the Capuchin order. With regard to Italian money for the Church
in Tunisia, Lavigerie denied there had been any to speak of. On
the contrary, the balance of payments was in Italy's favor, as
documented by letters from the Foreign Ministry thanking him for
earthquake and flood relief.[48]

By the time of this controversy Lavigerie had accomplished
most of his program in North Africa. Capable lieutenants at Algiers
and Tunis handled the routine details of supervising the White
Fathers and diocesan clergy, while he concentrated his attention
on two projects in central Africa and Europe: the Oeuvrage
Antiesclavagiste and the ralliement occupied a great deal of

Lavigerie's time during his last years. The campaign against the
slave trade was the last African enterprise of his career; to
resolve the tension between church and state within France was
his other compelling goal. Both of these projects require mention
in any analysis of his work.

In 1888 Lavigerie vigorously undertook to organize and coordinate a campaign against slavery in the African interior. It had
always horrified him, particularly the first-hand reports he received regularly from White Fathers in the mission field. Some
areas of the continent were being depopulated by the raids of
Arab slavers, who marched their caravans north along routes lit-
tered with skeletons. This hideous trade had increased during the
1880s, perhaps as a reaction to the European scramble for colonies
in Africa. In 1888 Lavigerie directed his talents as an orator
and politician to the Oeuvrage Antiesclavagiste. Lavigerie founded
this movement in order to coordinate programs in each of the major
European countries, for as a French patriot he realized that his
effectiveness depended on the extent to which he could channel
the nationalism of each country into this crusade. Between 1888
and 1890 Lavigerie travelled to rallies and conferences throughout
Europe, straining his health in the process.[49]

The large scale capture and selling of Africans did not end
until years after Lavigerie's death, but he deserves credit for
eliminating slavery in Tunisia. The beylic had forbidden it since
the 1840s in order to please the British, but the importation of
slaves into Tunisia continued on a small scale even after the
French invasion. Lavigerie spoke and wrote to French officials
about the problem several times. Finally a beylical decree of
28 May 1890 confirmed the prohibition of slavery, and it required
the "employers" of black domestics to give them notarized certifi-
cates of liberation. The authorities in Tunisia enforced this
decree completely.[50]

Lavigerie's efforts to establish an organization in Algeria
to fight slavery in the Sahara were less successful. In 1891 he
founded the Frères Armés du Sahara in the Algerian interior at
Biskra, where he lately spent considerable time nursing his
health. French officials had misgivings about the legal status of
such a semi-military project, as well as the risks of incidents
beyond the line of French control. But Jules Cambon, who had been
appointed governor general of Algeria partly on Lavigerie's recommendation, basically sympathized with the proposal. The ministers in Paris decided to wait and see if the project ripened. It
did not, partly because the founder of the Armed Brothers had
fallen seriously ill by the end of 1891.[51]

Lavigerie's physical deterioration during 1891 was substantially
attributable to the abuse which some French Catholics heaped upon
him for his role in the ralliement. One of the ironies of his
career is that the event for which the Primate of Africa is perhaps best known, the Toast of Algiers, related to French politics
and brought great harm to his projects in Africa. In the late
1880s Leo XIII had decided upon a concerted effort to resolve the
church-state conflict in France, and he chose the Archbishop of
Algiers for his spokesman. The Pope wanted to give monarchists
among the French clergy and laity a clear signal to abandon opposition to their lawful government. Lavigerie seemed best qualified
to make a public exhortation to all Catholics to give their
loyalty to the republic. Lavigerie delivered this call for
ralliement at a banquet which he hosted for forty officers of the
French Mediterranean fleet on 12 November 1890. It was the text
of a toast to the French navy. Making a group of conservatives
lift their glasses at the end of such a speech, and then subject-
ing them to a rendition of the Marseillaise, had a dramatic effect
on newspaper readers in France. Lavigerie expected the Holy See to
endorse his statement publicly, but because of the furor which it

caused among French Catholics, Leo let Lavigerie take the fire
alone.[52] The "hares in mitres" of the French hierarchy, who depended on monarchists in their dioceses for financial support,
likewise waited silently for the storm to subside.[53]

Historians debate the origin of the toast. In its aftermath
Lavigerie and his associates asserted that the Pope had imposed
this task upon him. Before rising to deliver the toast Lavigerie
supposedly told a colleague: "I am soon going to commit suicide."[54]
On the other hand, James E. Ward argues convincingly that the
toast was Lavigerie's own project, for which he obtained papal
approval in advance. Pierre Soumille's belief is that Vatican
support for the 1891 expulsion of the Capuchins from Tunisia was
Leo's part of a bargain he had made with Lavigerie the year before.[55] If so, the cardinal paid dearly for that favor. The post-
man brought him anonymous letters smeared with dirt, his old
friend Emile Keller withdrew from the Oeuvrage Antiesclavagiste,
and contributions from conservatives for the White Fathers declined substantially.[56]

The ralliement of 1890 was a failure in France. Yet on a
smaller scale in North Africa Lavigerie had shown during the previous decade that Catholics and the clergy could work loyally for
the republic without betraying religious principles. Lavigerie
was first of all a bishop and missionary, yet the contribution he
made to the development of a colonial empire for France merits
equal recognition. Théodore Roustan expressed his personal admiration in a letter to Lavigerie's biographer: "I had the honor to
be the Cardinal's collaborator; but I have always regretted not
having served under his orders, for he would have been for France
a new Richelieu."[57]

But Lavigerie had a different role in republican France, in
contrast to cardinal-prime ministers of the preceding two centuries. Although Lavigerie could not realize his project of

<u>ralliement</u>, he performed numberless services for his country be-
hind the scenes, helping Paul Cambon consolidate the protectorate, defending it against ambitious critics, and preventing
Mustapha ben Ismael from giving his name to another notorious
<u>affaire</u>. Lavigerie's relationship with Justin Massicault was
marked by something less than profound admiration, but they continued the basic partnership established under Roustan and Cambon;
Massicault appreciated Lavigerie's help in dealing with the
Italians even if he saw them as less than a peril. The last years
of Lavigerie's life did not bring him the satisfaction his efforts
deserved. The Toast of Algiers brought about a personal disaster
which laid a pall over his great achievements in North Africa.

VII
"Carthage Must Be Restored":
The Building of a French Diocese

Lavigerie's most visible contribution to the French position in Tunisia was the establishment of a diocesan staff completely sympathetic to France. The number of French citizens grew more rapidly than the other European populations in the regency, but Lavigerie still needed priests of various nationalities to serve them all. Lavigerie depended on Capuchin personnel until 1891, when he finally expelled the small number of them remaining. The churches, schools, and charitable foundations built during Lavigerie's term included a number of monuments to his personal power and to that of the French. Restoration of the ancient See of Carthage in 1884 officially made Lavigerie the foremost Catholic bishop in Africa, and he thereafter sought to increase the glory of the new archdiocese partly as a means of perpetuating his own.

During the first decade of the protectorate Lavigerie had participated closely in a wide range of administrative questions, but his primary responsibility was pastoral. His 1881 Christmas report to the Propaganda estimated the number of Catholics in Tunisia at 40,000.[1] Researchers at the archives of the Propaganda Fide routinely discount population statistics attached to appeals for money; the number of Europeans in Tunisia was not identical to the Catholic population. An estimate of 23,000 Catholics in Tunisia for 1881 is more precise. This still constituted a large responsibility, and the Catholic population grew rapidly thereafter. Catholics in Tunisia in 1886 numbered an estimated 40,000,

including French soldiers, and 75,000 by 1896.[2] Lavigerie had to
create facilities in Tunisia for his own clergy and for religious
orders which he invited there, largely at his own expense. The
apostolic administrator's first Christmas report noted that he
had only nine parishes, eight schools, and one small hospital to
serve the whole country.[3] Aside from the White Fathers at
Carthage, the clergy comprised eight Capuchins at the Parish of
Sainte-Croix in Tunis, and nine in the other towns.[4]

Mgr. Pons remarked of Lavigerie: "In the manner of United
States bishops, he built the schools before the churches."[5] He
encouraged Christian Brothers, White Sisters, and the Dames of
Sion to join in this. By 1883 twenty-four schools in Tunisia
taught multinational student bodies in the French language. Most
of these schools were Catholic. Louis-Pierre Machuel, who became
director of public instruction in 1883, soon negotiated an arrangement which integrated seventeen Catholic schools into the
system of public education. The Tunisian government paid the
salaries of their religious personnel. In return, the schools
submitted to official inspection, and they promised to bring
faculty credentials up to state standards. Negotiating with
Machuel, Lavigerie considered him to be "an essentially dangerous
and hypocritical man [who] makes the devil against us."[6] But they
worked together to cover the financial needs of Catholic education. Brothers, priests, and nuns directed twenty of the sixty-
seven French schools established in the regency by 1889.[7]
Lavigerie took special interest in the Collège Saint-Louis,
which he relocated in October 1882 and renamed after his patron
saint. In order to accommodate the regency's leading families
it was necessary to move the school to Tunis, where the Masons
planned another to compete with it. Lavigerie used the old
property at Carthage for the White Fathers' scholasticate.[8] The
government continued its subsidies to the Collège Saint-Charles,

although on one occasion its representative carried French support to excess: in Cambon's absence another official spoke at
the 1885 awards assembly who had the "unhappy inspiration" to
tell the students and their families that the Collège Saint-
Charles was "destined to form servants for France and for the
Republic." Lavigerie complained to the foreign minister that
"that truth was not a clever thing to say," for most of the
audience was not French. Forty-two students withdrew, and new
enrollments fell sharply.[9] Lavigerie's secondary school continued
to promote more discreetly the assimilation of foreign students
into their new mother country, but against the competition of
rival schools it lacked sufficient enrollment to break even fi-
nancially. An 1886 agreement with the government placed Saint-
Charles under joint direction, comparable to that of the Collège
Stanislas in Paris. This relieved Lavigerie of its operating
expenses, but the authorities interfered increasingly in its
administration. Three years later the cardinal sold the school
for the price of his initial investment, which he used to build
a minor seminary at Carthage.[10]

During the early 1880s Lavigerie rapidly built facilities for
worship, and he encouraged French congregations to establish
houses in Tunisia. When he took over the vicariate in July 1881,
almost all ecclesiastical property was in the possession of the
Capuchins. His circular to the clergy of Algiers declared:
"Carthage claims a cathedral worthy of its great memories" - as
well as one not owned by the Italians.[11] This had first priority.
Ground was broken at Tunis in November for the provisional Sanctuary of St. Vincent de Paul, a "simple hangar" built in eighty-
two days.[12] Lavigerie planned eventually to build a permanent
cathedral, including episcopal offices, two seminaries, and
twenty new parish churches with schools.[13] He soon moved the
hospital of the Sisters of St. Joseph from its miserable premises

into a larger barracks provided by the bey. He gave the hospital
a council of administration with representatives of the French,
Italian, and Maltese communities it served. During the 1880s the
Sisters of Bon Secours arrived, and the Carmelites opened a house
near Saint-Louis de Carthage. The Franciscans of Mary founded an
orphanage, and in 1886 Lavigerie's White Sisters opened a shelter
for poor girls who had trouble finding respectable employment.[14]

At the end of two years in Tunisia Lavigerie had established
the basic infrastructure needed for restoration of Carthage as a
regular see. The tenuousness of Lavigerie's provisional appointment as apostolic administrator still served a useful function in
wringing cooperation and partial support from the government for
meeting the vicariate's financial needs. Lavigerie always held in
reserve the threat of his own resignation or of a Vatican decision
to take the administrator's post away from him. But both Lavigerie
and the Pope who upheld his tenure suffered from poor health; the
security of a regular French bishopric at Carthage ultimately
seemed more important to Lavigerie than the marginal sums obtained
from the government by means of this bluff.

Having revitalized Carthage, Lavigerie prepared for its restoration. Jules Ferry's return to power in February 1883 assured
official cooperation. The prime minister replied to Paul Cambon's
inquiry of March 1883 that the government approved the restoration
of the See of Carthage, provided it place no financial obligation
on France. Lavigerie traveled to Rome two months later to broach
the idea to the Holy Father. He quoted to Leo XIII the testimonial
provided in 1053 by St. Leo IX:

> There is no doubt that, after the Roman Pontiff, the
> first archbishop and the greatest metropolitan of all
> is the Bishop of Carthage. He can not lose that privi-
> lege, received from the Holy Roman Apostolic See, in
> favor of any other bishop of Africa. That will obtain

until the end of the centuries as long as the name of
Our Lord Jesus Christ is invoked in Africa, whether
Carthage remains deserted or whether its glory revives
again. . . . Thus hold the decrees of our venerable
predecessors, the Roman Pontiffs.[15]

Leo XIII accepted the proposal in principle and told Lavigerie
to return after making sufficient material preparations.[16]

The political climate of the Vatican favored the project.
Although Bismarck had attempted to reconcile Italy with the Holy
See after her entrance into the Triple Alliance, the danger of
Italy's displacing France as the foremost Catholic power was eliminated in 1884 by an Italian court decision requiring the Propaganda to convert its endowment into government bonds. Lavigerie
warned Ferry, however, that Italy could thus control the salaries
of apostolic delegates in mission lands, thereby influencing
appointments. He urged the French government to summon a concerted
protest by major countries in the Propaganda's jurisdiction,
namely, Turkey, the Hapsburg Empire, Canada, and the United States.
In fact, Italy's latest anticlerical outrage actually increased
Simeoni's financial dependence on the Propagation de la Foi and
ended any sympathy he might have had for France's rival.[17]

Lavigerie's formal note to the prime minister in January 1884
proposing restoration of Carthage emphasized the importance of
ending completely the danger of the Italians' resuming control
of the vicariate. Cambon passed the word that Ferry "gives you
carte blanche," although he insisted on secrecy and no financial
obligation for the government. On 19 April 1884 Lavigerie sent
the Pope his formal petition, which the Propaganda and the
Secretariat of State considered during May and June. Ferry assigned
a navy vessel to carry the cardinal to Rome, and he obtained
Vatican approval in late June. All parties realized the importance

of secrecy until the final abolition of the capitulations by the
Italian Senate.[18]

   After the elimination of consular jurisdiction in July, there
remained only one area in Tunisia where the Italians could pos-
sibly resist French power, and they made a last-ditch attempt to
save the vicariate. The Pope's opinion of Lavigerie was too high
for his decision to be prejudiced by the struggles within France
regarding divorce and conscription of the clergy, but the Curia
found in church law an objection to the personal union of Algiers
and Carthage under one archbishop. Canonists considered a bishop
as being married to his see, and in that view Lavigerie's possession of two cathedrals would be bigamous. Leo swept away this
last obstacle with a dispensation from canon law. Ambassador
Lefebvre de Béhaine, who observed all of these struggles in Rome,
fully credited this decision to the cardinal's "predominant influence." He noted the peroration to which Lavigerie's proposal
had been so successfully keyed: It should not be said, "Carthago
delenda est!," ("Carthage must be destroyed!"), but rather,
"Carthago instauranda est!," ("Carthage must be restored!"). The
"Hussard" carried the Archbishop-elect of Carthage and Algiers
back to La Goulette in early August, after a two-week vacation
in Capri.[19]

   Having won the basic decision, Lavigerie had to work out the
details during the next few months. He had agreed to endow the
new archdiocese with properties worth 2 million francs. He im-
patiently wrote Jacobini several times requesting a proxy for
Fr. Deguerry to accept these Tunisian holdings in the name of
the Pope. Lavigerie periodically suffered crises of health because of overwork and the North African climate. In late October
he was stricken so severely with "cerebral phenomena" and marsh
fever that he received the Last Rites. Chronic bad health gave
him a somewhat morbid concern with death, and he wired the Vatican

several times urging promptness in preparing the papal bull. At
the same time he urged the resident to obtain quickly the government's approval of a coadjutor for the new see so as to secure
the succession of a Frenchman, for his grave condition threatened
"possible catastrophe." Cambon wired the Quai d'Orsay that Bishop
Barthélemy-Clément Combes of Constantine was a worthy candidate.
Although Cambon personally doubted Lavigerie was moribund, he
felt that the government's approval would have a therapeutic effect on his spirits. The Cults Ministry gave preliminary approval,
although Combes's promotion to Carthage did not actually take
place until 1893. Lavigerie rallied in the first week of November
and awaited the bulls which Jacobini said were on their way.[20]

When the document <u>Materna Ecclesiae Caritas</u> finally arrived
in mid-November, it nearly gave Lavigerie another shock. He wrote
to Jacobini that, although the text was rich in allusion to the
ancient glories of Carthage, there was a terrible error in the
heart of it. Rather than the whole territory of Tunisia, the new
diocese comprised only a few square kilometers around Saint-
Louis. He requested the prompt issuance of a decree of interpretation to clarify the paragraph which defined its boundaries.

> It would result from the paragraph, in effect, that
> the Apostolic Vicariate of Tunisia would continue to
> exist, and that the Archdiocese of Carthage would be
> reestablished at its side, with only five villages
> almost completely Muslim. Not only, I repeat, would
> such a supposed solution be absolutely contrary to
> what I have asked, to what has been deliberated by
> the Sacred Congregation of the Propaganda, and to
> what has been accorded by the Holy Father; but besides
> it would be <u>absolutely ridiculous</u>. Such a diocese
> would have no element of dignity nor of life.

How could such an editorial mistake have been
committed? I can explain it only by the distortion
of things otherwise very clear, caused when one
does not know them personally.[21]

Jacobini replied that the circumscription of his see was not an
error; it had been dictated by concern for the sentiments of a
portion of his clergy and the Tunisian faithful. Lavigerie's
enemies in the Curia had thus scored a temporary victory, but
Jacobini nonetheless promised to grant his request within a few
months.[22]

Lavigerie wrote to his friend Cardinal Simeoni in Italian
language which was less tactful than his letter to the secretary
of state: "I see that now in the Propaganda miracles are happen-
ing, but indeed, contrary to those of the Gospel. In the Gospel
water was changed into wine, and you on the other hand change
wine into water, which now pleases no one."[23] In the eyes of the
French government the two questions of transforming the vicariate
and transferring the 2 million francs in real estate were linked.
Paris had consented to restoration of Carthage on the basis of
an understanding which the Vatican had violated, at least in
spirit. Lavigerie delayed transferring the endowment for Carthage
to the Pope, for much of the property in question was located
outside the perimeter of the primatial enclave. In February
Lavigerie threatened to die if Simeoni did not help him straighten
out this mess. He insisted that the Vatican completely supress
the vicariate. He also wanted the promised papal brief to reserve
the Holy See's right to divide the regency into two additional
dioceses in order eventually to make Carthage an ecclesiastical
province. A papal brief of 31 March 1885 finally extended the
boundaries to include the whole vicariate.[24]

Restoration of Carthage enabled Lavigerie to proceed with a
plan to extend his episcopal influence to yet another jurisdiction, that of Malta. The agent for this was to be Antonio Buhagiar.
Fr. Buhagiar's appointment as Auxiliary Bishop of Carthage provided quick benefits to the French as part of the Maltese policy,
but Lavigerie failed to achieve his ultimate goal of making
him Bishop of Malta. Pope Leo had asked him in 1883 to suggest
a candidate, and Lavigerie sent the unsuspecting Curé of Sfax
on an errand to Rome for the Pope to judge his qualifications
personally. Proceeding with their plan, Lavigerie informed the
British consul on 5 August 1884 that he had chosen a British subject for his auxiliary bishop in Tunisia as a mark of his attachment to the Maltese people. Thomas Reade took the bait and
provided a whole-hearted endorsement of Buhagiar's fitness for
the episcopate, which Lavigerie saved until the time came to forward it to British authorities. The enthusiasm demonstrated by
the Maltese in Tunisia at Buhagiar's consecration has already been
described. This gave Buhagiar great personal stature at Malta
itself, which he visited a few months later. Lavigerie wrote the
Pope in September that it was unwise for him to escort Buhagiar
there himself, so he found a pretext by which the new bishop
might be "as if naturally and without premeditation, carried onto
the field of combat."[25] At the end of 1884 Lavigerie sent Buhagiar
on a French navy vessel to Malta "to find priests and monks for
Tunisia." The people welcomed him proudly and the authorities
received him warmly.[26]

Lavigerie's progress reports to the Pope during 1885 described
the state of the Maltese clergy in scandalous terms. The aged
Bishop Scicluna was infantile, and his greedy nephews ran the
diocesan treasury like a "veritable bank." Lavigerie accused the
lower clergy of passing their time in cafés while the faithful
crowded the churches. Some priests had concubines, and one of

them had openly engaged in whoring on a visit to Algiers. The
clerical factions chased after benefices, and there were five
openly declared candidates to succeed Scicluna, not counting the
eventual winner, Bishop Pace of Gozo. The people wanted Buhagiar,
and Lavigerie urged the Pope to make him coadjutor in order to
give him the authority necessary to correct this state of affairs.
Buhagiar soon became apostolic administrator of the diocese, but
his rivals at Malta opposed him. Some sent poison pen letters denouncing him to Lavigerie and to the Pope. But the real obstacle
came from the British, who did not want a French protégé for
Bishop of Malta. At the end of 1886 Lavigerie had to write to
Buhagiar that official opposition blocked his candidacy for coadjutor. In January 1889 Scicluna was succeeded by Mgr. Pace,
whose family Lavigerie considered to be "one of the most infamous
of the whole island." The former administrator, Mgr. Buhagiar,
went to Rome until the Pope could find him another post.[27]

Buhagiar's move to Malta in 1885 had left a gap at Tunis.
Lavigerie tried by various means over the next seven years to
place a French coadjutor there. He needed someone to supervise
the clergy on a daily basis, and he also realized the importance
of appointing a French coadjutor whose right of succession would
block the possibility of the see's reverting to an Italian. In
1885 Lavigerie tried to appoint Mgr. Lamothe-Tenet, rector of the
Institut Catholique de Toulouse, as coadjutor. The Holy See approved, but Lamothe-Tenet's royalist background drew government
objections. The Tunisian appointment was not itself governed by
the procedures of the Concordat, but a French priest who received
consecration without government approval could lose his rights of
citizenship. After the veto of Lamothe-Tenet's candidacy, Lavigerie
decided for the moment to settle for an auxiliary bishop to build
up the archdiocese while he pursued his other activities in Algeria
and Europe.[28]

The choice of Bishop Jourdan de la Passardière was a fiasco.
This man had solicited and received from the Holy See in 1884
the title of bishop in partibus without the approval of the
French authorities, who struck his name from the voting register.
He served Cardinal Caverot of Lyons as auxiliary, but Caverot's
successor did not want him. Jourdan needed a job, and the former
prefect at Lyons, Justin Massicault, recommended him to Lavigerie.
According to the story which Lavigerie and Massicault gave to
officials at Paris, Mgr. Jourdan de la Passardière's fluency in
Italian would be a great asset in Tunisia. They recommended giving
him a trial appointment at Tunis to see if his zeal and his health
qualified him for coadjutor. The candidate also hoped to earn the
restoration of his civil rights. There was no difficulty obtaining
the approval of Foreign Minister Flourens, Lavigerie's old friend,
nor that of Political Director Jusserand, a former Tunisian specialist at the Quai d'Orsay. The Archbishop of Lyons' desire to
be rid of Jourdan, and Massicault's strong support of him overcame objections at the Ministry of Cults, which completed the
arrangements in autumn 1887.[29]

Jourdan had agreed to Lavigerie's conditions for this appointment. The archives of the Prelature of Tunis do not indicate
whether even Massicault knew all of them. Officially the future
Coadjutor of Carthage was to supervise the see's clergy from the
archdiocesan office at Tunis. He was to make a complete financial
report annually and turn over one-third of his receipts from
quests in Europe. Lavigerie retained direct authority over the
district right around La Marsa and Carthage, where he had established his most cherished projects. This arrangement left
Lavigerie's time free to devote to the White Fathers and White
Sisters. The cardinal's letter of 1 July 1887 reviewed the secret
terms to which the auxiliary bishop had agreed in their meeting
at Lyons. This was really a term appointment of three or four

years, barring <u>force majeure</u>. In return for working in Tunisia
Lavigerie agreed to help him obtain restoration of his civil
rights. After his rehabilitation, Lavigerie promised to recommend
him for another see in France or Africa. In the meantime, his
primary responsibility was to create new works, particularly a
cathedral at Tunis. Lavigerie insisted that Jourdan not admit
that Tunis was a stepping stone to another diocese.[30]

The clergy and faithful of Tunisia awaited the new auxiliary
bishop's arrival in late October 1887. He appeared three days
late, acting as if nothing had happened. The rumor spread that
his family was mad. In fact, his brother in the navy had had a
breakdown at La Goulette and was still confined.[31] Lavigerie nonetheless decided to make the best of things. At the installation
ceremony on All Saints' Day he presented Jourdan to the people as
"a new father. . . . But I claim the right to love you even more,
in my quality as grandfather."[32] "The Cardinal conducted him to
his throne, gave him the cross, insignia, of jurisdiction, and
made him sit to the chant of 'Ecce Sacerdos Magnus.' Then His
Eminence addressed to the faithful one of those brilliant impro-
visations of which he alone has the secret. Its paternal accents
touched all hearts. . . . [Jourdan de la Passardière's own expression of thanks] well justified his reputation as a great
orator."[33]

Four months later President Sadi Carnot restored Jourdan's
civil rights. He immediately went to Lavigerie at Algiers to say
that bad health forced his return to France. Lavigerie coldly re-
proached Jourdan for compromising him in this "comedy," and he
sent him back to Tunis. The bishop went to Europe on quest during
the summer of 1888, but he preached without raising money. In
February 1889 Jourdan again pleaded a medical excuse for leaving
Tunisia permanently, which the cardinal accepted on 2 March as a
resignation. Lavigerie himself was crippled with rheumatism at

Biskra in the Algerian interior. He composed another letter to
Jourdan, not sent, which expressed the regret that because of
his neglect, not one church had been built in Tunisia for the
previous eighteen months. Lavigerie denied having any personal
rancor.[34]

Jourdan recovered his health quickly upon his return to France,
and he started looking for a diocese. Massicault recommended his
old friend to the foreign minister for another post. Lavigerie
sent the cardinal-secretary of state a summary of the facts,
stating that the candidate was ill indeed, mentally. The irony
of this man's career is that a decade later the French anti-
slavery movement, which Lavigerie founded in 1888, had Mgr.
Jourdan de la Passardière, Bishop of Rosea, as organizing secretary of its committee.[35]

After Jourdan's departure from Tunis Lavigerie entrusted the
archdiocese to Mgrs. Gazaniol and Tournier, for whom he obtained
at Rome the rank of protonotary apostolic. Gazaniol supervised
the clergy and Tournier managed the finances. These two "creatures
of His Eminence [were] absolutely in his hand." The Archbishop
of Carthage chose for his next auxiliary Carmel Brincat, the young
Franco-Maltese who had replaced Charmetant as procurator at Paris.
Mgr. Brincat became Auxiliary Bishop of Carthage in name only,
for the Oeuvrage Antiesclavagiste kept him working at Paris.
Gazaniol and Tournier remained in charge at Tunis.[36]

Lavigerie knew he was dying in 1891. He sought for the last
time to arrange the Carthaginian succession. His choice was Mgr.
Léon Linvinhac, the first bishop to be consecrated at Carthage in
eight centuries. The former Apostolic Vicar of Nyanza had received
word in Uganda on 31 March 1890 that the general chapter of the
White Fathers had elected him vicar general, under Lavigerie's
control. After making Linvinhac the "coadjutor" of the Society,
Lavigerie tried to conscript him for Carthage as well in order

to assure the coordination which had been so useful in the past.
Lavigerie wrote to Leo XIII in November 1891 that Linvinhac's
only fault was his excess of humility and dislike of great responsibility. The Pope did not grant Lavigerie's request that
he order Linvinhac to accept the Coadjutorship of Carthage. But
early the following year Lavigerie got permission from the Vatican
for Brincat to consecrate his three vicars general, Gazaniol,
Tournier, and the Maltese Paloméni. Lavigerie wanted to make them
bishops in preparation for dividing Tunisia into three dioceses.[37]
He hoped by creating suffragan sees to increase further the prestige of Carthage.

Lavigerie attached great importance to his title as Primate of
Africa, and he reacted angrily when Mgr. Pace of Malta challenged
it in 1889. Having dispossessed Lavigerie's protégé and the Pope's
choice for bishop there, the British added insult to injury in
August of that year. The Foreign Office sent a delegation to Rome
to propose the elevation of Malta to an archbishopric with ecclesiastical primacy over African offshore islands and all British
possessions on the continent. This proposal could set a precedent
for Italian and German prelates to follow. It enraged Lavigerie,
who told Massicault he had the means to destroy his enemy's credit
at Rome: "Mgr. Pace has just confided the temporal administration
of his diocese to one of his nephews, a layman, who is in a state
of declared bankruptcy at Tunis, and against whom civil suits are
going to be brought before our tribunals."[38] The cardinal wrote a
letter to the Pope's private secretary, in which he outlined the
British proposal's canonical irregularities. He threatened to resign Carthage, whose restoration was one of the glories of
Leo XIII's pontificate, rather than permit the see to be despoiled
during his own term. The Primate of Africa stressed the eleventh-
century theme: "He can not lose that privilege. . . . Thus hold the
decrees of our venerable predecessors, the Roman Pontiffs." Rome

rejected the British challenge to France's ecclesiastical hegemony
in the Mediterranean and to Lavigerie's rank.[39]

   The symbol of his primacy was the Basilica of Saint-Louis de
Carthage, which one can see on a clear day from Tunis. Lavigerie
broke ground for this monument in May 1884 in anticipation of
Leo XIII's restoration of the see. He devoted himself to financing
its construction and supervising the details of its lavish deco-
ration. He gave special attention to the crypt, where his remains
lay for seventy-two years.[40] He dedicated the basilica on Ascension
Thursday, 15 May 1890, with a primatial council of North African
bishops and honored guests from the French hierarchy. Bishop
Buhagiar was invited, Pace was not.

   The decrees which Lavigerie prepared for the council's approval
asserted the primacy of Carthage in terms which made officials at
the Quai d'Orsay wonder if they might offend sensibilities at
Rome. Massicault replied that the texts were less substantive
than they seemed. They were specifically intended as a reply to
the recent British challenge. Lavigerie based all of his claims
on St. Leo IX's words from the eleventh century, and Leo XIII
approved the draft decrees. Massicault believed that it was in
the interests of France that Lavigerie's affirmations prevail.[41]
The government approved Massicault's request for military and
naval honors at the ceremony, insisting that it have a national
character: the tricolor was to be prominently displayed, and the
fleur-de-lis of St. Louis must not appear as a flag. Fifteen
thousand people crowded and surrounded the basilica for the dedication.[42] The sixty bishops and theologians participating in the
Council of Carthage approved the cardinal's three sets of proposals: they ratified the ancient canons of the first See of
Carthage, particularly those asserting papal authority against
heresy; they endorsed all of Leo XIII's pronouncements, stressing
his condemnation of slavery; and they adopted for Carthage the

rules of the Archdiocese of Algiers. Lavigerie reported to
Leo XIII that the agenda of the council went exactly as planned,
with no dissent.[43] The dedication of the Basilica of Saint-Louis
was a triumphal event in Lavigerie's career. It celebrated his
nominal leadership of the Church in Africa and his authority
over the Catholic community of Tunisia. After the initial defiance of the Capuchins in 1881 Lavigerie had only occasional difficulties with the Italians.

One source of chronic tension was the cardinal's plan to move
the Cemetery of Saint-Antoine to another tract, which he purchased
in 1882 outside the city limits at Bab-el-Khadra. On this issue
the Italians repeatedly stirred up opposition among the Maltese.
Both groups traditionally buried their dead in Saint-Antoine's,
which faced the French residence across the Promenade de la Marine.
The beylic had originally donated a large plot of land for the
gratuitous use of the Christian community, but the fee system of
the Capuchins became almost a scandal in the opinion of the
French. The procedures of common graves and shallow burials were
a menace to public health.[44] The disgusting state of the tombs
at Saint-Antoine's, as well as the cardinal's desire to use this
prime real estate for other purposes, made Lavigerie and Cambon
wish to forbid additional burials downtown. In June 1883 Lavigerie
advised Cambon to take advantage of a wave of cholera that was
on its way from Cairo: "If it arrives in July or August, it will
be a real disaster."[45] The Italians and Maltese had such a horror
of cholera that, with proper timing, a ban on burials within 500
meters of the city limits should give them a sense of relief.
Lavigerie provided Cambon with the "Draft of a Beylical Decree."[46]

This was not used until the "Fondati Affair" of May 1885. The
diocese refused to permit burial of a relative of the former director of the vicariate's goods. The Fondatis had never actually
paid for their plot at Saint-Antoine's, but the municipality

reversed the decision against them. During the disorders which
occurred at the cemetery, the mourners tore down a wall. Lavigerie
wrote Cambon that this was one of the "thousand deeds in that
daily war which has been going on for three years."[47] Its result
was a municipal decree of 7 October forbidding further burials at
Saint-Antoine's.[48]

The city had bought Lavigerie's new cemetery on 26 July for
80,000 francs to be paid over five years. At the end of this time,
in 1890, Lavigerie could legally build his Tunis cathedral on part
of Saint-Antoine's and sell the rest of it, provided he transport
the old graves to Bab-el-Khadra or to the crypt of the future
cathedral of Tunis. The cathedral's co-patrons were to be
St. Vincent de Paul, a former slave in Tunisia, and St. Olive, a
Sicilian virgin martyred there. The Italian Curé of Sainte-Croix
went home to raise money for St. Olive's monument, but more than
a hundred Maltese and Italians signed petitions protesting removal of their dead. Vicar General Gazaniol's report to the residence stated that many of the signatures were obtained by incredible means from minors, women, persons with no title to the
graves, and illiterates who did not know what they were signing.
The Italian and British consuls tried to persuade their constituents to permit removal of the graves at the Church's expense. By
the end of this episode only a minority of the petitioners still
objected. Some of the others even subscribed money to the Cathedral of St. Vincent and St. Olive, which was begun in 1890 and
completed seven years later.[49]

The other source of recurring Franco-Italian tension in Tunisia
was the community of Capuchins, "who conserve here vis-à-vis us
an independent and absolute power."[50] Lavigerie finally sent them
all home exactly one decade after getting control of the vicariate.
Despite the Capuchins' initial defiance of his authority, their
outward behavior was correct. But they resented his regime, and

by late 1883 only eleven Italians remained. This was barely half
the number of Capuchin priests and brothers in Tunisia on
Lavigerie's arrival. Some friction developed between them and the
French and Maltese confreres whom Lavigerie imported in order to
dilute their nationalism. Lavigerie claimed it was difficult to
find French and Maltese monks willing to serve under an Italian
superior. Because of this shortage of personnel Lavigerie sought
to place non-Capuchin clergy in charge of some of the nine pre-
protectorate parishes. Friction developed between Lavigerie and
the Prefect Salvatore da Napoli, who decided to leave at the end
of 1883. Lavigerie wanted the Capuchins' mission to stay, for he
needed them to serve the large Italian community in Tunisia. He
especially wanted to prevent the uproar among the laity which the
departure of their confessors would cause. Salvatore stayed until
1884, when Lavigerie arranged for him to became a bishop.

Despite the moderating influence of Fr. Felice of Malta within
the Capuchin community,[51] by 1887 their differences with Lavigerie
had resulted in the departure or replacement of twenty-one Italians (fourteen priests and seven brothers). The Capuchins retained
only four parishes in the country. Their superior general at Rome
therefore proposed to the Propaganda in March 1887 a complete
withdrawal from Tunisia. The pretext for this was a shortage of
men resulting from French and Italian government measures against
religious congregations. Lavigerie opposed the Capuchins' decision
to withdraw because of the recrimination it would cause among the
Italian laity. He also warned Simeoni and the Pope that the
Capuchins' "collective departure" would provoke criticism in the
liberal press of Italy against the Holy See for betraying national
interests. Lavigerie obtained at Rome a direct order from the Pope
that the Capuchins remain in Tunisia. In 1888 only four of the
community were Italian. By September of that year their relations
with Lavigerie had deteriorated so much that he gave to the nuns

of the Italian hospital the gold clock which the Capuchins had
just presented to him for his twenty-fifth anniversary as a
bishop.[52]

It is not absolutely clear what finally provoked Lavigerie in
1891 to expel the Capuchins. There were difficulties regarding
the choice of personnel for parishes at Tunis, Bizerta, and La
Goulette.[53] Friction developed after the visit in February of the
new superior general of the Capuchin order. The father general
had placed Fr. Vincenzo in charge of the Capuchin community without the approval of Lavigerie, who had a right to be consulted on
such an appointment. Lavigerie wrote to the superior general at
Rome protesting the Capuchins' disregard of diocesan authority.
Because of that disregard he announced his decision to renounce
earlier objections to the departure of the twelve Capuchin priests
and brothers still in Tunisia. Lavigerie's procurator at Rome,
Fr. Louis Burtin, was assigned to work with the Capuchin authorities in orchestrating their quiet repatriation. Lavigerie suggested the Capuchins' shortage of personnel as a pretext for
their withdrawal from Tunisia.[54]

The Capuchin procurator general replied that, since they remained in Tunisia by the Pope's direct order, only the Pope could
rescind it. On 21 May the appropriate order for withdrawal went
from the Propaganda to the Capuchin superiors, who transmitted
the order to the Province of Malta on 8 June. Three days later
Burtin told the Capuchin superiors at Rome that their confreres
in Tunisia had leaked the news, forcing Lavigerie to announce it
publicly. Lavigerie also sent a French priest to take over the
parish at La Goulette with no warning, which greatly offended
Italians in the Tunis area. The Capuchins at Rome denied any indiscretion on their part, and they blamed Lavigerie for acting
before they could carry out an orderly withdrawal. The Capuchin
secretary general of missions detailed all of this in a memoir

to Simeoni. The Capuchins were prepared to document their account, and they requested its publication.[55]

The whole affair caught French diplomats at Tunis, Paris, and Rome by surprise. Cardinals in the Curia shared the Quai d'Orsay's astonishment and irritation.[56] Lavigerie's decision to change the original schedule for the Capuchins' withdrawal seemed to relate to the French navy's refusal to let him use the "Hirondelle" to go from La Goulette to Algiers. Lavigerie was sick, and he dreaded a rough journey by rail. The government's "act of public cruelty" enraged him. He took the train on 15 June. Upon arriving at Algiers he sent a letter to Massicault, who was on vacation. Lavigerie demanded "under pain of finally giving my resignation" that the government underwrite his episcopal expenses in Tunisia.[57] The abrupt expulsion of the natural heirs to Lavigerie's mitre seemed intended to make his resignation threat more credible; the expulsion would enable him to quit Carthage without leaving the Capuchins behind to make trouble for France. Lavigerie claimed to have rendered this service to France without consulting any officials because he did not want them to take the blame for it. Massicault's letter of 23 June to Foreign Minister Ribot noted that getting rid of the Capuchins was basically a gain. But he feared that, even under those circumstances, Lavigerie's resignation would diminish French influence in Tunisia.[58]

The storm at Tunis continued for another month, during which Lavigerie wired his instructions to Tournier and to Burtin from Algiers. At Lavigerie's insistence, the Maltese father provincial, Bernardo, arrived at La Goulette on 19 June to try to ease the crisis. His orders from Rome were to close down the Capuchin community in Tunisia with a minimum of disorder. This was not easy. The editor of L'Unione, Sig. Fabri, and Count Raffo, discreetly supported by the Italian consul, organized a public meeting of 800 Italians and Maltese to protest Lavigerie's action. For

freethinkers and Jews at the meeting, Lavigerie had provided an
occasion to vent their hostility to France. Ten thousand Italians,
Spanish, and Maltese signed a protest petition, which a delegation took to the Vatican. La Riforma in Rome stated that this
would not save the Capuchins, for their expulsion was part of a
larger rapprochement between France and the Holy See. From Algiers
Lavigerie himself exhorted the delegation to work at Rome for
repeal of the anticlerical laws which had forced the Capuchin
order to bring their men home.[59]

He wrote to Massicault on 19 June: "This morning I received
from Rome a dispatch which informs me that the Pope will not let
himself be shaken, and that all will soon be finished. It is but
a question of days."[60] The Pope at first refused to receive the
delegation from Tunis, but he relented and met with two of them
on 3 July. They realized, despite Leo's courtesy and warmth,
that he would not repudiate the cardinal. Nonetheless, Ambassador
de Béhaine reported to Paris the Pope's "surprise and fatigue" at
the trouble precipitated by Lavigerie. L'Unione stated that there
had been a tumultuous meeting at the Propaganda attended by twenty
cardinals, who divided for and against Lavigerie. The pro-Italian
faction reportedly blamed openly the Holy See's "sort of alliance"
with France, so embarrassing to the Church in a time of war
against the Italian government. But the Vatican's instructions
for Bernardo were still to send the Capuchins from Tunis one or
two at a time. Lavigerie wired Tournier that they were not leaving
soon enough. The first pair left on 10 July, and most of their
confreres soon followed. Italian and Maltese supporters were restrained and dignified in their farewell demonstrations of sympathy. The last of the Capuchins left in October.[61] Because of
their expulsion Lavigerie lost his great popularity among the
Maltese, but it did not seem to worry him; he had eliminated the
Italian fifth column from his clergy.[62]

This essentially completed Lavigerie's work in Tunisia. His loyal clergy numbered more than sixty priests. They served in fifteen new parishes, many schools, a hospital, an old-age home, a provisional cathedral with episcopal offices, and the primatial basilica at Carthage. In addition to these diocesan facilities, the White Fathers trained their missionaries at the Scholasticate of Saint-Louis, and a novitiate for White Sisters was located nearby. "Vin de Carthage," produced at the White Fathers' vineyards, won a grand prize at the 1889 Paris Exposition. The Society later established another scholasticate and vineyard at Thibar, and during the 1890s an agricultural settlement accommodated the orphans whom they had raised. Lavigerie was careful to keep the distinction between diocesan facilities and his own mission establishments in order to facilitate the government's financial assistance to the former.[63] Obtaining help from the government was a constant struggle; the "Hirondelle" contretemps was one of many such episodes over the years. Lavigerie's patriotic motive for building the Archdiocese of Carthage made official ingratitude harder to bear, especially considering the way in which he served as a lightning rod for anti-French sentiment in Tunisia.

He wanted as much as possible to glorify Africa's primal see in anticipation of the continent's conversion to Christianity. By force of personality he accomplished a great deal in that regard, raising scores of buildings, eliciting Vatican reinforcement of his claims, and surrounding his throne in the basilica with a court of prelates. But Linvinhac refused to maintain after him the personal union of Carthage and Maison-Carrée. Lavigerie bequeathed the primatial trappings of Carthage to worthy successors who continued its momentum of growth until the end of the protectorate.

VIII
The Struggle for Funds

Lavigerie's least complicated problem, finances, remained the most intractable one from 1881 until his death eleven years later. By the end of Cambon's term he and Lavigerie had "successively demolished the principal obstacles"[1] to the French regime - except for one. Lavigerie could satisfy only a portion of Carthage's needs from Catholic contributions and his own investments. He rigorously avoided deficit spending in his projects, with one exception: he mortgaged himself to the hilt in 1881 to buy real estate in Tunisia right after the invasion. His memoir of Christmas 1881 to Cardinal Simeoni stated his conviction that starting construction before raising funds was bad business. When he died, he left the White Fathers little cash for an endowment, but the Society and the Sees of Carthage and Algiers were solvent.[2]

In order to meet his requirements he kept steady pressure on the government, but even the support of cabinets headed by Ferry and Gambetta was limited. Neither leader of the domestic program against the Church could justify making an official exception of the Cardinal of Carthage and Algiers on the basis of an expansionist design which many deputies and citizens condemned. Some politicians used Lavigerie as a target for attacking government policy in Tunisia.[3] On issues which clearly touched the national interest he could appeal to French citizens over the government's head. Lavigerie created a particular uproar in 1885 over suppression of the Algerian seminary credit. In this constant struggle for funds he juggled a situation in which republican leaders, Tunisian officials, Vatican prelates, Catholics in the métropole, and French patriots who were not practicing Catholics, each had an influence.

Managing these different factors, Lavigerie stressed his credentials as an imperialist and as a missionary.

The financial aspect is perhaps where Lavigerie's contribution
to French power in North Africa appears most sharply. A few statistics provide the background. During the twenty years before
Lavigerie's arrival in North Africa monarchist regimes had spent
an average of 1,119,000 francs annually to build churches,
schools, and seminaries there. During the decade of 1867 to 1876
the "first colon of Algeria" built 49 places of worship and accommodated 11 congregations, dispensing nearly 9 million francs.
These facilities were in place at the time of the first annual
attack on the cults budget in 1876.[4] When Lavigerie imposed his
religious protectorate on Tunisia, he could count on little government support for operating expenses, and the task of finding
6 million francs for construction of the new diocese fell completely on him.[5] Without him that amount of capital would never
have been raised.

The Propagation de la Foi had set the pattern for routine fund-
raising which Lavigerie adapted so successfully. These efforts
annually produced hundreds of thousands of francs. Lavigerie circulated written appeals in France and acknowledged large contributions with commemorative literature and handwritten thanks.
He sent White Fathers on quest in Europe and North America.
Charmetant regularly toured the chateaux of France, sometimes en-
countering hostility. The Bishop of Laval threatened to appeal to
the police against him: "Algeria was a pit that swallowed up
money without result."[6] Fr. Delattre made a tour of Canada
before going to Tunisia in 1875. Lavigerie spurred his priests
on with letters which sympathized with their discouragement. He
wrote to Delattre in Marseille at the end of November 1878, scold-
ing him for not keeping to his rounds. Lavigerie himself had been
turned away many times, and he emphasized to Delatttre that

sometimes the hardest tours resulted in the greatest contributions.[7]

The Society's organ, Missions d'Alger, developed a wide circulation in France and kept the White Fathers' work in the public
eye. Lavigerie's talent for getting secular press coverage enabled him to publicize his patriotic endeavors beyond the circle
of readers who responded to apostolic appeals. Lavigerie often
published signed articles in Missions d'Alger, Propagation de la
Foi, and other periodicals, emphasizing the missionaries' noble
task among the natives and the manner in which such work enhanced
the grandeur of France.

There were many patriotic French Catholics willing to contribute to his early program at Saint-Louis de Carthage. The shrine
offered monarchists an ideal means of supporting French national
policy without compromising their politics. Nothing seemed more
likely to revive the glory of the old regime in that area than
an expanded chapel with shelters for orphans and the aged.
Lavigerie wrote to several pastors of churches in France named
after St. Louis, requesting gifts to equip the sacristy. The descendants of the nobles who had accompanied St. Louis on crusade
could have their family names inscribed in the new monument by
contributing to it. Chambord led the nobility's subscription,
and even the wife of President MacMahon donated an ornament to
the chapel. By 1876 Charmetant and Count de Buisseret, head of
the committee to restore Saint-Louis, had raised 300,000 francs.[8]

There were occasional millionaires who sought a noble title.
Lavigerie wrote Charmetant that in exceptional cases he could
ask the Pope to give the title of count to a generous contributor
who showed the "most honorable sentiments." Charmetant later got
into a dispute with a Mme Martinet, who had pledged 25,000 francs
for the seminary at Carthage in return for a papal title for her
son. She misunderstood the terms and balked at paying the Vatican

an extra 8,000 francs for the fees. "In all of this there is a very unbecoming haggling on the part of these parvenus."[9]

For his operating expenses Lavigerie received help from two French mission organizations, the Sainte-Enfance and the Propagation de la Foi. Lavigerie's relationship with the Sainte-Enfance was not always harmonious. Soon after Pope Leo XIII gave the White Fathers missionary jurisdiction in equatorial Africa in 1878, Lavigerie obtained a blunt letter from the Propaganda Fide "requesting" the council of the Sainte-Enfance to give him 200,000 francs for this new territory. The members of the council were prepared to submit to a direct papal order to subsidize one of Leo's favorite projects, but they intended to publicize it in a manner as disagreeable as possible. Charmetant reported to Lavigerie that they hated him and were prepared to make a scandal in the press. After the leadership of the Sainte-Enfance changed, they finally agreed to give 50,000 francs per year. Lavigerie had a better rapport with the Propagation de la Foi, which provided large subsidies to the White Fathers in equatorial Africa, and later in Tunisia. In 1882 its allocation of 260,000 francs for Lavigerie's various projects included 60,000 for the protectorate.[10]

But such amounts were negligible in the face of Lavigerie's need for construction capital in Tunisia. During the first year of the protectorate he estimated 3.5 million francs as his requirement for "the moral conquest of the land."[11] At Paris in August 1881 Lavigerie met with the political director of the Quai d'Orsay, who was sympathetic but not encouraging. Courcel stated candidly that military questions took priority over those of administrative reorganization. The effect of additional troop assignments to suppress the rebellion made the government cautious. Ferry could not press for any substantial appropriation which would offend anticlerical moderates and further erode his

tenuous majority. The radicals had informers in all the ministries, which kept officials from giving Lavigerie large amounts
by administrative means. Roustan urged Foreign Minister Barthélemy
to give Lavigerie additional help, but the ministers dared not
act in the summer of 1881.[12]

All they offered was moral support for an appeal in August to
the bishops of France. Barthélemy willingly put his name to the
text of a letter composed by Lavigerie which recommended the
appeal to Flourens in terms of the national interest. The director
general of cults distributed copies of it to the hierarchy, while
Lavigerie's own private circular asked them to stress in public
the religious importance of his work rather than its political
implications. But the appeal was unhappily timed at the height
of the electoral campaign. Tunisia was closely identified with
the republicans, and monarchist contributors were hostile to
French involvement there. Some Catholics still held against
Lavigerie his willingness the previous year to compromise with
the anticlericals regarding the March Decrees. Dependent on monarchist contributors themselves, some bishops were very timid in
their endorsements, and a few gave almost no support at all. Yet
others like the Archbishop of Rheims commended Lavigerie's appeal
in terms which expressed their own approval of the occupation as
well: "The Church and France are involved in the success of this
peaceful mission; religion and patriotism invite us to cooperate
in it."[13] But the 1881 appeal yielded only 300,000 francs.

During the first year of the protectorate Lavigerie received
only small amounts of direct aid from the French government.
Earlier chapters have mentioned some of the subventions and furnishings provided by various ministries. In addition, the Ministry
of Cults approved the assignment of members of Lavigerie's
Algiers staff to assist him at his other headquarters. There was
no objection to his using extra cathedral vestments and ornaments

on his travels in Tunisia. The international commission, charged
in autumn with compensating Europeans for damage done during the
pillage and shelling of Sfax, gave favored status and quick action to the claims of the Sisters of St. Joseph and the Catholic
parish. The Post Office approved Lavigerie's request for a telegraph franchise to cover his wires to French officials and to
his clergy in Paris and Algiers. But none of these measures
helped build new churches, and they provided only a small frac-
tion of the estimated 75,000 francs which Lavigerie needed for
clerical salaries in Tunisia.[14]

His ingenuity was limitless in suggesting various resources
for the government to use on his behalf. The apostolic administrator's first memoir to the government emphasized the importance
of obtaining French control over the parishes. He outlined the
means for acquiring the right of patronat: France should obtain
from the regency beylical properties which could be sold for the
costs of constructing new parishes or given to contractors in
exchange for building them. Canon law upheld the government's
right as donor to control the appointment of pastors. Lavigerie
also suggested this device for endowing the existing parishes so
as to control their future appointments. "Here is a simple and
practical means of changing the present situation swiftly and
without violence, in rendering useless the precautions taken by
the Italian Capuchins to remain masters, and even in turning their
precautions against them."[15] Roustan endorsed this idea in principle, although he expressed his doubts to Lavigerie and to the
foreign minister concerning the resources of the bey, who had
difficulty covering his own expenses.[16]

Considering the damage done to Church property during the rebellion, it seemed reasonable that for the first year a part of
the Sfax and Kairouan indemnities be assigned to him. Roustan
endorsed his appeals, urging Gambetta to include Tunisia under

the cults budget for Algiers, inasmuch as the occupation troops
had been attached to the Algerian Nineteenth Corps. "The clergy
represent another sort of occupation, which has as much importance in regard to the special conditions of this land."[17] But
government officials in Paris pointed out to Charmetant that the
press would be watching closely the use of the war indemnity.
They preferred the idea of using property owned by the bey.[18]

The apostolic administrator reviewed his requirements and
prospects for the coming year (1882) in a Christmas report to
Cardinal Simeoni at the Propaganda. Lavigerie asked Simeoni's
recommendation for help from the Propagation de la Foi, and he
suggested a scenario by which the Vatican might pressure the
French government to underwrite part of the vicariate's capital
expenses: he would write to Simeoni requesting a certain sum.
The prefect should reply informing him that the money was not
available and noting the obligation tacitly accepted by the government. On this basis Lavigerie could state his own case from
Tunisia while the Vatican worked through the French ambassador
at Rome and the Paris nuncio. Lavigerie expected that such a combination of pressure would be effective.[19]

He took off the velvet glove on 10 January 1882 in a letter
to Premier and Foreign Minister Gambetta. Since the military period was over, it was timely to consider the government's responsibility for the support of Tunisia's clergy. The succession of
an Italian prelate was clearly possible if France should fail to
meet her obligation. The Holy See had insisted on maintaining
the rights of the Capuchins, who lived on the alms of their own
flocks. Lavigerie had recently learned that the British government planned to subsidize Maltese priests as a means of countering
French influence, and Italy would doubtless follow that example.
It was hard enough to control these foreign priests, but salaries
from their governments would make them "a state within a state."

Roustan's report supported Lavigerie's argument: "The only government existing in their eyes will be that which pays them."[20] With
reference to the Chamber, Lavigerie's letter to Gambetta noted
the example of Bismarck. During eleven years of Kulturkampf,
while the Iron Chancellor was jailing German bishops and priests,
he augmented the salaries of clergy in Alsace-Lorraine who got
nothing from French politicians but anticlerical speeches. "To a
lesser extent the situation is the same in Tunisia. In foreign
pay the clergy there can create a grave embarrassment by their
influence on a population whose religious ardor often verges on
fanaticism. The Holy See can take their side, since it has frankly
reserved to itself the right of nominating to the apostolic ad-
ministratorship an Italian or an Anglo-Maltese bishop."[21]

Lavigerie's threat, reinforced through Vatican channels, had
its effect. He visited Paris and discussed Tunisian affairs with
Gambetta, who agreed to provide Lavigerie with 50,000 francs from
special funds of the Ministry of Cults. The cabinet fell in late
January before this allocation was completed, but Freycinet approved his predecessor's decision. This evaded an immediate accounting to the Chamber, although the day of reckoning came in
November.[22]

This amount was hardly adequate, especially considering Italian
and Maltese proposals to set up lay schools in competition with
Lavigerie's. Italian consular agents spared no pressure on parents
to enroll their children. Lavigerie prepared an extensive report
for Roustan on the educational needs of the European community,
urging the improvement of existing primary schools and the addition of nineteen more. He estimated an annual payroll of 83,600
francs. In order to bypass the Chamber, he suggested this be obtained through the Foreign Ministry budget, which provided
1,113,000 francs in 1882 for overseas religious and educational
establishments. Lavigerie's 60,000 francs, by far the largest

subvention under that heading, continued until his death.[23] He
still felt a strong sense of grievance that the ministers would
only grant funds under discretionary headings in small amounts
which did not require legislative review. These totalled 110,000
francs for 1882 and 123,000 for 1883, but he needed much more.[24]

During his trip to Paris in spring 1882 to receive the cardinal's biretta, Lavigerie tried to get more help from the Ministry of Cults. He urged the use in Tunisia of reliquat appointments, clerical posts which fell vacant during the year and were
available for assignment at large. An alternative was suggested
by the decree of 22 April 1882 which attached Tunisia's administrative services to respective ministries in Paris. In keeping
with the attachment decree, a marginal note in the cults budget
could authorize the use of unspecified funds in Tunisia while
evading debate in the Chamber over particular listings. In July
Lavigerie threatened to leave Tunis if the ministers would not
help him. They considered his suggestions but held back for fear
of triggering an uproar. Jules Roche and others of the extreme
left had revived the issue that year of separating church and
state, as well as suppressing the orders completely.[25]

The hostility which Freycinet had attempted to evade finally
erupted during the ministry of Charles-Théodore-Eugène Duclerc
(August 1882 to January 1883). In connection with Roche's interpellation of 16 November, the radicals attacked Premier and Foreign Minister Duclerc's predecessor for Lavigerie's 50,000-franc
grant. The new minister of cults, Armand Fallières, lamely responded in terms of French interests in the regency and the importance of the clergy; but he did not dare to specify the
republic's financial commitment as the Vatican's price for a
French ecclesiastical regime. Paul Bert accused the cardinal of
leading "Tunisian vespers" against the republic. Clemenceau cried
scandal, demanding to know why the Archbishop of Algiers neglected

his see. Only Bassetière defended him, repeating Il Diritto and
Crispi's ironic tribute: "That bishop is worth an army to us,
M. Clemenceau!" The radical leader claimed not to understand.
Two days later Fallières answered Roche's interpellation with
more vague remarks about Lavigerie's sacrifices and the strict
legality of the cults subvention. Only Jules Ferry spoke directly
to the issue, declaring that the apostolic administrator's nomination had engaged the honor of France for his support. This
fueled another barrage, although the radicals could not rally a
majority for the order of the day condemning Freycinet's ministry.[26]

The press debated the question vigorously. La Solidarité
charged the prelate with ambitiously exploiting a patriotic cause
in order to extend his influence. Le Constitutionnel criticized
Duclerc for letting such a storm develop when a brief explanation
would have dampened the controversy. In any event, accusations
in November that White Fathers had gone among the tribes evangelizing Arabs destroyed any chance of a marginal note to the
budget of cults for attachment. Lavigerie sent to the current
director of the Ecoles d'Orient an open letter strongly denying
that his priests in Tunisia were employed outside of parish,
school, or hospital ministry to European Christians. Turning to
the broader issue of overseas expansion, he defended the government program in Tunisia. He lamented the sorry contrast between
French criticism of overseas policy and British public support
for the Foreign Office's venture in Egypt. In keeping with government policy, the White Fathers refrained from any ministry to
the "fanatical" Arabs, and Lavigerie denied rumors that several
of them had been killed at the gates of Kairouan - his half-dozen
martyrs were buried in equatorial Africa and the Sahara![27]

Another letter urged Prime Minister Duclerc to set the record
straight during Senate debates on the budget. Lavigerie claimed

that the basic problem was the government's unwillingness to explain the issue fully to the legislature. He threatened to
resign. He stated also to Fallières: "It is not acceptable, indeed, either for the government or for us, to see renewed on the
part of the opposition, attacks which a noisy minority has raised
this year."[28] Duclerc privately expressed to the Ministry of
Public Instruction his high opinion of Lavigerie's schools in
Tunisia, and he told Charmetant that he would "scrape all the
drawers of the ministry" to find Lavigerie's 50,000 francs. But
Duclerc gave top priority to Tunisia's administrative reorganization, and his government would not fight for Lavigerie in the
Chamber. The 50,000-franc subsidy from Cults was finally struck
in June 1883 from the budget for 1884.

Lavigerie still pressed for support, pointing out to the foreign minister that government aid amounted to only one-tenth of
the 1.1 million francs he had spent in 1882. But the republican
Chamber responded by totally suppressing the scholarships for
seminarians in Algeria. Lavigerie's letter to the members of the
Senate Budget Commission noted that French colons who originally
had required government assistance to settle in Algeria were
hardly able to finance the education of their sons. Stipends for
these seminarians were vitally important in terms of national
security in the colonies, for French pastors had great influence
in North African parishes of mixed populations. Lavigerie noted
the possibility of a future war with Spain, Italy, or Britain,
and he urged the senators to reconsider: "The suppression of
scholarships in the seminaries of Algeria is, in effect, the complete suppression, in the near future, of all French clergy in
North Africa. The suppression of French clergy in North Africa is
a peril for the influence of our country."[29]

Such considerations were restored to a high priority in February
1883 with the return to power of Jules Ferry, who had increased

his following among the opportunists after the recent death of
Gambetta. As the foremost exponent of overseas expansion, Ferry
was Lavigerie's patron even while the anticlericals chopped away
at the budget of cults. He wrote to his wife in August 1883 that,
having subdued the clergy and the orders, "we can now pursue a
moderate policy."[30] In the Chamber the new minister of cults
had unsuccessfully supported the attachment of Tunisian clergy
to the Algiers budget, and Lavigerie's conferences in Paris during June and July produced a combination of 135,000 francs in
various government grants. At Tunis the new director of public
instruction, Louis Machuel, negotiated the agreement to pay most
of the vicariate's religious teachers from the beylical budget.

Cambon wrote from Paris in June 1884 that Ferry's opinion of
Lavigerie was so high that he would give him whatever he wanted.
He asked that twenty-five of his priests be salaried under the
Ministry of War as chaplains. The need of French troops in Tunisia
could be documented, for in a strict canonical sense the nearest
French parish was in Marseille or Algeria. This means of subsidiz-
ing the clergy continued long after the bulk of French troops
were withdrawn. Following the restoration of Carthage as a regular diocese, Lavigerie applied to the Ministry of Cults to subsidize the twenty-one of his French priests who still received
nothing from any government source. A decree of 5 January 1885
awarded 500 francs per year to each of them. Thus in 1885 the
government managed by some means to support all forty-five Frenchmen in Lavigerie's diocesan staff of sixty-one. This willingness
to assist him by executive devices was partial compensation for
legislative cuts in the budget of cults.[31]

The protectorate's anomalous status facilitated a looser application of such subsidies, once obtained, than was permissible
in the métropole, but the cults minister, Goblet, admonished the
cardinal to reserve government appointments for French nationals.

He emphasized the necessity of following bureaucratic norms so
as not to jeopardize credits for future years. More important,
this was an indispensable preliminary to permitting the consolidation of Tunisia into the regular cults administration. Lavigerie
promised all deliberate speed in conforming to French procedures,
but he noted the extraordinary situation in the regency, and he
refused to compel his Italian and Maltese priests to become
French citizens. This problem resulted in the elimination of two
chaplaincies in late 1888.[32] Ten chaplaincies were maintained
into the twentieth century, and five of these tenures extended
several years after the 1905 renunciation of the French
Concordat.[33]

French control of several churches and hospices in the Holy
City enabled the government to help Lavigerie in another manner
which avoided any parliamentary incident, but which caused some
resentment at Rome. Lavigerie had requested a rector's appointment
in September 1882 in order to maintain a procurator for his business with the Holy See, but the project did not receive serious
consideration until Ferry's return to power. France enjoyed the
right of patronat over these churches, and a dispute developed
over the use of one of them for the White Fathers. In Rome the
Abbé Puyol, superior of Saint-Louis des Français, strongly objected on the grounds that the French Pious Establishments were
a prerepublican heritage held in trust by the national Church,
and not to be administered as plums in the gift of the Quai
d'Orsay. Desprez's successor, Ambassador Lefebvre de Béhaine,
agreed with Puyol in opposing this subsidy for the White Fathers.
Béhaine joined with Lavigerie's enemies at Rome, who included the
former nuncio to Paris, Cardinal Czacki. Part of their hostility
no doubt derived from resentment at the way in which Lavigerie
had himself become a sort of ambassador-nuncio between French
ministers and the Pope. But Premier Ferry backed Lavigerie: "The

more I examine this question, the more it seems to me that there
would be real political advantage in establishing at Rome a community of Algiers Missionaries."[34]

The prime minister decided to have six White Fathers assigned
to chaplaincies paying 2,400 francs per year. During his visit
to Rome in May and June of 1884, Lavigerie worked on the details
of these appointments to the Church of Saint-Nicolas des Lorrains.
Ferry impressed Béhaine with the importance of aiding the recruitment of these patriotic missionaries. The ambassador asked the
cardinal-secretary of state to inform Mgr. Puyol that "his duty
is to protect loyally, rather than to attack, the community which
he directs under the high patronage of the Ambassador of France
to the Holy See."[35] After wrangling over the terms and duration
of the lease for Saint-Nicholas, Lavigerie obtained the appointments he wanted in order to support his procurator Louis Burtin,
and other White Fathers who were studying at Rome for advanced
degrees.[36]

Jules Berry's support encouraged Lavigerie to persevere in his
Tunisian projects, particularly the restoration of Carthage. So
long as Lavigerie had the prime minister's complete confidence
he could tolerate routine vexations like Italian press slanders
and anticlerical inroads on the cults budget for North Africa.
Beginning with an attack on the 1876 budget of 850,000 francs,
over a ten-year period the anticlericals had reduced the annual
appropriation for the Church in Algeria by 578,000 francs. Part
of this loss was included in the 4.8 million francs cut from the
national cults budget voted in spring 1884. French press attacks
on Lavigerie were taken up by Italian papers on the theme that
Lavigerie was not a bishop, but a "political agent of France."
He declined the government's nomination for the Legion of Honor
so as not to compromise his appearance of independence before
foreigners.[37] After such selfless devotion to France, the Chamber's

decision in May 1885 to strike the 100,000-franc credit for North African seminaries was outrageous. Ferry's ministry had fallen because of the Tonkin issue, and Henri Brisson became premier (April 1885 to January 1886). The suppression of the seminary credit was the last straw.[38]

Lavigerie went on a rampage, stirring up the voters so much that the government was forced to buy him off. He toured France's major churches, calling upon the faithful to support his work after this scandalous "act of official atheism." He contrasted the influence of religion in Tunisia with the Mahdi rebellion in the Sudan. His priests extended French influence farther into Africa than the French army; King Mtesa of Uganda had asked White Fathers there to place his country under the republic's protection. At a sensational Paris lecture given on 10 May in the Church of the Madeleine Lavigerie apologized for his "simple missionary's" lack of eloquence. He relied, instead, upon the gesture of a prince of the Church walking among the congregation, passing the plate for patriotism. At Saint-Sulpice he wept from the pulpit, dissolving his audience in tears.[39] Later he preached at the biggest church in Lille: "If the government cuts off our funds we will be abandoning North Africa to foreign clergy and to the contempt of foreign flocks."[40] The public responded to these appeals with tens of thousands of francs.

The prefect of the Nord, Jules Cambon, whose predecessor and brother was the Tunisian resident, wrote to the minister of interior and cults that this tour was beginning to affect the government's popularity. Lavigerie's priests did not always follow his example of moderation in avoiding direct attacks upon the republic. Precisely by his own restraint Lavigerie gained sympathy from beyond clerical circles. Criticism of the Chamber's unpatriotic decision did the republicans great harm; the moderate press joined Catholic and conservative journals in sympathy.

Jules Cambon urged the minister to negotiate an end to this barn-
storming. The minister forwarded the report to Ferry, vouching
for its accuracy and requesting that Lavigerie be persuaded to
calm down. The government offered secret compensations for part
of the 578,000-franc reductions, but the cardinal insisted upon
a public vindication. He continued to preach and beg, setting up
an organization of dames patronesses for wealthy women who assisted
his work. These activities began to complicate the campaign for
October elections.[41] Finally the secretary of the nunciature asked
Lavigerie in the name of Rome to bargain with Brisson's cabinet.
The moderate press urged Cults Minister Goblet to give his seminaries the 100,000 francs, which the Chamber restored on
8 August.

This eliminated one election issue just as the campaign intensified. The prefect of Algiers reported to Goblet that the archbishop's attitude and behavior during the elections was "absolutely
correct," although at the request of the Pope he issued a circular
to his clergy in mid-August on "Justice and Liberty." He asked his
priests to avoid politics but called upon Catholics to stand together to protect the Church against the atheists. This letter
was very moderate in tone, claiming only the right of bishops to
speak in defense of the Faith under attack. It was followed, however, by more provocative pastorals from other bishops within
France.[42]

After the elections Goblet, who congratulated himself for recovering Lavigerie's 100,000 francs, complained before the
Chamber: "In truth I have been ill recompensed! I regret to say
it is the Cardinal-Archbishop of Algiers who gave the signal for
that campaign of episcopal circulars against the Republic." The
minister's attempt to play the role of unrecognized protector
drew a retort in the Senate from M. Buffet: "In truth, Cardinal
Lavigerie can believe that he has largely paid his debt in advance;

and far from being your debtor, he remains your creditor. Do you
know any man who has rendered more eminent services to the mother
country in Africa?" Challenging Goblet to find anything objectionable in the pastoral, Buffet quoted Lavigerie's request for his
priests to thank the country for restoring part of their credits
and to renew their devotion and loving prayers for France: "And
this, Mr. Minister, is the letter that you denounce from the
height of the tribune like an armed insurrection against the
Republic!"[43]

By this time, however, the radicals were less menacing than
their public utterances. The fall of Ferry had given rise to
Catholic fears, but in secret conferences several radical leaders
disclosed to Lavigerie that their public positions were more extreme than their actual intentions. In time the republicans became increasingly wary of driving Catholics to the support of the
man on horseback, Boulanger.[44]

Whether Goblet's sense of grievance had been a genuine expression of dismay or a political bid for sympathy, he was more cooperative with Lavigerie the following year. The Freycinet government favored renewal of the cults subvention for seminaries,
but in 1886 the Budget Commission rejected this recommendation.
Parliamentary debate on cults appropriations for North African
seminaries always provoked bitter attacks on Lavigerie, who protested to Premier and Foreign Minister Freycinet. He was willing
to bear Italian slanders patriotically, but to receive such
abuse from the French in full view of foreigners was unacceptable.
He again threatened to leave Tunisia to the Capuchins. Mme Paul
Minck had created a great stir with the charge that Lavigerie was
personally a millionaire, and he decided not to endure further
degradation. His open letter in Missions d'Alger explained that,
after the intolerable demonstrations in Parliament which had
marked his previous struggles for support, he preferred to avoid

"an agony which prolongs itself without honor." The clergy of
Algiers supported this decision to renounce absolutely the
100,000 francs, stating that they "would rather die of hunger
than of shame." Goblet privately assured Lavigerie that the ministry would try to help in other ways. He told the Council of
Ministers that he intended to fix a seminary appropriation of
50,000 francs in the Tunisian budget, which at that time was
around 20 million francs. Lavigerie had long requested help from
that source, but Massicault reported again that it simply was
not possible. To support the Catholic clergy from the beylical
budget without providing similar support for the Muslim and Jewish
faiths would make an outrageous distinction.[45]

Lavigerie continued to pressure Massicault and the Quai d'Orsay
for that form of assistance, but they could not yield. Lavigerie
greatly resented having to "wage war at his own expense,"[46] for
until the end of his life Lavigerie had to wring assistance from
the government in order to run the Archdiocese of Carthage on a
hand-to-mouth basis. Most of the capital for building it came
from private sources.

The nobility's generosity applied generally to projects of a
memorial nature. Lavigerie depended on this source particularly
in his plans for the magnificent basilica and monastery at
Carthage. He had addressed an appeal "A la noblesse française"
in November 1882, proposing to build an armorial for the old
knights. A thousand francs entitled each contributor to a place
for his standard and engraving of the family name in gold.
Chambord led the subscription, which raised 250,000 francs. This
reliance upon the monarchists imposed some prudence in republican
times, particularly in 1883 when Chambord died leaving 100,000
francs for the African missions. Lavigerie promptly notified
Flourens lest some deputy find in his silence a mystery or evidence
that he was organizing "an army of blacks to reestablish the

monarchy."[47] Lavigerie's fund-raising program involved a political
juggling act of sorts, which he managed to keep going until the
Toast of Algiers in 1890, six months after the dedication of the
basilica. The first stone of the shrine was turned in May 1884,
and the next year Lavigerie appealed to the descendants of St.
Louis to build the altar and reliquary for the remains of their
ancestor. He offered to engrave the names of other generous
Frenchmen in the marble of a canon's stall in return for endowing
the prebends of the cathedral chapter.[48]

Construction of the basilica slowed down, and raising the
800,000 francs needed for its completion required the rest of the
decade. In 1886 Lavigerie created two orders for its benefactors.
He established a house and rules for the Canonesses of Carthage,
mostly rich widows and spinsters who followed a regime of light
prayer and good works. Charmetant delivered Mlle Louise Roustan's
membership certificate, and Lavigerie invited the Empress Eugénie
to be honorary head of the organization.[49] The Canons of Carthage
were priests "who added generosity to their other merits."[50] Pope
Leo agreed to entitle them as members of his household. These
monsignors could wear purple cassocks and mitres - with the local
bishop's permission. Each Canon of Carthage donated 30,000 francs
to endow the basilica and received 1,500 francs annual revenue
until his death. A White Father could represent him at Carthage
as his coadjutor. Massicault reported on the eve of the basilica's
dedication that Lavigerie had given ten of these titles to priests
in various French sees.

> One of them, of the Diocese of Rouen, has encountered
> a disappointment. His Archbishop, Mgr. Thomas, forbade
> him to carry the episcopal insignia, and he claimed
> from the Cardinal either his intervention or the res-
> titution of 30,000 francs; but the Cardinal has let
> him know that he does not intervene in the administration

of his Colleagues, and that he does not return money
received.

Two canons were dead almost as soon as named. The
Cardinal replaced them, by [White Fathers], to whom
has now devolved the annual prebend of 1,500 francs.
And it will be done likewise with other losses.[51]

Carthage had a special appeal for French nobles, canonesses,
and would-be monsignors; but Lavigerie needed money for the rest
of Tunisia as well. Soon after taking the vicariate he planned
a lottery. He expected it to yield 3.5 million francs for his
capital projects, but it met with difficulties from the start.
The bey and Prime Minister Freycinet were persuaded to approve
it only by threats, respectively, of assigning the vicariate's
expenses to the beylic and of resigning Tunis. Even then
Lavigerie's name could not appear in the advertising for the
Grande Loterie Tunisienne. Lavigerie established committees, and
Charmetant had to add to his other chores that of organizing the
lottery at Paris. Charmetant went to Gambetta to request support,
or at least silence, from the opportunist press.[52] He hired the
expertise of a M. Avenel to supervise the printing, numbering,
and marketing of 6 million tickets. "You did not know, or else
you concealed from me, that M. Avenel was a Jew, consequently a
man of whom it was doubly necessary to beware for a work like
ours."[53] At the same time Avenel was promoting another lottery
to which he gave a higher priority, and he passed this task on
to a M. Destrée. Because of this conflict of interest, French
economic conditions, and public opinion against the Tunisian
invasion, only seventy-two percent of the tickets were sold.
Lavigerie was furious at Charmetant's "veritable betrayal of the
interests so sacred and so grave which I entrusted to you."[54]
Charmetant wrote Lavigerie a long letter of explanation, asserting the need to have strawmen and expert consultants in a

venture of this kind, and it seems to have ended Lavigerie's
recrimination. The lottery netted 1,041,285 francs, less than
a third of Lavigerie's expectation. And it could not be repeated.[55]

Lavigerie's greatest source of money by far came from profitable real estate ventures. From their arrival at Carthage the
White Fathers discreetly purchased property around Byrsa for
archeological diggings and for expansion of the mission there.
Baron E. de Sainte-Marie at the consulate eagerly passed on real
estate tips to Fr. Bresson or to Lavigerie. Sainte-Marie intervened with owners on the priests' behalf. The latter negotiated
the transactions according to Lavigerie's instructions from
Algeria or Europe. Their correspondence during the 1870s contains
many references to opportunities, pending deals, and strawmen.

> I ask you for information and you send me only the
> names of fractions! Can you not give me the approxi-
> mate area of each of the parcels? Can you not tell me
> their nature? What interest do you have in making me
> bargain with my eyes closed?
>
> And those people of Tunis, are you sure of them?
> Are they associated with the sellers to cheat you?
> At Tunis that is something to beware. . . . How is
> it that you have not bought the amphitheater after
> having asked for the money so long ago? . . . Truly,
> you grieve me by your carelessness.[56]

Roustan thanked Lavigerie on another occasion for informing him
of recent purchases, noting his priests had been so discreet that
he would otherwise not have known about them.[57]

In 1881 Lavigerie made a killing. At the beginning of the
French invasion a number of Tunisians, particularly court favorites, reacted to the uncertainties of the moment by selling property. Lavigerie instructed Bresson on 27 August:

At this moment it is necessary to think seriously of
profiting from favorable circumstances for purchases
according to the instructions I have given you.

. . . As soon as there is no more danger in going
about, you will see a flock of harpies descend on
Tunisia, and it will no longer be the time. What is
necessary is to put hands on the lands near Tunis or
the rail lines of the type which will have a rapid
appreciation.[58]

Lavigerie and Charmetant worked to raise the cash needed to con-
clude the bargains negotiated by Bresson. Lavigerie planned to
buy land in Tunisia by means of a joint-stock corporation, a
project which reminded Charmetant of Richelieu's program for
developing Canada along the St. Lawrence River. Lavigerie wanted
rich practicing Catholics to join in this multimillion-franc
project for Tunisia's economic and spiritual development. The
million for his own participation was to come from mortgaging
properties he and the White Fathers already held.[59]

But French investors, who considered the Tunisian venture to
be a government bid for popularity, were nervous. They had little
confidence in the security of Tunisian land titles, particularly
after the Enfida affair. Kheredine had sold his 96,000-hectare
domain, along with other properties, for 2.5 million francs to
the Société Marseillaise de Crédit. His successor, Prime Minister
Mustapha ben Ismael, joined with British and Maltese enemies of
France in exploiting a Muslim loophole to abbrogate the sale.
Lavigerie had declined the Société Marseillaise's initial invitation to participate in the Enfida's development, and the French
title to it was not safe until sometime after the invasion. In
such a climate Paris bankers rejected Lavigerie's joint-stock
proposal, and they would not even lend him money for mortgages on
Tunisian property.[60]

Lavigerie and Charmetant had to raise capital by other means.
They had some securities in Paris, although Lavigerie instructed
Charmetant on 7 May to hold on to his Tunisian bonds until they
climbed higher. The White Fathers' properties in Algeria were
worth more than 2 million francs. The Société Civile des
Orphelinats Agricoles, which owned them, received title to much
of the Tunisian property financed by mortgaging its farms, vineyards, and orphanages. Officially, this wealth was transferred
to Tunisia in order to put it beyond the anticlerical republic's
reach. In fact, it was the source of capital for speculation on
a grand scale. New acquisitions in Tunisia were to be mortgaged
in turn for further purchases. On the basis of Algerian loans
and Charmetant's financial report from Paris, Lavigerie instructed
Bresson to go as high as 1 million francs if opportunities were
sufficiently attractive. Lavigerie's purchases were customarily
made secretly through agents or strawmen like Amedeo Volterra,
but on 2 June he ordered Bresson to suspend them because they
had been discovered through some leak in their correspondence.[61]

Lavigerie soon directed Fr. Bresson to pursue discussion with
the Société Marseillaise of a purchase of between five and ten
thousand hectares of the Enfida, preferably land near the shore.
The consortium's proposal was based on the condition that
Lavigerie would undertake to provide completely from his own resources facilities for worship and education. Obviously French
promoters shared Roustan's appreciation of Catholicism's contribution to the development of French interests in Tunisia. An establishment of his missionaries would enhance the value of all
land in the area for settlement, and Lavigerie confidently insisted that the terms should involve a purchase at no greater
than the original price. Except for the fact that by 1884 Lavigerie
had established a parish at Enfida, one cannot cite evidence that
these preliminaries led to a sale.[62]

Lavigerie's accumulation of land continued through the 1880s.
He persuaded French authorities to use the bey's right of eminent
domain in helping him purchase several enclaves within his other
tracts at La Marsa and Sidi Bou Said.[63] A parcel near the cardinal's house at La Marsa caused a nasty feud. Sheik Tahar Chebil
had agreed to sell Lavigerie his one-third hectare, and Lavigerie
closed off a nearby path to keep out marauders. Chebil then
raised the asking price, which Lavigerie refused to pay. Chebil
befouled the area with excrement in an "attempted blackmail of
the grossest type. . . . One can add to this that, probably toward the same end, Sheik Chebil has rented his little house to
women of a special category, whose shameful cries continually
make a scandal under the windows of the Cardinal's house."[64]

La Justice of Paris accused Lavigerie the following year of
pressuring Muslims into selling him lands cheap. Lavigerie's
accumulation of properties gave him a reputation for vast wealth,
which struck Edward White Benson, Archbishop of Canterbury, when
he visited Tunisia: "He is a genius in finance." One aspect of
Lavigerie's Maltese policy had been to purchase much of his land
through Maltese agents, who profited from the commissions. By 1892
much of Lavigerie's property was up for sale. The British consul
Drummond Hay told Benson, "He has the face of a banker."[65] Numerous critics noted his deliberately impressive standard of living;
the cardinal's palace and profitable vineyards at La Marsa alone
had cost 600,000 francs.[66]

Lavigerie's reputation for wealth was justified in the sense
that he handled great sums of money, although he stated that they
were "neither millions nor mine."[67] The personal union of
Lavigerie's many projects made them a sort of ecclesiastical
conglomerate. He held personal title to some properties and controlled others through ecclesiastical corporations. He invested this
wealth as a means of protecting and increasing it. His frenzy in

autumn 1884 at the thought of dying in Tunisia before a papal
proxy arrived for settling Carthage's archdiocesan endowment
expressed his sense of stewardship.

But Lavigerie was an absolute autocrat in controlling this
wealth. Priests who questioned his disposal of assets they administered for him were put in their place. Although the White
Fathers' first vicar general for current affairs, Fr. Deguerry,
usually enjoyed the title of superior general, the Vatican had
approved Lavigerie's authority over the Society as superior for
life. When he sold the Collège Saint-Charles at Tunis for 500,000
francs, several of the White Fathers wanted to recover the money
for their Société des Orphelinats; but Lavigerie intended to
spend it on a diocesan seminary at Carthage. He was challenged
at the Société des Orphelinats' meeting of 5 January 1890.
Lavigerie rebuffed the White Fathers' protests on the grounds
that the structure of giving his various works corporate autonomy
was a legal fiction for safeguarding their property against third
parties; they were not to use these precautions against himself.[68]

Lavigerie's testament of 8 June 1890 specified how this wealth
was to be divided. It listed his various works: the Sees of
Algiers and Carthage, the Oeuvrage Antiesclavagiste, the Apostolic
Vicariate of the Sahara, the Société Agricole de l'Algérie, and
the vineyard at Kouba. Lavigerie appointed four executors repre-
senting these interests. They were to settle his debts, determine
the fair division of his property, and arrange ten thousand Masses
for his soul. His widowed sister, Mme Kiener, had the right to
choose from his personal effects; and each executor could select
an object from his sacristy. In the event that any of his executors should claim part of his estate before a tribunal, the property in dispute would go to his sister.[69]

A few days after making this will at Tunis, Lavigerie took the
train to Algiers for the last time, leaving the storm he had

created by abruptly ordering the Capuchin mission out of Tunisia.
He was physically broken from years of overwork and months of
monarchist abuse following the Toast of Algiers. The following
spring, on 7 May 1892, the news of persecution of Catholics in
Uganda brought on a severe stroke which crippled him and left
him bedridden in Algiers. He was too sick to return to Tunisia
alive.[70] One project at Carthage demanded his immediate attention, and that was the completion of his crypt in the basilica.
He dictated a letter to Delattre on 6 August, directing him to
get bids from the Italian marble sculptors; there was no time to
lose.[71] After several very painful months he died on 26 November.
The French government authorized full military honors for the
cardinal, and Governor General Jules Cambon gave the eulogy at
the naval dock of Algiers. While sailors hoisted the casket onto
the "Cosmao," it spun around, impressing one of the bereaved
priests: "He is dead for certain. If he were alive, he would be
screaming at this."[72]

IX
Epilogue and Conclusion

Lavigerie's death came after a decade of French rule in Tunisia.
Mgr. Jean-Joseph Tournier served as apostolic administrator of
the See of Carthage during the greater part of 1893, while the
French government negotiated the appointment of another archbish-
op.[1] The first choice of Lavigerie and the government had been Mgr.
Linvinhac, but after the cardinal's death the superior general
instructed Fr. Louis Burtin, the White Fathers' procurator at
Rome, to broadcast his unfitness for Carthage.[2] Linvinhac told
Jules Cambon at Algiers that he wished to die as a missionary on
some river in the African interior, "for the Faith and for
France."[3]

Officials at Tunis, Algiers, and Paris reviewed the qualifications of the cardinal's other associates. The new resident
minister at Tunis, Charles Rouvier, wired the Quai d'Orsay on
5 January 1893 that it would be a mistake to divide Tunisia into
three sees under the mediocrities whom Lavigerie had made arch-
deacons for that purpose. Rouvier wanted a man who was well
regarded at Rome and who knew how to raise money: "We need here
a prelate with a French heart, who is a politician more than an
apostle, who dreams not of making converts in the Muslim world,
which would be an evil and a mistake, but of strongly establishing
his authority and his prestige as a bishop on the Catholics established in the Regency."[4] Jules Cambon reported a few days later
from Algiers that, although the prelates of North Africa were all
skilled in the details of administration, they had little initiative. Lavigerie, "like many men of will, liked to find in his
collaborators an almost absolute subordination."[5]

One of them, Mgr. Dusserre, had chafed under this yoke as
Coadjutor of Algiers. Upon inheriting the see, Archbishop Dusserre
expressed his resentment to the clergy of Algiers in an episcopal
letter which Jules Cambon reported later to Paris. "In this extraordinary document this prelate blamed in an explicit fashion
the works and life of the Cardinal, and the formulas of ecclesiastical style did not disguise the bitterness of his thought."
This privately circulated letter had scandalized the clergy of
Algiers and Tunis, alienated the White Fathers, "astonished the
Propaganda, and wounded the Holy Father." After the official
honors wich the republic had provided for Lavigerie's funeral,
Dusserrre had also criticized the government as "the source of
all our evils."[6] Dusserre's letter destroyed his candidacy for
the See of Carthage.

The nominal Auxiliary Bishop of Carthage, Mgr. Carmel Brincat,
actually worked at Paris for the Oeuvrage Antiesclavagiste.
Brincat's youth and his Maltese origin disqualified him in the
government's opinion. The saintly Bishop of Constantine, Mgr.
Barthélemy-Clément Combes, had been Lavigerie's second choice
after Linvinhac. But his health was poor, and Combes seemed likely
to bring with him his large, "absorbent" family from the Midi.[7]
Brincat and Linvinhac recommended Fr. Charmetant to Jules Cambon,
who agreed that Charmetant was "made for public life."[8] But some
officials suspected him of Jesuit connections,[9] and the Holy See
was reluctant to promote a priest to primate in one move. Enemies
of France at the Vatican did not want another talented French
patriot appointed to Carthage. They exploited the question of
financial support as a delaying tactic. French officials were
prepared to bargain for regularizing the status of the see. They
wanted control over its appointment, and they wanted it placed
under the Secretariat of State instead of the Propaganda. Negotiations continued through the summer and fall resulting in an

agreement dated 7 November 1893, "for the duration of the so-
called Protectorate."[10] The government promised to pay an annual
subvention of 75,000 francs, and the Holy See agreed to name the
Archbishop of Carthage "after accord with the French government."[11] The man finally chosen under this "concordat" was the
Bishop of Constantine.

Mgr. Combes inherited two dozen parishes ministering to some
50,000 Catholics in Tunisia. During his three decades as archbishop the number of both grew steadily. At first Combes easily
maintained the clergy's good rapport with civil and military
authorities. He often preached patriotic sermons in the cathedral
of Tunis, which faced the French residence. The symbolic way in
which these two buildings together dominated the most important
avenue of the city was obvious to a population which vividly remembered the "Grand Cardinal" for many years after his death.
The resident minister after Rouvier, René Millet, was a practicing Catholic. The 1890s were a calm period of church-state relations in Tunisia, although the Dreyfus Affair caused some increase
in antisemitism. Freemasonry was very active, and anarchism was
strong among the Italians in Tunisia, but most Europeans kept
the externals of religion.[12] Church-state tension increased after
the turn of the century. Although the 1901 Associations Law and
the 1905 abolition of the Napoleonic Concordat did not directly
apply to Tunisia, the resident, Stephen Pichon, obtained a beylical decree in 1903 which caused most church schools to be
laicized by 1906.[13] Anticlericalism within the métropole carried
over into Tunisia until the First World War, during which the
"fellowship of the trenches" effectively resolved the church-state
problem once and for all.

Authorities in Tunis observed Lavigerie's centenary in 1925 by
placing a statue of the cardinal at the Porte de France. Some
accounts mistakenly note that it faced the Arab quarter as if

leading a crusade. It actually looked away from the Medina toward
the harbor, but Lavigerie's majestic pose holding a cross and
Bible was still so offensive that troops had to protect the statue
from demonstrators.[14] Five years later at Carthage, the Catholic
Church held a Eucharistic congress which coincided with the centenary of the French invasion of Algeria. This celebration com-
memorated the return of Christianity after North Africa's "Arab
parenthesis." The bey and other Muslim dignitaries attended its
opening ceremony, a fact which Tunisian nationalists still recall
with bitterness.[15]

After national independence in 1956 the Church withdrew from
Tunisia as rapidly as French power. The government permitted the
White Fathers quietly to dismantle Lavigerie's statue at Porte
de France. They also transferred his remains from the basilica
in Carthage to their recently built Mother House at Rome.[16] The
"concordat" of 1893 was obsolete, and secret negotiations between
the Bourguiba government and the Vatican replaced it with the
Modus vivendi of 1964. The Church ceded most of its properties to
the government for "ends of public interest compatible with their
former distination."[17] All but five of the many churches built
during the protectorate are now libraries, cultural centers, and
museums. The Cathedral of Saint-Vincent and the Parish of Sainte-
Jeanne d'Arc still serve foreign Catholics at Tunis.[18] In 1975,
a century after Lavigerie's priests arrived at the Chapelle
Saint-Louis, a few clergy and nuns in Tunisia still engaged in
works of charity and scholarship. But they respect the official
prohibition against making converts. The government permits other
activities which do not challenge the nation's Muslim identity.

The Catholic parenthesis in Tunisia's modern history is finished. The statues of Christian saints and the banners of French
nobles are gone from the Carthage basilica. Lavigerie's episcopal
coat of arms is still on the inside back wall, and the Latin words

of St. Leo IX confirming the primacy of Carthage in Africa remain
in large letters on the museum's inside and outside walls. But
there is little else to remind the visitor of the cardinal's influence or of his ambitious plans.

Primate of Africa capped his many titles: Archbishop of
Carthage and Algiers; Apostolic Delegate for the Sahara and the
Soudan, and for Equatorial Africa; Superior General for life of
the White Fathers and the African Sisters; leader of the Oeuvrage
Antiesclavagiste.[19] Lavigerie's personal influence extended into
Asia Minor, where Eastern Rite Christians looked to him as the
personification of French protection against Turkish oppression
and of cultural ecumenism in the Roman Catholic Church. He was
the greatest ecclesiastical pluralist of modern history, coordi-
nating these many activities from his French base in North Africa.
He dreamed of the eventual Christianization of the continent's
vast population. In Lavigerie's pastoral and patriotic design,
this was the most important goal of the French "civilizing mission" in Africa.

The statement, "I believe in the resurrection of Christian
Carthage," expressed his faith for the future. He dreamed of restoring a modern city, both European and French, as the regency's
new capital.[20] But Lavigerie's grandest dreams in North Africa
did not materialize. He never fully appreciated the sincerity and
moral power of Muhammad, and his indirect strategy for converting
Islam's believers failed to make any real dent in their number.
Like the fewer evangelical Protestant missionaries in French
North Africa, the White Fathers touched the lives of individuals
through schools and medical stations.[21] But the Muslims were not
susceptible to conversion in significant number during the period
of the protectorate. One can only speculate how soon they ever
would have been. Lavigerie's great impact was on the Europeans
of Tunisia. This Catholic contribution to France led the resident,

Charles Rouvier, to call for a rabbi of Lavigerie's mold to organize the native and European factions of the Jewish community.[22]
Neither faith produced another man to extend such a program.

For an evaluation of Lavigerie's work in Tunisia it is easiest
to summarize his methods. Implementation of his plans required
shrewd statesmanship with the Holy See and the Paris government
alike. He obtained the Vatican's support for French colonial policy, in spite of Italian opposition, in large measure because of
his friendship with Pope Leo XIII. He was an indispensable agent
of the government in Gallicizing the clergy. Yet in the negotiations which established the French ecclesiastical regime he was
his own man, bargaining as much for support from the government
as from the Vatican. Lavigerie's dual diplomacy occasionally
involved playing Paris and Rome against each other "according to
my knowledge of men,"[23] and he was not above coaching one in the
tactics of exploiting the other's fear. This ability to orches-
trate diplomatic pressure was an important factor in his success.

But the rapport he enjoyed with Paris officials was fundamental.
After a brief period of opposition to the republic in the early
seventies, Lavigerie recognized that its authority was legitimate.
Regardless of whether he would have preferred a return to the
monarchy, he saw no possibility of turning back. He admired many
of the republic's leaders, and he served it enthusiastically
overseas. Yet on some occasions when the government neglected its
obligation to help with expenses, Lavigerie's outrage led to
threats of resignation. His violent temper, calculated sense of
timing, and intuitive diplomatic skill confuse the historian's
attempts to distinguish the genuine threats from bluffs. But
French politicians knew that a resignation was his highest card.

Despite these tantrums and the anticlerical climate within
France, relations between the Paris government and the Church in
North Africa were fundamentally harmonious. Algerian authorities

relied on the clergy as a stabilizing influence on foreign populations. The prudence of Lavigerie and his coadjutor, Dusserre,
was something which the Prefecture of Algiers took for granted
during the cardinal's lifetime: "Of affable characters, these
gentlemen manifest no opinions. Their influence from the religious
point of view is great on the foreigners and next to nothing on
the French. . . . Their political attitude has always been correct
and their relations with the administration are very courteous."[24]
Lavigerie's coadjutor and suffragan bishops were under his thumb.
In negotiations with the Algerian administration and the Paris
government he could confidently guarantee their good conduct. If
more of the great prelates of France had shared his tact and moderation, and if they likewise had been able to pledge discipline
and restraint on the part of their suffragans, the history of
church-state relations in France would be quite different. The
ralliement would have come earlier and it would have succeeded.

Lavigerie's role in the "new imperialism" is harder to summarize than his role in the Church or in French domestic politics.
The personal influence of individuals was decisive in the first
stages of this expansion, for generally European governments
developed an imperialist policy later after beginning an empire
through haphazard commitments.[25] Roustan and Courcel were the
diplomats who persuaded the ministers to impose the protectorate.
Yet a close examination of Lavigerie's involvement in Tunisia
establishes that he ranked with them in terms of the contribution
he made to the consolidation of French control in the regency and
in terms of the influence he exercised upon the decisions of
Gambetta and Ferry in the government.

The archbishop's analysis of the Muslims' "fanatical" resentment of French rule had much to do with his views on secular
policy in North Africa. However distorted his larger perception
of Islam, his sources of current information were excellent.

Reports of German contacts with the heads of the interior tribes
gave him chronic anxiety about the danger of a rebellion should
occupation troops be withdrawn to fight a war in Europe.[26] This
nightmare strengthened Lavigerie's conviction that Tunisia required an enlightened and benevolent policy of governing the
Muslims through a beylical regime under the French resident's
supervision. Rather than openly attack Boulanger and other ambitious officers and civil servants who favored annexation,
Lavigerie insisted in more general terms that abandoning the
natives to their abuse would nurture resentment which could ex-
plode at the wrong time and destroy French power in North Africa.
Recalling the Druse massacres of Maronite Christians in the
Levant, he knew the consequences of a French collapse for his
missions. Lavigerie believed that Africa required the continuing
presence of European troops, but he always opposed giving the
French army control of colonial policy. He supported the army's
advancement into Africa as an umbrella under which French missionaries could advance with greater safety.

Lavigerie's patriotism appears clearly in his many letters
and speeches, yet it is difficult to assess the precise relationship between his devotion to France and his commitment to the
Church. Although he was a strong supporter of French influence
in Palestine and North Africa, his policy in central Africa indicates that his enthusiasm for French power in a given area was
inspired primarily by the advantages which it offered to the
missions. In North Africa these advantages were obvious, but his
primary concern in equatorial Africa was pastoral. When the Quai
d'Orsay refused a request for French protection relayed by
Lavigerie in 1879 from King Mtesa of Uganda, Lavigerie did not
attempt further to engage the government in the area.[27] He sent
Charmetant to Brussels several times to negotiate with Leopold II
for the establishment of a White Fathers' seminary there to train

Belgians for the Congo.[28] In 1886 Lavigerie asked for German
protection of his missionaires in central Africa during a conversation at Tunis with the German consul, Julius Eckardt.
Bismarck's policy of encouraging the German East Africa Company
did not extend to direct government intervention of that sort.
The episode produced nothing but irritation on the part of French
officials, who only learned of it when Bismarck suggested a joint
declaration to the Freycinet government.[29]

On the other hand, the fact that the central African apostolate was, by circumstances, not mixed with the politics of France
does not prove conclusively an apostolic interpretation of
Lavigerie's motive. Elsewhere the Christian apostolate was wedded
with French interests, and many of Lavigerie's public utterances
and private letters imply that his patriotic motive was fundamental and coordinate with his missionary spirit. As Fr. Jacques
Durant observed, one should expect this in a man of the nineteenth
century: "It would deny the mentality of the times to separate the
two motives or to subordinate one to the other."[30] Lavigerie
testified to his deep patriotism in hundreds of statements, many
of them given from the pulpit.

But it is still difficult to resolve the question of whether
his commitment to the expansion of French power sprang from an
ultimate loyalty independent of apostolic considerations, or
whether it followed from the beneficial partnership between church
and state overseas. A quotation from an 1875 discourse delivered
in the cathedral of Algiers places the issue in better perspective.
Speaking on "The Mission of France," Lavigerie addressed the
Eldest Daughter of the Church, whose genius it was

> to transmit, at the price of sacrifice, your sentiments
> and your enlightenment. That you have done for so many
> centuries for truth; that you have done even for your
> errors; that you still do by your writings, by your

word, by your language which remains that of the
civilized world. That is what you have come to do in
this barbarous Africa. You have come here not to
found your power on the servitude and the destruction
of the vanquished, but to form here a free and
Christian people.[31]

Lavigerie was first a pastor, but his motives were complex.
The commitment of the men who served under him sprang from a
simpler vision, yet their sacrifice reflected the spirit of their
leader. Though Lavigerie had sophisticated assistants like
Charmetant and Linvinhac who shared his thoughts and actively
advanced his overall design, the average White Father was a dedicated priest who simply labored in the field. These men cooperated with local officials and obeyed the founder's special
instructions, but most of them were not particularly aware of
advancing French power except for Lavigerie's utterances on the
subject. Since Delattre many members have brought prestige to
the Society in mission-related sciences, but most of the early
White Fathers were steady wheel horses.

The toughening regime of Lavigerie's seminaries gave an early
idea of the physical hardships they faced in the years ahead.
Their life expectancy in the African interior was less than forty
years.[32] But they risked attacks from slavers and languished
from unaccustomed food because of a vocation to carry Christianity
into Africa. They reflected the spirit of their founder, whose
fundamental commitment was to the religious life he had entered
as an adolescent. He eagerly acquired political power, and his
patriotism was genuine. But his last major program was the
Oeuvrage Antiesclavagiste, an international enterprise enlisting
the support of many countries. His final grand gesture was the
Toast of Algiers, an attempt to end the division crippling the

Church to which he devoted his life. Its apostolate was the
deepest force within him, reinforced by the national interests
of France.

The Abbé Lavigerie had first drawn public attention in the
1850s for his Sorbonne lectures in ecclesiastical history. During
the next three decades he influenced the direction of affairs
in the Church and in French politics. A century later one seeks
to explain Lavigerie's wholehearted commitment to French imperialism in terms which accord with his vocation as a priest. He anticipated the Christianization of Africa by White Fathers and
other missionaries as European soldiers and explorers opened
the continent to them. Lavigerie viewed this new era of Europe's
expansion as a glorious stage in the history of the Church.

Notes

PREFACE

1. Mgr. Baunard, Le Cardinal Lavigerie, 2:482.

2. Archives Nationales, Paris (AN), F19, 2487, "Mgr. Lavigerie," 154; Baunard, 1: 438, 439, 522.

3. Arthur Marsden, British Diplomacy and Tunis, 1875-1902, p. 99.

4. François Renault, Lavigerie, l'esclavage africain, et l'Europe 1868-1892; Xavier de Montclos, Le Toast d'Alger: Documents 1890-1891; Xavier de Montclos, Lavigerie, le Saint-Siège, et l'Eglise, 1846-1878; James Edward Ward, "Franco-Vatican Relations, 1878-1892."

5. Baunard, Le Cardinal Lavigerie; J. Tournier, Le Cardinal Lavigerie et son action politique, 1863-1892; J. Mercui, Les Origines de la Société des Missionnaires d'Afrique.

6. Jules Cambon, "Souvenirs sur le Cardinal Lavigerie," Revue des Deux Mondes 32 (1926): 277-89; another article by Jules Cambon bearing the same title appeared in Revue d'Histoire des Missions 3 (1926): 1-6; Georges Goyau, "Le Cardinal Lavigerie," Revue des Deux Mondes 26 (1925): 310-43, 579-609, 775-807; 27 (1926): 149-86; also published in book form, Georges Goyau, Un Grand missionnaire.

CHAPTER I

1. AN, F19, 2487, "Mgr. Lavigerie," 102; Baunard, vol. 1, chap. 1; Glenn D. Kittler, The White Fathers, chap. 2; Fr. Jacques Durant, interview, 18 April 1969.

2. Georges Picot, Le Cardinal Lavigerie et ses oeuvres dans le bassin de la Méditerranée et en Afrique, p. 3. This little book is item 517 in AN, F19, 2487, "Mgr. Lavigerie."

3. Montclos, Saint-Siège, p. 143n.

4. Archives du Ministère des Affaires Etrangères, Quai d'Orsay,
Paris (AE), Correspondance politique, Tunis (T), 54:250-53, Noailles
to Barthélemy, 19 January 1881.

5. Ibid.; Picot, pp. 3, 4; Jacques Gadille, La Pensée et
l'action politiques des évêques français au début de la IIIe
République, 1870-1883, 1:120-22.

6. Bernard de Lacombe, "Le Cardinal Lavigerie," Correspondant
200 (1909): 891-921, 895; Kittler, pp. 21-25.

7. Montclos, Saint-Siège, pp. 324-28; Fr. Jacques Durant,
interview of 2 August 1971; Kittler, pp. 10, 11.

8. Montclos, Saint-Siège, p. 332.

9. Kittler, p. 12.

10. Ibid.; Picot. p. 6.

11. Montclos, Saint-Siège, pp. 344, 345; René Pottier, "Cardinal
Lavigerie," Encyclopédie Mensuelle d'Outre-Mer (Paris) 1, no. 27
(November 1952): 325-28, 325.

12. Kenneth J. Perkins has written two articles on the Arab
Bureaus and their policy, "The Bureaux Arabes and the Colons," and
"Pressure and Persuasion in the Policies of the French Military in
Colonial North Africa."

13. J. Bouniol, ed., The White Fathers and their Missions,
pp. 17-23; Vincent Confer, France and Algeria, pp. vii, 3, 4-7;
Montclos, Saint-Siège, pp. 346-48; Gen. Georges Spillmann, "Controverse entre Napoléon III et MacMahon au sujet du Royaume arabe
d'Algérie," pp. 162-67.

14. Spillmann, pp. 159, 160.

15. Raymond F. Betts, Assimilation and Association in French
Colonial Theory, 1890-1914, pp. 19, 20; Confer, pp. 3-6, 123
(n. 10); Spillmann, pp. 157-67.

16. Montclos, Saint-Siège, p. 331, also pp. 346-48.

17. R. P. de Préville, Un Grand Français, pp. 229, 230.

18. Montclos, Saint-Siège, p. 333n; quotation from Mgr.
A[lexandre]. Pons, La Nouvelle Eglise d'Afrique, ou la catholicisme

en Algérie, en Tunisie, et au Maroc depuis 1830, pp. 133, 134.

19. Picot, p. 7, letter of 17 May 1868.

20. Bouniol, pp. 17-41; Kittler, chap. 3; Lavigerie's loathing
of MacMahon is described by Paul Cambon, Correspondance 1870-1924,
vol. 1, 1870-1898, pp. 184-86. See also Tournier, Action politique,
pp. 45, 46, and particularly 46n for this anecdote:

One one occasion MacMahon's harassment of Lavigerie boomeranged.
When Algiers's suffragan See of Oran fell vacant, MacMahon told the
minister of cults to name the most disagreeable choice Lavigerie
could have. The appointment was expedited without proper staff
work, giving Lavigerie the last laugh: "I had to wire the minister
of cults that M. Compte-Calix, languishing for several months, had
died eight days before, and I marveled that one could name as bishop a cleric of my diocese without finding out not only what he was
but even if he were."

21. Picot, p. 7; Claude-Maurice Robert, "Lavigerie L'Africain,"
pp. 80, 81. After Lavigerie's death the official name of the order
became Society of Missionaries of Africa. Renault, 1:156n. The name
White Fathers of Africa is also used officially. The word Soudan as
used here is a "vague and elastic expression . . . used by European
explorers from the eighteenth century upon their penetration of the
continent; it refers especially to former French West Africa." Paul
Robert, Dictionnaire universel des noms propres (hereafter cited as
Petit Robert 2), p. 1729.

22. Goyau, "Le Cardinal Lavigerie," 27:585; Baunard, 1:326-33;
A.-C. Grussenmeyer, Vingt-cinq années d'épiscopat en France et en
Afrique, 1:233-48, 2:298n.

23. The quotation is from two letters in Montclos, Saint-Siège,
p. 476. See also p. 476n. AE, T 57:403-15, Lavigerie to Charmetant,
24 April 1881; Archives de la Prélature-Tunis (APT), Lettres du
Cardinal Lavigerie (LCL), 251-62, documents concerning laicization
proposals in Algiers, late 1860s; Baunard, 1:349-54; Betts, pp. 20,
21; Confer, pp. 8, 9; Montclos, Mission universelle, p. 188;
Spillmann, p. 167. Lavigerie still continued to prefer a civilian

regime in Algeria, and he argued strongly against imposing a military administration on the Regency of Tunis in the 1880s.

24. Kenneth J. Perkins, "The Bureaux Arabes," pp. 99, 100;
Mercui, p. 174; Préville, pp. 121, 134, 135; Montclos, Saint-Siège,
p. 476n.

25. Archives Lavigerie, White Fathers of Africa Generalate,
Rome (AL), B3, 594, Broglie to Lavigerie, 7 November 1873.

26. Mgr. Charles Lavigerie, "Saint-Louis, roi de France et son
tombeau sur les ruines de Carthage, Lettre de Mgr. l'Archevêque
d'Alger au missionnaires de son diocèse," p. 15; E. de Sainte-Marie,
"Essai sur l'histoire religieuse de la Tunisie," 9:472.

27. AL, B3, 108, "Lettres Tunisiennes," background news release
written by Lavigerie; Henri Cambon [son of Paul Cambon], Histoire
de la Régence de Tunis, p. 269; Le Diocèse de Carthage, "Notice
Historique" par L'Abbé Bombard, Curé de la Cathédrale; Jean Ganiage,
"Etude demographique sur les Européens de Tunisie au milieu du XIXe
siècle," 5:168n; Goyau, "Le Cardinal Lavigerie," 26: 605, 606;
Sainte-Marie, 9:469-72; le Baron Robert de Billing, Le Baron Robert
de Billing, Vie, notes, correspondance, pp. 387, 388.

28. AL, B3, 594, cited above.

29. AL, AC818, Roustan to Lavigerie, 19 February 1875.

30. Baunard, 1: 416, 429-31, 486-91.

31. L'Archivo Storico della Sacra Congregazione de Propaganda
Fide, Piazza di Spagna, Rome (APF), "Scritture Riferite nei Congressi,"
Barbaria, vol. 20 (1867-1877):826, letter of 10 May 1875.

32. APF, Barbaria 20:833, Lavigerie to Propaganda, 10 June 1875.

33. AL, B3, 51, 52, and 53, letters of Lavigerie to Roustan
dated 10, 14, and 21 May 1875; quotation taken from B3, 53; AL,
"Diaire de Saint-Louis de Carthage, 1875-1881," enties for June
1875. Hereafter, this notebook and its continuation, the "Diaire de
Saint-Charles, 1881-1886," will be cited as "Diaire."

34. AL, B3, 210(1), Lavigerie to Bresson, 15 June 1875.

35. R. P. J. Cussac, Un Géant de l'apostolat, le Cardinal Lavigerie,
p. 80.

36. Ibid.; Montclos, Saint-Siège, pp. 549-51; AL, vol. 35, copy 457 of C4, 71, Lavigerie to Charmetant, 12 February 1877.

37. Charles Cardinal Lavigerie, Oeuvres choisies de son Eminence, le Cardinal Lavigerie, Archevêque d'Alger, 1:370-73. Prosper-Auguste Dusserre eventually became coadjutor. He succeeded Lavigerie as Archbishop of Algiers in 1892, by which time he thoroughly despised the cardinal.

38. This memoir is summarized in Mercui, pp. 262-65. Lavigerie had made a bid to become Patriarch of Jerusalem in 1872, but the Vatican appointed an Italian, Mgr. Bracco. Montclos, Saint-Siège, pp. 532-36. In the late 1870s Lavigerie wanted to send Pontifical Zouaves to central Africa to stamp out the slave trade, "for my secret design is really to try to found a Christian Kingdom in the center of equatorial Africa. Two hundred rifles do not seem exaggerated to me." AL, 35:1382 / C4, 88, Lavigerie to Charmetant, 25 March 1879.

39. Bouniol, pp. 52, 53; Baunard, 1:viii; AL, "Charmetant au Cardinal" 1:5945 / C4, 417, 14 January 1878; "Charmetant au Cardinal" 1:4950 / C4, 423, 3 February 1878.

40. Ward, "Franco-Vatican Relations," p. 34; Tournier, Action politique, p. 119. The author's article, "Cardinal Charles Lavigerie: The Politics of Getting a Red Hat," appeared in The Catholic Historical Review 63, no. 2 (April 1977): 185-203.

41. Alan Scham, Lyautey in Morocco, pp. 3-17.

42. AN, F19, 2487, "Algérie," 32, "Extrait d'un rapport de M. le Procureur Général près la Cour d'Appel d'Alger" 1887.

43. Among many conversations with White Fathers at Rome, I particularly benefitted from a chat with Fr. Gerald Lachance on 3 August 1971.

44. In a conversation at Rome on 2 August 1971, Fr. Jacques Durant shared many of his insights based on research in Lavigerie's work in Algeria.

45. For a Protestant's impression of Lavigerie's grandeur, see Rev. J. C. Bracq, "Cardinal Lavigerie and his Anti-Slavery Work," pp. 721-25.

46. See J. Néré's review of Montclos, Saint-Siège, in Revue Historique 239 (1968): 444-46.

47. Later in Tunisia Lavigerie confided to Paul Cambon his opinion of Pius IX, "one of those whom God, in his wrath, sends to chastise humans." The length of his reign (1846-78) was a tremendous source of harm, in Lavigerie's opinion. Secretary of State Giacomo Antonelli, the last layman to wear a cardinal's hat, was "one of the most immoral men of the century." The Pope's entourage of "imbeciles and scoundrels," led by Antonelli, "made him think the moon was made of green cheese." Paul Cambon, Correspondance, pp. 209-11, letter to Mme Cambon, 27 December 1883. Lavigerie had given a rather half-hearted welcome to the Pope's Syllabus of Errors in 1864, but at the Vatican Council of 1869-70 he endorsed publicly and fully the ultramontane concept of papal authority. In the council sessions he worked as a member of the "third party" to moderate the definition of papal infallibility so as to make it more acceptable to the "inopportunists," who opposed it on practical grounds. Baunard, 1:309; Montclos, Mission universelle. pp. 32, 195; Montclos, Saint-Siège, pp. 584, 585; Lacombe, pp. 895, 898.

48. Lavigerie wanted to make the College of Cardinals representative of other countries, "un sénat véritablement modérateur." Montclos, Toast, pp. 36, 37; Xavier de Montclos, ed., Le Cardinal Lavigerie: La mission universelle de l'Eglise, p. 78; Montclos, Saint-Siège, p. 535; William Burridge, Destiny Africa, pp. 37-39.

49. John McManners, Church and State in France, 1870-1914, p. 68.

50. Montclos, Toast, pp. 36-39; Montclos, Saint-Siège, pp. 206-10, 540-49, 557, 558, 584, 585. Quotation from p. 547, original emphasis.

51. Paul Cambon, Correspondance, pp. 184-86, 209-11. Lavigerie repeatedly dismissed the idea of electing a non-Italian pope, particularly whenever journalists suggested him as a candidate, on the grounds that it would risk a schism. He proposed instead that one could provide for election of a foreigner in the distant future by making the Sacred College more representative. But it would take a

hundred years. AL, 38:1075 / B2, 229, Lavigerie to Charmetant,
8 January 1888. In 1890 Lavigerie suggested to the Pope another reform as a means of increasing the number of clergy in Africa. His
idea of letting native priests marry was rejected out of hand by
the Holy Office. Renault, 1:228.

52. Charles P. Groves, The Planting of Christianity in Africa,
2: 211, 212; Montclos, Mission universelle, p. 29.

53. Montclos, Saint-Siège, pp. 578-80.

54. Abdeljelil Temimi, "Rôle des missionnaires dans l'expansion
du christianisme en Tunisie, 1830-1881," p. 115.

55. A more ecumenical analysis of Islam from the Christian perspective is provided by Rev. Kenneth Cragg in The Call of the Minaret,
p. 189; Un Père Blanc [Joseph Mazé], "Les Idées principales du
Cardinal Lavigerie sur l'évangélisation de l'Afrique," pp. 360-72.

56. Lavigerie, Oeuvres choisies, 1:5, quoted from chap. 1,
pastoral letter of 1867 titled "Le passé, le present, et l'avenir
de l'Algérie."

57. Cragg, pp. 255, 256.

58. Mgr. Charles Lavigerie, "Missions d'Afrique," pp. 200, 201.

59. For a discussion of the controversy caused in 1888 by
Lavigerie's public remarks implying that the institution of slavery
was a logical consequence of Islamic teachings, see Renault, 2:363
and thereafter. I refer to this also in chap. 6, n. 49.

60. Un Père Blanc, pp. 367-72.

61. Lavigerie, Oeuvres choisies, vol. 2, chap. 22, "Lettre sur
des accusations de fanatisme," pp. 520, 521. The emphasis is mine.
See also vol. 1, chap. 2, "L'Armée et la mission de la France en
Afrique," discourse given in the cathedral of Algiers, 25 April 1875.

62. AN, F19, 6243, "Religieux Protectorat," clipping of article
by Prince Ferdinand Tyan in Figaro, 26 September 1904.

CHAPTER II

1. Jacques Gadille, "La Politique de défense républicaine à
l'égard de l'Eglise de France, 1876-1883," Bulletin de la Société

d'Histoire Moderne, 1 (1967): 2-9.

2. Missions d'Alger 45 (January 1883): 1-6.

3. Gadille, La Pensée, 1: 120-22, 214-17.

4. Baunard, 1:447-51; Néré, pp. 444-46.

5. McManners, p. 56.

6. Evelyn M. Acomb, The French Laic Laws, 1879-1889, p. 236; McManners, ch. 2; Ward, "Franco-Vatican Relations," ch. 1, part 2.

7. AN, F19, 6243, "Religieux Protectorat," quotation from clipping of Petite République, 4 October 1904; Ward, "Franco-Vatican Relations," chap. 1, part 3. The Eastern Protectorate should not be confused with the Far East Protectorate, which derived from the 1858 Treaty of Tientsin with China.

8. William L. Langer, ed., An Encyclopedia of World History, p. 728.

9. AN, F19, 6243, "Religieux Protectorat," P. Magny, Sub-Director of Cults, "Note pour M. le President du Conseil sur le Protectorat de la France sur les Chrétiens d'Orient," 29 August 1904.

10. Ibid.; AE, Correspondance politique, Rome, Saint-Siège (SS), 1067:358-60, Desprez to Freycinet, 29 May 1880.

11. André Retif, "Les Evêques français et les missions au XIXe siècle," Etudes, 295 (December 1952): 362-72; Ward, "Franco-Vatican Relations," pp. 13-15, 35, 36.

12. Goyau, "Le Cardinal Lavigerie," 27:183n.

13. Denis W. Brogan, The Development of Modern France, 1870-1939, pp. 89, 90, 132; Alexander Sedgwick, The Ralliement in French Politics, 1890-1898, pp. 3, 4; James Edward Ward, "Leo XIII: 'The Diplomat Pope,'" Review of Politics 28, no. 1 (January 1966): 47-61.

14. Ward, "Franco-Vatican Relations," ch. 1, part 4. The Lateran Treaty of 1929 restored 109 acres to papal sovereignty.

15. AE, Correspondance politique, Turquie, Poste consulaire de Beyrouth (B), 26:363-66, Patrimonio to Duclerc, 19 September 1882.

16. AE, SS 1067:358-60, Desprez to Freycinet, 29 May 1880.

17. Montclos, Saint-Siège, pp. 540-46; Montclos, Toast, p. 39.

18. Paul Cambon, Correspondance, p. 184-86, quotation from p. 186.

19.   James Edward Ward, "Leo XIII and Bismarck: The Kaiser's Vatican Visit of 1888," Review of Politics 24 (July 1962): 392-414.

20.   AE, B 26:363-66, Patrimonio to Duclerc, 19 September 1882.

21.   AE, B 26:76-80, Patrimonio to Freycinet, 10 March 1882; B 26:363-66, Patrimonio to Declerc, 19 September 1882.

22.   AL, "Charmetant au Cardinal," 3:5179 / C4, 644, report from Beyrouth of 30 January 1887.

23.   AN, F19, 2487, "8 Lettres," 5, Lavigerie to minister of interior and cults, 15 October 1880. Leaders in the White Fathers were apprehensive regarding the Scholasticate of St. Anne of Jerusalem, lest it distract the Society from its commitment to the apostolate in Africa.

24.   AE, B 27:103-8, Patrimonio to Challemel-Lacour, 8 May 1883; SS 1075:270-72, Béhaine to Challemel-Lacour, 30 April, 1883; quotation from SS 1076:45-49, Sous-Direction du Midi to Béhaine, 10 May 1883. The original draft of this document contains a reference, crossed out, to "the clear patriotism with which he [Lavigerie] has helped make France loved in the lands where he has successively been called."

25.   Mercui, p. 320; quotation from Ward, "Franco-Vatican Relations," p. 38.

26.   AE, B 27:333-35, Patrimonio to Ferry, 18 November 1884. Italy's influence within the Curia, however, remained sufficient to withstand French pressure to have Piavi removed or "kicked upstairs" - until 1889, when he became Patriarch of Jerusalem. At that, his successor at Beyrouth was another Franciscan. Ward, "Franco-Vatican Relations," p. 165.

27.   AL, 28:3205(39) / D5, 139 and 3205(41) / D5, 143, Lavigerie to Noailles, 5 July and 6 August 1885; "Charmetant au Cardinal" 3:5175 / C4, 654, 14 July 1886.

28.   Montclos, Toast, p. 38.

29.   Montclos, Saint-Siège, pp. 527-29.

30.   Jacques Gadille distinguishes three groups among the anti-clericals. The "opportunist" majority wanted to maintain the

Concordat. They included Jules Ferry, Charles-Théodore-Eugène
Duclerc, Jules Barthélemy-Saint-Hilaire, and Jean-Antoine-Ernest
Constans, as well as the director of cults, Léopold-Emile Flourens.
The radical left, including Jules Simon and Georges Clemenceau,
urged separation of church and state. Between these two groups were
anticlericals like Léon Gambetta and Paul Bert, who aimed to curtail the Church within the Concordat system. The budget of cults
served them as an annual target. Gadille, "Défense républicaine,"
pp. 3-5.

    31. Ward, "Franco-Vatican Relations," p. 2. McManners (p. xvii)
credits Alphonse Peyrat with saying it in 1863.

    32. Baunard, 2:232; Ward, "Franco-Vatican Relations," p. 3;
quotation from Henri Cambon, Histoire, p. 268.

    33. Paul Cambon, Correspondance, p. 182.

    34. Acomb, pp. 70-72, quotation from p. 72.

    35. Goyau, "Le Cardinal Lavigerie," 26: 597.

    36. Ferry was minister of public instruction and fine arts in
most of the cabinets until the middle of his own second ministry
(February 1883 to March 1885). He gave up that portfolio in November
1883 in order to take over foreign affairs from ailing Paul-Armand
Challemel-Lacour. Baunard, 2:35-39; Jules Cambon, articles titled
"Souvenirs," Revue des Deux Mondes, p. 286, and Revue d'Histoire des
Missions, p. 5; Jean Ganiage, L'Expansion coloniale de la France
sous la Troisième République, 1871-1914, pp. 45-47.

    37. Acomb, pp. 136-43; Tournier, Action politique, pp. 49, 50.

    38. Tournier, Action politique, chs. 3 and 4, quotation from
p. 82.

    39. Montclos, Toast, p. 30.

    40. Acomb, pp. 143, 144. President MacMahon signed the decree
of 31 August 1878, authorizing the White Fathers. Mercui, p. 281.

    41. Ernst Helmreich, ed., A Free Church in a Free State?,
pp. 86-92; Tournier, Action politique, chs. 3 and 4; APT, LCL, 88,
résumé of Lavigerie's audience with the Pope, 28 May 1880.

    42. Acomb, pp. 144-46; Helmreich, pp. 86-92.

43. AE, SS 1067:194, Freycinet to Desprez, 9 April 1880; AN,
F19, 2487, "Algérie," 31, "Lettre Confidentielle de Mgr. L'Archevêque
d'Alger à MM. les Curés de son diocèse," 9 September 1880; Tournier,
Action politique, pp. 111, 112.

44. AN, F19, 6075, "Execution of the 1880 Decrees," Lavigerie
to Dusserre, 17 June 1880, 2:56 p.m.; minister of interior to governor general, 17 June 1880, 6:10 p.m.; governor general to minister
of interior, 18 June 1880, 2:11 p.m.

45. Ibid., governor general to procurator general, Ministry of
Justice, 19 June 1880, 8:38 a.m.; minister of interior to governor
general, 19 June 1880, 12:30 p.m.; governor general to minister of
interior, 23 June 1880, 9:41 a.m.; minister of interior to governor
general, 23 June 1880, 4:25 p.m.; Baunard, 2: 47-49, 60; Tournier,
Action politique, pp. 111, 112.

46. AN, F19, 2487, "31 Lettres," 13, Lavigerie to Flourens,
4 August 1880; Baunard, 2:50-52.

47. AN, F19, 2487, "31 Lettres," 14, Lavigerie to minister of
cults, 5 August 1880.

48. AN, F19, 2487, "8 Lettres," 4, Lavigerie to director general
of cults, 10 September 1880.

49. Tournier, Action politique, pp. 105-12.

50. Ibid., p. 102.

51. AE, SS 1067:186, cable from Freycinet to Desprez, 6 April
1880.

52. AE, T 49:285-300, Courcel to Roustan, 16 April 1880, quotation from pp. 298, 299.

53. Lavigerie sent a copy of this letter to the Ministry of
Cults. See AN, F19, 2487, "8 Lettres," 3. Most likely this letter
merely summarized and recorded the context of a request already
granted by the premier-foreign minister in an interview.

54. AN, F19, 2487, "31 Lettres," 17, Lavigerie to "Conseiller
d'Etat," 30 November 1880.

55. AN, F19, 2487, "8 Lettres," 5, Lavigerie to minister of
interior and cults, 15 October 1880, already cited. The importance

of this testimonial is evident, yet both Goyau ("Le Cardinal
Lavigerie," 26: 796, 797) and Tournier ("Le Cardinal Lavigerie,"
p. 849) mistakenly cite it as having been written in 1882. The
original at the Archives Nationales refers at the beginning to
Lavigerie's planned trip to Tunis to open the Collège Saint-Louis
and to the request just made for a coadjutor. These references confirm the earlier date as correct.

56. Ibid.

57. Ibid.

58. Baunard, 2: 39, 40, 144.

59. Ward, "Franco-Vatican Relations," pp. 34, 35.

60. AL, 36:1574(13) / T, 539, Lavigerie to Charmetant, 21 November
1881.

61. Ibid.; Tournier, Action politique, ch. 6.

62. AE, SS 1071:183-87, Desprez to Barthélemy, 9 October 1881.
Conscription of seminarians, a "crippling" measure affecting
Lavigerie's missions, finally passed the National Assembly in 1889.
APT, LCL, 835, press release, n.d., concerning the Military Law of
15 July 1889.

63. Gadille, "Défense républicaine," p. 8.

64. APT, LCL, 94, Lavigerie to Jacobini, 26 January 1883.
Lavigerie urged Jacobini to counsel Chambord not to signal such a
catastrophic uprising. If the clergy joined such a cause, separation
of church and state would inevitably result.

65. APT, LCL, 96, Lavigerie to Jacobini, 18 December 1883.

66. APT, LCL, 97, Lavigerie to Jacobini, 8 July 1883.

67. APT, LCL, 96, 97, and 108, Lavigerie to Jacobini, 18 December,
8 July and 23 March 1883; AL, 28:3144(59) taken from Lefebvre de
Béhaine papers, Lavigerie to Lefebvre de Béhaine, 18 May 1883;
37:552 / C4, 207, Lavigerie to Charmetant, 24 July 1883; 38:1427 /
C4, 316, Lavigerie to Charmetant, 27 July 1885. A particularly provocative critic of the government was Mgr. Freppel, Bishop of Angers,
elected to the Chamber of Deputies as a conservative in 1880.
Petit Robert 2, p. 697. Lavigerie wrote to Jacobini, "I do not know

a single French bishop who does not consider unfortunate Mgr.
Freppel's presence in the Chamber." APT, LCL, 103, 7 July 1883.

68. AL, 37:1417 / C4, 265, Lavigerie to Charmetant, 7 December
1884.

CHAPTER III

1. Pons, p. 258, quotation from Il Diritto.

2. Not counting Talleyrand, who was an ex-cleric.

3. Montclos, Saint-Siège, p. 550.

4. Pierre Soumille provides a good assessment of available population statistics, including an estimate of 708 French in 1880.
Pierre Soumille, "Les Européens de Tunisie et les questions religieuses de 1893 à 1914: Etude d'une opinion publique, Tome Premier
1893-1901" (Unpublished third cycle thesis, Université de Provence,
Aix-Marseille I, 1973), ch. 1, part 2. Citations refer to this manuscript, which is even more lavish in footnotes than the published
work, Pierre Soumille, Européens de Tunisie et questions religieuses,
1892-1901.

5. APT, LCL, 2017, Lavigerie to Roustan, 12 June 1880(?).

6. Soumille, "Les Européens," p. 18n; Dwight L. Ling, Tunisia
from Protectorate to Republic, pp. 6, 7; Leon Carl Brown, The
Tunisia of Ahmad Bey, 1837-1855, "Appendix 3: A Note on Population."
Realizing the difficulties of evaluating population figures, Brown
considers 1 million to 1.5 million to be a good "conservative estimate" for Tunisia's population in mid-century. Ling estimates the
population for 1828 at 5 million. Epidemics, economic disorders, and
famine reduced this number considerably in half a century. The
present population is around 6 million. A community of indigenous
Jews lives on the island of Djerba, where their ancestors settled
sometime during the last 2,500 years. "Of the 80,000 residents in
1956, some 800 and 280 now remain in Hara Kebira and Hara Seghira
respectively. The reason is the pull of Israel, not any local anti-
Semitism," Michael Tomkinson, Tunisia: A Holiday Guide, p. 95.

7. Brown, introduction, ch. 1, pp. 46, 92, 353, 363, and 380.

The Tunisia of Ahmad Bey, 1837-1855 provides a superb analysis of
Tunisian society and politics. Brown describes Tunisia much as
Lavigerie found it twenty years later. Many of the same leaders
of the political elite were still active.

8. Ibid., ch. 7; Ganiage, L'Expansion, pp. 60-64; Jean Ganiage,
"Les Européens en Tunisie au milieu du XIXe siècle, 1840-1870," pp.
398-400.

9. The practice of extending consular protection to large num-
bers of people in the beylic became a major problem. By way of comparison, Leland Louis Bowie has published a brief paper on "The
Impact of the Protégé System in Morocco, 1880-1912," which distills
the findings of his doctoral research on "The Protégé System in
Morocco, 1880-1904." Bowie concludes that the inevitable French
takeover in Morocco (1912) was facilitated by the immunities granted
to thousands of Moroccan subjects. The protégé system had an adverse
effect on revenues of and claims upon the Sultan's treasury, it
eroded his ability to levy militia for his army, and foreign loyalties compromised the dedication of local Moroccan officials. In
Tunisia the "capitulation" treaties did not undermine the central
government so grievously as in Morocco, but they caused serious
problems. Later chapters discuss Lavigerie's advice and assistance
to French officials in eliminating this form of "state within the
state."

10. Ganiage, L'Expansion, pp. 65-68, quotation from p. 68;
Abdurrahman Cayci, La Question tunisienne et la politique ottomane,
1881-1913, p. 14. Many beylical officials without military qualifications used the title of general.

11. Théodore-Justin-Dominique Roustan (1833-1906) served at
Cairo, Beyrouth, Damascus, and Alexandria, before replacing Baron
de Billing at Tunis. Jean Ganiage, "Une Affaire tunisienne: L'Affaire
de L'Enfida, 1880-1882," Revue Africaine 99 (1955): 341-78. Roustan
later served at Washington and Madrid. "Tenacious, energetic, but
with much suppleness, Roustan was at his ease in the milieu of
intrigues of an oriental court," Gilbert Gehring, "Les Relations

entre la Tunisie et l'Allemagne avant le protectorat français,"
Cahiers de Tunisie 71-72 (1970): 11-155, p. 92.

12. Ganiage, L'Expansion, pp. 67, 68; AE, T 50:114, Roustan to
Courcel, 18 May 1880; AL, "Diaire," entries of June 1875 and July
1877.

13. Ganiage, "L'Enfida," p. 349n; Ganiage, L'Expansion, p. 68.

14. Ferdinand de Lesseps in 1874 promoted a feasibility study
for the "Project of an African Interior Sea." Many geographers and
scientists stated that the chotts, or salt lagoons, in the south of
Tunisia were below sea level and could be connected by a canal to
the Mediterranean in order to create an inland waterway closer to
the Sahara. Estimates of the cost grew from 25 million francs (1874)
to 75 million (1880). The Tunisian government lately reconsidered
this project as a means of increasing rainfall for farmers north of
the chotts. Military considerations still oppose dividing the country in two by flooding the chotts, as well as the fact that the
largest of them, the Chott Djerid, is several meters above sea level.
Andre Martel, Les Confins saharo-tripolitains de la Tunisie, 1881-
1911, 1:167-71, 2:147-59; Tomkinson, p. 8; Chris Wright, seismic
surveyor, interview, July 1975.

15. AL, B3, 339, Bresson to Lavigerie, 27 August 1878; AE,
T 52:12-15, Roustan to ministry, 2 October 1880.

16. AL, B3, 381, Delattre to Mother House, 11 March 1878; B3,
446, Notes; "Diaire," January 1876.

17. AL, B3, 55, Lavigerie to Roustan, 15 June 1875.

18. AL, B3, 24 (identical to B3, 439), Roustan to Lavigerie,
3 September 1876.

19. AL, B3, 210(4), Lavigerie to Bresson, 2 August 1875; B3,
264, Lavigerie to Delattre and confreres, 3 May 1876; B3, 365, Roger
to unnamed, 4 June 1877; B3, 442, "Note."

20. AL, B3, 596, 22 May 1876.

21. AL, B3, 25, Roustan to Lavigerie, 27 December 1876; B3, 265,
Lavigerie to Delattre, 23 July 1876.

22. Lavigerie rigorously ruled out baptism despite the childrens'

requests, fearing both Arab protests and later apostasy. In the
case of the young blacks, the archbishop forbade Europeanization,
for he hoped that they would return to the interior eventually as
missionaries. He directed the priests to instill a pride in their
race and to feed them simple food of the sort which they would have
on their return. AL, "Diaire," 29 October 1876; B3, 210(4),
Lavigerie to Bresson, 2 August 1875; B3, 340 and 345, Bresson to
"Mon Très Rév. Père," letters dated 10 December 1878 and 28 January
1880; B3, 319, "Carte de Visite," 29 May 1879. La Vigie Algérienne
charged the White Fathers with buying "legions of blacks" from their
parents in an article on "Le Recrutement des néophytes nègres." In
fact, the priests had rescued them from the captors who had murdered
their parents. This anticlerical slander was typical of the peren-
nial attacks which Lavigerie and his priests had to bear. Delattre's
vehement defense against La Vigie's slander threatened a lawsuit and
emphasized that shelters for ransomed black children were operated
in Italy as well as North Africa by several congregations besides
the White Fathers. AL, B3, 438, Delattre to Procurator of the Republic in Algiers, 1 November 1877. Lavigerie moved his school for
blacks to Malta in summer 1881, so that they could attend medical
school there. Other leaders of the White Fathers resisted this project, and after Lavigerie's death it was phased out. Renault, 1:213-
36.

23. Grussenmeyer, 2:132-34.

24. AL, B3, 453, Sainte-Marie to Lavigerie, 22 June 1875; B3,
484, Delattre to Catteville, 16 November 1875; B3, 268, Lavigerie
to Fathers of Carthage, 19 March 1879; B3, 221, Lavigerie to Bresson,
3 May 1881; quotation from B3, 506, Delattre to Catteville, 18 May
1880, Delattre's emphasis of Lavigerie's pun on the name of a
northern constellation; Petit Robert 2, p. 432.

25. AL, B3, 272, Lavigerie to Delattre, 12 June 1880.

26. Nouvelle biographie générale, 41: 1010, 1011.

27. AL, B3, 276, Lavigerie to Delattre, 11 August 1880.

28. AL, B3, 282, Lavigerie to Delattre, 29 March 1881.

29. AL, B3, 277, Lavigerie to Delattre, 22 August 1880; Mgr. Charles Lavigerie, De l'Utilité d'une Mission Archéologique Permanente à Carthage: Lettre à M. le Secrétaire Perpétuel de l'Académie des Inscriptions et Belles-Lettres par l'Archevêque d'Alger.

30. AL, B3, 399, Delattre to Mother House, 6 May 1881; B3, 608(1), Fr. Bridoux to Superior at Saint-Louis, 5 July 1882; B3, 408, Delattre to Lavigerie, 26 May 1883; quotation from B3, 417, Delattre to Mother House, 26 February 1885; Dictionnaire universel des contemporains, p. 433.

31. Fr. Louis-Alfred Delattre was born in Belgium in 1850. Lavigerie appointed him curé of his primatial basilica at Carthage, where he served until his death in 1932. Delattre continued in the twentieth century to develop the Musée Lavigerie at Carthage, which became a national museum after Tunisian independence. Delattre joined the Academy of Inscriptions, and by the end of his life he had published more than 250 notices, articles, and books. The National Museum of the Bardo, which now shares the former beylical palace with the National Assembly, is considered by many to be the world's finest collection of mosaics.

Despite the great prestige which archeological work brought to Lavigerie and his priests, they sometimes faced criticism for their construction program at Carthage. Salomon Reinach (1858-1932) and Delattre found themselves in a difficulty concerning authority over land being developed by White Fathers. Reinach advised the Commission of Scientific Missions in Paris that Lavigerie's planned basilica might pave over archeological treasures. Regarding the land under the basilica, Lavigerie commented that the 45 m. by 14 m. foundation would be dug a sufficient 10 m. deep to rescue artifacts. In an area of some 500 hectares, that should leave approximately 4,999,370 square meters at Reinach's disposal. Lavigerie resented his projects for doubling the cost of labor overnight. He told Reinach that to excavate Carthage in the same manner as Pompeii would cost over 100 million francs.

Presently the Tunisian government has halted construction of new hotels or other major projects in the area. Several American and European archeological teams continue to work there. Local residents excavating in their backyards come across ancient carvings eagerly sought by amateur collectors, and tourists can buy original Roman or Byzantine coins on site. The oil lamps peddled on the street are replicas, sometimes cast from original molds.

Louis Bertrand, "Le centenaire du Cardinal Lavigerie," Revue des Deux Mondes 30 (1925): 578-80; Robert Streit and Johannes Dindinger, Bibliotheca Missionum, 7:738-50; Soumille, "Les Européens," p. 292n; AL, "Charmetant au Cardinal" 3:5112 / C4, 599, 25 May 1884; AL, 37:1411 / C4, 248, Lavigerie to Charmetant, 31 May 1884; Petit Robert 2, p. 1537; Tomkinson, pp. 31, 56, 57; Jean Perraudin, "Le Cardinal Lavigerie et Léopold II," Zaïre 11 (1957):901-32; 12 (1958): 37-64, 165-77, 275-91, 393-408, reference to Delattre from 11:912.

32. Goyau, "Le Cardinal Lavigerie," 26:607; Cussac, pp. 97, 98; Mercui, p. 240.

33. AL, B3, 366, Roger to unknown, 24 July 1877; B3, 378, Delattre to Mother House, 17 July 1877.

34. AL, B3, 211, Lavigerie to Roger, 1 August 1877; "Diaire," entries for July 1877.

35. AL, B3, 368, Roger to unknown, 27 November 1877.

36. AL, B3, 60, Lavigerie to Roustan, 4 December 1877; B3, 27, Roustan to Lavigerie, 20 December 1877.

37. AL, B3, 601, Lavigerie to Roustan, 4 December 1877.

38. AL, B3, 603, Roustan to Lavigerie, 24 December 1877.

39. AL, B3, 61, Lavigerie to Roustan, 4 December 1877.

40. Roustan provided a glowing testimonial in a dispatch to the foreign minister, dated 27 April 1880, in AE, T 49:339-40.

41. Quoted in Goyau, "Le Cardinal Lavigerie," 26: 783, 784; and in Tournier, "Le Cardinal Lavigerie," p. 843.

42. Baunard, 2:131.

43. Goyau, 26:783-84; Carlton J. H. Hayes, A Generation of Materialism, pp. 30-34; L. C. B. Seaman, From Vienna To Versailles,

pp. 126, 133.

Gilbert Gehring's monograph, "Les Relations entre la Tunisie et l'Allemagne avant le protectorat français," previously cited, documents the December 1874 reversal of Bismarck's attitude toward French interest in Tunisia, and his subsequent support for Paris against the objections of other governments.

During the period right after the Franco-Prussian War Bismarck's policy was to isolate France and to call Europe's attention to any French aggression. Documents of 20 December 1874 and 10 January 1875 explain his change of mind, respectively, to German embassies abroad and to Hohenlohe: "For us there is nothing inconvenient in French policy seeking in North Africa a field for its activities" (p. 90). "The absorption of forces which France would employ there and fix there, and the difficulties which that would create there, constitute a distraction from her aggressive tendencies against Germany" (p. 91). If Bismarck did not intend to stir up trouble between France and Italy, he did not mind it (pp. 106n, 107n).

The German consul general at Tunis, Charles Tulin, had a very cordial rapport with Roustan. After Licurgo Maccio's arrival in October 1878, Tulin and his Austrian colleague stayed neutral during the "War of the Two Consuls" (p. 115).

On 4 January 1879 Bismarck told the French ambassador to Berlin, Saint-Vallier: "Well, I think that the Tunisian pear is ripe and it is time for you to cut it. . . . My desire is to give you proof of good will in questions which touch you and where there are no German interests opposed to yours" (p. 110).

44. AE, T 50:47-52, draft treaties dated 11 February 1879 and 4 May 1880; Ganiage, L'expansion, pp. 11-15, 70.

45. André Raymond, "Les libéraux anglais et la question tunisienne, 1880-1881," Cahiers de Tunisie 3 (1955): 422-65, pp. 424, 425. The picture of careless administration and corruption in the consular tribunal permitted to develop under Reade is presented in great detail in Jean Ganiage, "L'Enfida," previously cited. This article is typical of Ganiage's thoroughness in biographical

background. For the lengthy footnote on Thomas Fellowes Reade (his father's third successor in the Tunis consulate), see p. 357. Reade became "soon celebrated at Tunis for his long strolls on the Avenue de la Marine" (renamed Avenue Jules Ferry, now Avenue Habib Bourguiba), Gehring, p. 110.

46. AE, T 51:191-93, Roustan to ministry, 5 August 1880; see also his reference to Reade in T 54:240-41, dated 25 January 1881; Ganiage, "L'Enfida," p. 351n. Transferred from Beyrouth in October 1878, Maccio "arrived on a gunboat and entered the consulate between two lines of marines." William L. Langer, "The European Powers and the French Occupation of Tunis, 1878-1881," American Historical Review 31: 55-78 (1925), and 251-65 (1926).

47. Baunard, 2:142.

48. Gehring, p. 115.

49. Paul Cambon, "Lettres de Tunisie," pp. 136, 137; Ganiage, "Les Européens," pp. 395-97, 416; Ganiage, L'Expansion, pp. 296, 297; Joan Gardner Roland, "The French Role in the Modernization of Jewish Communal Organizations in North Africa, 1880-1918," pp. 2-8, 13.

50. AE, T 49:97-98, Roustan to Courcel, 3 February 1880; T 51:330-81, Roustan to Courcel, 14 September 1880; T 56:238, wire, Roustan to ministry, 26 March 1881; AL, quotation from AC823, Roustan to Lavigerie, 29 September 1880; AC824, Roustan to Lavigerie, 12 October 1880; B3, 112, Lavigerie to Bresson, 6 October 1880; Ganiage, "les Européens," pp. 416, 417.

51. Ganiage, "Les Européens," pp. 416, 417; Ganiage, L'Expansion, pp. 70, 71. Paul Cambon wrote to his wife in January 1882, while being briefed by officials at the Quai d'Orsay in preparation for taking over Roustan's post, that they had stressed the importance of his seeing "Madame Elias," for she "exercises at Tunis an absolute preponderance." Paul Cambon, "Lettres de Tunisie," pp. 129, 130. She seems to have lost her intimate role in French policy after Roustan's departure in 1882.

52. "That's all right," according to one French priest at Rome.

53. APF, Barbaria 21:206-09, copy of Roustan to "M. le Ministre,"
25 March 1879.

54. AE, T 54:257, digest of Italian Foreign Minister Cairoli's
report to the Chamber on overseas education subsidies, 19 January
1881; AL, B3, 343, Bresson to "Mon Très Rév. Père," 3 March 1879;
Victor Guérin, Les Missionnaires catholiques dans le Nord de
l'Afrique, pp. 63-69; Brown, pp. 292-95; Joan Gardner Roland, "The
Alliance Israélite Universelle and French Policy in North Africa,
1860-1918," pp. 138, 144, 276, 277; Roland, "The French Role in the
Modernization of Jewish Communal Organizations in North Africa,
1880-1918," pp. 1, 2, 9. At the turn of the century a native group
known as the Young Tunisians started a program of modern Qur'anic
schools, free of direct government control. These "free schools"
emphasized Western languages, science, and other subjects. At the
same time they transmitted the Islamic heritage to children whose
parents hesitated to break with tradition. These schools qualified
many graduates for admission to the Collège Sadiki. The Young
Tunisians' free schools exemplified a pattern which developed in
colonial territories from Morocco to Indonesia. In Tunisia the promoters were Western-oriented, whereas in Algeria, for example, the
founders aimed at developing a strong sense of Algerian identity.
See John James Damis, "The Free-School Phenomenon: The Cases of
Tunisia and Algeria." Damis prepared his Ph. D. dissertation on "The
Free School Movement in Morocco, 1919-1970."

55. AL, "Diaire," 25 May 1879; B3, 210(10), Lavigerie to Bresson,
7 May 1879; quotation taken from an extensive memorial in B3, 319,
"Carte de Visite," 29 May 1879.

56. AL, B3, 319, "Carte de Visite."

57. AL, B3, 65, Lavigerie to Roustan, 13 September 1879.

58. AL, B3, 605, Waddington to Lavigerie, 10 June 1879; B3, 64,
Lavigerie to Waddington, 7 August 1879; quotation from B3, 388,
Delattre to Mother House, 9 September 1879; B3, 448, Roustan to
Lavigerie, 6 October 1879.

59. AL, B3, 344, Bresson to "Mon Très Rév. Père," 9 November 1879.

60. AE, T 60:142-43, Roustan to Barthélemy, 9 July 1881.

61. AL, B3, 66, Lavigerie to Roustan, 23 November 1879.

62. The White Fathers were to double that total within two years of Lavigerie's 1881 takeover. Grussenmeyer, 2:125.

63. AE, SS 1069:249-51, "Note sur l'Administration du Vicariat Apostolique de la Tunisie" [April 1881].

64. AL, B3, 66, cited above, Lavigerie to Roustan, 23 November 1879.

65. AL, B3, 346, Bresson to "Mon Très Rév. Père," 1 June 1880; "Diaire," April and May 1880; Pottier, p. 327; APT, LCL, 2017, Lavigerie to Roustan, 12 June 1880(?).

66. AL, B3, 70, Lavigerie to Roustan, 10 May 1880; B3, 347, Bresson to "Mon Très Rév. Père," 6 July 1880.

67. Baunard, 2:143.

68. AL, B3, 30 and 454, two copies filed of Freycinet to Roustan, 10 May 1880.

69. AL, B3, 71, Lavigerie to Freycinet, 23 June 1880; B3, 33, Moüy (at Quai d'Orsay) to Lavigerie, 3 August 1880; B3, 34, ministry to Lavigerie, 18 September 1880; B3, 454, contains other copies of this correspondence; Guérin, Les Missionnaires catholiques, p. 25.

70. AL, B3, 234, Lavigerie to Deguerry, 4 August 1881.

71. AL, B3, 210 (items 18 and 19), Lavigerie to Bresson, dated 20 and 18 August 1880; B3, 80, Lavigerie to Roustan, 3 December 1880.

72. AL, "Diaire"; B3, 80, Lavigerie to Roustan, 3 December 1880; B3, 398, Delattre to Mother House, 12 October 1880.

73. AE, T 53:68-70, Roustan to ministry, 21 November 1880; AL, AC824, Amed Volterra to Roustan, 21 September 1880.

74. AE, T 51:61, Roustan to Courcel, 7 July 1880; T 52:12-15, Roustan to Barthélemy, 5 October 1880; Roland, "The Alliance Israélite Universelle," p. 276, 277.

75. AL, B3, 31 and 31 bis, Roustan to Lavigerie, 15 May 1880.

76. AE, T 50:114, Roustan to Courcel, 18 May 1880; reference to consular organ from T 50:202, 1 June 1880.

77. Quotation from AL, B3, 32, Roustan to Lavigerie, 18 May 1880;

see clipping from <u>L'Avvenire di Sardegna</u> of 6 May, B3, 31; also AE, T 50:15 and 159, Roustan to ministry of 14 May 1880 and translation of Arabic clipping from <u>L'Indépendent</u> of 9 May 1880.

78. Ganiage, <u>L'Expansion</u>, pp. 71-73; Jean Ganiage, <u>Les Origines du protectorat français en Tunisie, 1861-1881</u>, p. 570n.

79. AE, T 50:107-11, Roustan to Freycinet, 10 May 1880.

80. Ganiage, "L'Enfida," pp. 349, 350; AE, T 49:341-43, Roustan to ministry, 27 April 1880.

81. Raymond, pp. 425-32; quotation from Archivio Storico, Ministero degli Affari Esteri, Rome (Farnesina), "Archivi di Gabinetto, 1861-1887," Busta 233, "Affari d'Africa in genere, 1886-1887" (mislabeled, should read "1868-1887"), fas. 6, v, H. S. Wardonnel? to Cte. Maffei, 17 August 1880, relaying substance of a dispatch from Reade to British embassy in Rome.

82. AE, T 54:62-66, Roustan to Barthélemy, 11 January 1881.

83. Ganiage, <u>L'Expansion</u>, p. 73.

84. AE, T 54:62-66, Roustan to Barthélemy, 11 January 1881, previously cited.

85. AE, T 53:77, 78, coded cable from Roustan to ministry, 24 November 1880; AL, "Diaire," 18 and 20 November 1880; AN, F19, 2487, "31 Lettres," 17, Lavigerie to "Conseiller d'Etat," 30 November 1880.

86. AE, T 53:79, coded cable from Roustan to ministry, 25 November 1880; T 53:82, coded cable from Roustan to ministry, 26 November 1880; T 53:87-88, particular letter, Roustan to Courcel, 26 November 1880; T 53:163, Lavigerie to Roustan, 12 December 1880, refers to "crackbrain"; AL, B3, 78, Lavigerie to Roustan, 26 November 1880.

87. AE, T 53:97, cable from Alexandre to Augustin, 27 November 1880; quotation from AL, B3, 81, Lavigerie to Roustan, 6 December 1880, original emphasis.

88. AE, T 53:89, Lavigerie to Roustan, 26 November 1880.

89. AE, T 53:101, Barthélemy to Constans, 2 December 1880; T 53:167, "for Constans" to Roustan, 15 December 1880; T 53:168, Barthélemy to Roustan, 16 December 1880; T 54:119, Lavigerie to

Roustan, 12 January 1881.

90. AE, T 53:111-12, Roustan to Foreign Ministry, 7 December
1880; T 54:20-21, Lavigerie to Roustan, 29 December 1880 (found
also in AL, B3, 83); T 54:22, Augustin to Roustan, 20 December 1880
(found also in AL, B3, 124); T 54:84, ministry to Roustan, 13
January 1881; T 54:119, Lavigerie to Roustan, 12 January 1881.

91. AE, T 54:10, coded cable from Roustan to Foreign Ministry,
2 January 1881; SS 1069:8-9, Desprez to ministry, 5 January 1881;
SS 1069:38-42, Desprez to Barthélemy, 15 January 1881.

92. AE, T 56:244, cable from Barthélemy to Roustan, 28 March
1881; quotation from T 56:263, Roustan to Courcel, 29 March 1881.

93. AE, SS 1069:207-8, and 241, reports of Desprez to the ministry dated 27 March and 12 April 1881.

CHAPTER IV

1. In Algeria the French had optimistically undertaken programs
of education, vaccination, clinic services, etc., in order to promote evolution of the natives' way of life. Although the Arab-Berber
masses outwardly yielded to French military power after 1848, they
never accepted the benefits of the infidels' "superior" civilization,
suspecting that French clinics and schools were an attempt to undermine their culture and faith. "For the Muslims refusal became an
arm of defense," in the words of Yvonne Turin (p. 100). Her book,
Affrontements culturels dans l'Algérie coloniale: Ecoles, médecines,
religion, 1830-1880, studies the developing official awareness that
the basic evolution of Muslim society was not within sight. Resentful
native teachers tried to keep students from French influence. Traditional healers temporarily lost patients to French doctors only
insofar as someone desperately ill overcame his distrust for the
sake of a quick cure. The natives questioned the motives behind
colonial programs, and they resented French cultural advances.
MacMahon recognized in 1869 that the Muslim population was more
hostile to the French than in 1844 (p. 197). Lavigerie blamed this
fact on the army's mismanagement of the situation, although Turin's

research suggests that he deceived himself about the potential of
Catholic charitable and educational projects to do better. In order
to reach the middle- and upper-class Algerians with educational
programs the government promoted a system of Franco-Arab schools.
But by 1880 the French authorities all recognized the Muslims' deep-
seated resistance to the French idea of progress.

2. AL, 36:1392 / C4, 145, Lavigerie to Charmetant, 29 March 1881.

3. Ibid.; Kittler, p. 64; Mercui, pp. 297, 298, 404; Fr. René
Lamey, interview, summer 1972; AE, T 66:240, Lavigerie to Freycinet,
4 February 1882; AN, F19, 2487, "Mgr. Lavigerie," news clippings 110
and 125; AL, "Charmetant au Cardinal" 1:4951 / C4, 424, 5 February
1878; 35: 935(16) / T, 211, Lavigerie to Charmetant, 29 January
1878; 36: 1396 / C4, 156 and 528 / C4, 169, Lavigerie to Charmetant,
24 August and 24 December 1881; 38: 3160(121) / C4, 365, Lavigerie
to Charmetant, 8 October 1886.

4. AL, "Charmetant au Cardinal" 2:5023 / C4, 506, 26 April 1881;
36:524 / C4, 164, Lavigerie to Charmetant, 5 December 1881;
38:1600(3) / C4, 324(bis) and 1600(4) / C4, 325(bis), Lavigerie to
Charmetant, 6 and 20 November 1885.

5. Ganiage, L'Expansion, pp. 74, 75(quotation); Billing, pp. 395,
396; Raymond, p. 435; Cayci, pp. 25-28.

6. Ganiage, L'Expansion, p. 75; Tournier, "Le Cardinal Lavigerie,"
p. 843; Langer, "European Powers," p. 259n.

7. Baunard, 2:150, 151; Ganiage, L'Expansion, p. 76; Raymond,
p. 425. "In every quarter could be felt the strong hand of Bismarck,
who practically cut short all schemes of intervention," Langer,
"European Powers," p. 262.

8. AE, T 52:12-15, Roustan to ministry, 2 October 1880.

9. AL, AC824, Roustan to Lavigerie, n.d.

10. AL, B3, 74, Lavigerie to minister (Ferry or Barthélemy),
6 October 1880.

11. AE, SS 1069:38-42, Desprez to Barthélemy, 15 January 1881;
1069:55-57, ministry to Desprez, 24 January 1881; APF, Barbaria
21:426-27, Father Innocenzo to Propaganda, 19 June 1880.

12. AE, T 54:117, Roustan to Courcel, 16 January 1881; AE, SS
1068:99, Flourens to Freycinet, 3 August 1881; Tournier, Action
politique, pp. 119-24.

13. AE, SS 1069:67, ministry to Desprez, 29 January 1881; SS
1069:80-83, Desprez to Barthélemy, 6 February 1881; Tournier,
Action politique, pp. 119-24.

14. AL, B3, 90, Lavigerie to Roustan, 15 January 1881; also
found in AE, T 54:120-22. The punctuation and emphasis is Lavigerie's.

15. AL, B3, 91, Lavigerie to Roustan, 4 February 1881;
"Charmetant au Cardinal" 2:5019 / C4, 501, 6 March 1881; AE, SS
1069: 101, 207-8, and 221, cables from Desprez to ministry dated
12 February, 27 March, and 2 April 1881.

16. AL, 36:935(41) / T, 466, Lavigerie to Charmetant, 10 April
1881. The emphasis is Lavigerie's. Covering letter for this message
to the government is 36:935(43) / T, 472.

17. AE, T 59: 301, 302, Charmetant to Courcel, 13 June 1881.

18. APF, Barbaria 21:639-40, Lavigerie to Simeoni, 10 April 1881.

19. Ibid.

20. AE, SS 1069:285-88, Desprez to Barthélemy, 29 April 1881;
Goyau, "Le Cardinal Lavigerie," 26:787n.

21. AE, T 57:156-58, Lavigerie to Charmetant, 11 April 1881.

22. Ibid.

23. AL, B3, 89, Lavigerie to Roustan, 1881.

24. AE, T 59:44-45, Roustan to ministry, 24 May 1881; Baunard,
2:152-54.

25. AL, "Diaire," 19 June 1881.

26. AL, B3, 220, Lavigerie to Bresson, 27 April 1881.

27. AE, SS 1070:67, Barthélemy to Desprez, 20 May 1881; SS
1070:187-91, Desprez to Barthélemy, 28 June 1881, T 59:34, Barthélemy
to Roustan, 22 May 1881; T 59:64, Charmetant to Courcel, 25 May 1881;
APF, Barbaria 21:643-44, Lavigerie to Simeoni, 8 May 1881.

28. AE, T 59:65-66, Lavigerie to Charmetant, 24 May 1881.

29. AE, SS 1070: 81-86 and 95, Desprez to Barthélemy, 27 and
29 May 1881; SS 1070: 92 and 108, ministry to Desprez, 29 May and

3 June 1881; T 59:150, Lavigerie to Charmetant, 2 June 1881; AL,
"Charmetant au Cardinal" 2:5026 / C4, 509, 25 May 1881.

30. AE, SS 1070:82-86, 114, and 125-27, Desprez to Barthélemy,
27 May, 7 and 8 June 1881; duplicate of 8 June 1881 in AL, B3, 41;
AL, 36:935(54) / T, 529, Lavigerie to Charmetant, 26 May 1881.

31. Quotation from AE, SS 1070:197-200, Desprez to Barthélemy,
1 July 1881; other reports dated 17, 28, and 30 June are found in
SS 1070: 158-59, 187-91, and 193.

32. AE, T 59:383-86, printed memoir by Barthélemy, 20 June 1881;
Paul Cambon, "Lettres de Tunisie," pp. 127, 128.

33. AE, T 59: 65, 66, Lavigerie to Charmetant, 24 May 1881.

34. Ibid.; AN, F19, 2487, "31 Lettres," 20, Lavigerie to
Flourens, 8 July 1881; "8 Lettres," 6, Lavigerie to Flourens, 21
July 1881; Tournier, Action politique, pp. 119-24.

35. AL, "Charmetant au Cardinal" 2:5025 / C4, 508, 4 May 1881.

36. AE, T 59: 301, 302, Charmetant to Courcel, 13 June 1881; AL,
"Charmetant au Cardinal" 2:5027 / C4, 510 and 5028 / C4, 511 of
29 May and 7 June 1881.

37. AE, T 59:598, cable from Roustan to ministry, 29 June 1881;
T 60:138-39, Lavigerie to Roustan, 7 July 1881; AL, "Diaire"; B3,
222, Lavigerie to Bresson, 29 May 1881; R. P. Anselme des Arcs,
Mémoires pour servir à l'histoire de la mission des Capucins dans la
Régence de Tunis, 1624-1865, pp. 138-40. Sutter retired to Italy and
died 30 August 1883.

38. AL, 36:3142(95) / T, 507, Lavigerie to Charmetant, cable,
4 June 1881.

39. AL, B3, 85, "Court exposé de la conduite des Pères Capucins
de Tunis vis-à-vis de nouvel Administrateur Apostolique et measures
à prendre pour faire cesser cette situation," 1881.

40. Ibid.

41. Quotation from AL, B3, 84, cable from Lavigerie to Roustan,
July 1881; AE, T 60:184, Roustan to ministry, 12 July 1881; Baunard,
2:162; Mercui, p. 308.

42. Request in AL, B3, 84, cited above; French compliance is

confirmed in AE, T 60:359, Roustan to ministry, 28 July 1881.

43. AE, SS 1070:311, Desprez to ministry, 26 July 1881; AL, B3,
5, 6, and 7, letters from Lavigerie to Jacobini, Simeoni, and
Leo XIII, dated 24, 24, and 27 July 1881; "Diaire," 15 August 1881.

44. AL, B3, 86, cited above; APF, Barbaria 21:882, memorandum
of the congresso of 29 July 1881.

45. AE, T 61:13-14, Roustan to Courcel, 1 August 1881; AL, B3,
234, Lavigerie to Deguerry, 4 August 1881.

46. APF, Barbaria 21:678, Liborio to Simeoni, 27 July 1881;
AL, B3, 1, Lavigerie to Jacobini and Simeoni, 1881; B3, 44, Courcel
to Lavigerie, 27 August 1881; B3, 235, Lavigerie to Bresson, 10
August 1881; AE, SS 1071: 15, 92-95, 98, 105-6, and 129, correspondence between the Quai d'Orsay and Bâcourt from 4 August to 6 September 1881; AL, 36:3142(97) / T, 513, Lavigerie to Charmetant,
28 September 1881.

47. AE, SS 1071: 164 and 168, Lavigerie to Charmetant, 28 and
29 September 1881; SS 1071:170-71, Barthélemy to Bâcourt, 29 September 1881; T 62:288, Barthélemy to Roustan, 29 September 1881,
AL, B3, 9, Lavigerie to Simeoni, late September 1881; B3, 86,
previously cited.

48. AL, 36:1397 / C4, 160, Lavigerie to Charmetant, 11 October
1881.

49. Ibid.; AE, SS 1071:172, Bâcourt to ministry, 30 September
1881; T 63:181-82, Roustan to Barthélemy, 13 October 1881; Baunard,
2: 163, 164; APF, Barbaria 21:736, Salvatore to Simeoni, 7 October
1881; Barbaria 21:763, Lavigerie to Simeoni, 19 October 1881.

50. AE, SS 1073:36, Desprez to ministry, 13 June 1881; Goyau,
"Le Cardinal Lavigerie," 26:790; APF, Barbaria 21:767, Liborio to
Propaganda.

51. AL, B3, 92, "L'Oeuvre de Francisation," dated July 1881.

52. APF, Barbaria 21:710-12, Salvatore to father general of the
Capuchins, 18 January 1882.

53. APF, Barbaria 21:713-19, Lavigerie to Simeoni, 21 January
1882, also found in AL, B3, 3; Barbaria 21:883, memorandum on

congresso of June 1882; Barbaria 21:933-34, Lavigerie to Simeoni,
14 December 1882; AN, F19, 2487, "Algérie," 32, "Extrait d'un
rapport de M. le Procureur Général près la Cour d'Appel d'Alger,"
1887.

    54. AE, T 54:120-22 (also AL, B3, 90), cited above.

CHAPTER V

1. Jules Ferry, Les Affaires de Tunisie, p. 29.
2. Ferry, pp. 98, 99, 114, 115.
3. AL, "Charmetant au Cardinal" 2:5023 / C4, 506, 26 April 1881.
4. AL, "Charmetant au Cardinal" 2:5045 / C4, 528, 11 February
1881.
5. Richard Macken, "Louis Machuel and Educational Reform in
Tunisia during the Early Years of the French Protectorate," Revue
d'Histoire Maghrébine 3 (January 1975): 45-55.
6. AL, 36:3142(78) / T, 467 and 524 / C4, 164, Lavigerie to
Charmetant, 28 April and 5 December 1881.
7. AE, T 57:156-58, Lavigerie to Charmetant, 11 April 1881;
AL, B3, 49, n.d., a list of nineteen questions or points of information to be investigated, addressed to the fathers in Tunisia;
Goyau, "Le Cardinal Lavigerie," 26:786; Tournier, "Le Cardinal
Lavigerie," pp. 844-46. The White Fathers had a very small presence
at Tripoli, but the Quai d'Orsay Archives for Tripoli have no
documents concerning them or Lavigerie. Renault, 1: 215, 215n.
8. France, Ministère des Armées, Service Historique de l'Armée,
Chateau de Vincennes, Val de Marne (Vincennes), Section Outre-Mer,
Tunisie, Series 3H, "Fonds Tunisie, 1831-1920," Sub-series 3OH1,
notebook "Mission Sandherr," entry for 19 April 1881.
9. Gehring, pp. 25-30; Vincennes, 3OH1, folio "Documents con-
cernant la Tunisie 1864 à 1888," item "Rapport du Lieut. Rouguerol
sur Tunisie," 15 November 1880. For a comment on the importance of
religious fervor in Algerian political resistance during the mid-
nineteenth century, see Turin, pp. 110-12.

Islam inspires a strong conviction that, ideally, Muslim society is one, without any separation between culture and doctrine, between the political and the religious. The Call of the Minaret, written by a Protestant missionary, Kenneth Cragg, provides an excellent treatment of Islam and Muslim culture. Several other books on Islam and the history of the Arabs have been written by Philip Khuri Hitti, Abdallah Laroui, and Bernard Lewis. I have listed them in the bibliography.

10. AL, "Charmetant au Cardinal" 2:5019 / C4, 501, 6 March 1881. Quotation from Vincennes, 30H1, "Mission Sandherr," 15 June 1881. This also refers to a letter from Fr. Deguerry enclosed with Sandherr's report.

Nicholas-Jean-Robert-Conrad-August Sandherr (b. 1846) was considered to be an extremely capable officer, and he rose to colonel. His working notes on Tunisia, the "Succession Sandherr" (Vincennes, 32H33), are interesting for their marginal designs of crowns, kings, and fleurs-de-lis. These monarchist doodles accord with Sandherr's later role as chief of the Intelligence Service at the time of the General Staff's accusation and first conviction of Captain Alfred Dreyfus. With glowing recommendations Sandherr retired from the army for reasons of health and died in 1897. Brogan, pp. 305, 330, 768; Vincennes, Ministry of War's personnel dossier on Sandherr.

11. Vincennes, 30H1, "Mission Sandherr," 27 June 1881.

12. AL, B3, 219 and 223, Lavigerie to Bresson, 12 April and 31 May 1881; Vincennes, 30H1, "Mission Sandherr," 7 June 1881.

13. AL, 28:3142(79) / T, 470, "Note sur la situation d'esprit des indigènes en Afrique du Nord," April 1881.

14. AL, 36:3142(78) / T, 467, Lavigerie to Charmetant, 28 April 1881.

15. AL, 36: 935(53) / T, 523, Lavigerie to Charmetant, 1 May 1881.

16. AL, "Charmetant au Cardinal" 2:5022 / C4, 505, 13 April 1881.

17. AL, "Charmetant au Cardinal" 2:5021 / C4, 503, 23 March 1881.

18. AL, "Charmetant au Cardinal" 2:5023 / C4, 506, 26 April 1881.

19. AE, T 57:403-15, Lavigerie to Charmetant, 24 April 1881.

20. AL, "Charmetant au Cardinal" 2:5023 / C4, 506, 26 April 1881.

21. Today Kheredine Pasha is one of Tunisia's greatest heroes.
This devout and incorruptible reformer lamented the decline of
Muslim civilization and worked throughout his life for its renewal.
Circassian-born (around 1820), Kheredine was one of the mamluks
(slaves) taken from their families at an early age and trained in
the beylical court. He served as one of Ahmad Bey's trusted officials, and he married one of Ahmad's sisters. In 1867 he wrote a
treatise on reform of Islamic society. Kheredine used the Qur'an as
the starting point for a pragmatic program emphasizing science and
political reforms. He signed his name in French: Khérédine. In Arabic,
Khayr al-Dîn means "Good of Religion." See Brown, pp. 220-22;
Gehring, p. 26n; Ganiage, "L'Enfida," p. 342n; Marsden, British
Diplomacy, pp. 40, 41; Martel, 1:362. White Fathers A. Demeerseman
and J. Fontaine have recently given Kheredine the praise which his
contribution to Muslim civilization merits. See A. Demeerseman,
"Au Berceau des premières réformes démocratiques en Tunisie," IBLA
20 (1957): 1-12; idem, "Doctrine de Khéreddine en matière de politi-
que extérieure," IBLA 21 (1958): 13-29; idem, "Indépendence de la
Tunisie et politique extérieure de Khereddine," IBLA 21 (1958):
229-77; idem, "Un Grand témoin des premières idées modernisantes en
Tunisie," IBLA 76 (1956): 349-74; J. Fontaine, "Khéreddine, Réformiste
ou moderniste?," IBLA 117 (1967): 75-81. An English translation of
Kheredine's program is by Leon Carl Brown, The Surest Path: The
Political Treatise of a Nineteenth Century Muslim Statesman, a
translation of the introduction to the Surest Path to Knowledge Concerning the Condition of Countries by Khayr al-Dîn al Tûnisî,
Harvard Middle Eastern Mongraphs 15 (Cambridge: Harvard University
Press, 1967). After his service as beylical prime minister (1873-77)
Kheredine eventually went to Turkey, where briefly he became Ottoman
grand vizier. At the request of the Tunisian government, the remains
of Kheredine (d. 1889) were brought from Turkey for reburial in
1968. Dr. M. Fadhel Jamali published a review of Dr. Brown's translation in Cahiers de Tunisie 65-67 (1969): 274-76. With regard to

the sincerity of Kheredine's religiosity, Dr. Jamali stated in an
interview at La Marsa, 25 May 1975, that Kheredine was "a devout
reformist."

22. AE, T 57:403-15, Lavigerie to Charmetant, 24 April 1881.

23. AL, 36:3142(78) / T, 467, Lavigerie to Charmetant, 28 April
1881; Betts, pp. 126-28.

24. AL, 38:1426 / C4, 314, Lavigerie to Charmetant, 9 July 1885.

25. AE, T 57:403-15, Lavigerie to Charmetant, 24 April 1881.

26. AE, T 57:156-58, Lavigerie to Charmetant, 11 April 1881.

27. AE, T 57:403-15, cited above. When general war came in 1914,
Tunisia and Algeria loyally contributed tens of thousands of Muslim
troops, many of whom died in defense of French territory.

28. Ibid. In comparison, Alan Scham mentions Lyautey's belief
in the need for free exchange in Morocco. See p. 17.

29. Al, 36: 935(50) / T, 519, Lavigerie to Charmetant, 29 April
1881.

30. Vincennes, 30H1, "Mission Sandherr," 15 June 1881.

31. Ibid., 6 July 1881; Ferry, pp. 51, 122.

32. Vincennes, 30H1, "Mission Sandherr," 14 July 1881. My colleague William L. Ochsenwald observes that this passage reflects a
poor understanding of Muslim civilization. The califate was the
succession to Muhammad. This leadership of the Muslim community was
civil and administrative rather than prophetical. It continued
through vicissitudes until Turkey's abolition of it in 1924. Cragg,
pp. 6, 94.

33. Cayci, pp. 91-98.

34. Ferry, p. 122.

35. Breton noted that by invoking a Muslim sovereign's authority
against his own subjects, the French complicated the situation, for
French support discredited the bey before his own people. The task
was "to constitute a party which, if not attached to the French, at
least will not be hostile," Vincennes, 30H1, 14-1, "La Question de
Tunisie," Commandant Breton to Col. Richard (tutoyant), 11 October
1881. The Jihad, or call to battle, was not an aggressive program

of Islam in the modern period. But a direct attack against Muslim
shrines could have provoked otherwise docile Tunisians to a holy
war of defense.

36. AL, 36:1397 / C4, 160, Lavigerie to Charmetant, 11 October
1881. Thomas-Robert Bugeaud was governor general of Algeria from
1840 to 1847. Petit Robert 2, p. 302. Lavigerie always distinguished
between the fanatical nomads of the desert and the docile natives
fixed in agriculture or trade. In a press interview he described the
latter as hard-working and monogamous, except for local magnates
who followed the Turkish style. Baunard, 2:169; Le Monde, 7 May 1885,
clipping in AN, F19, 2487, "Mgr. Lavigerie," 211. Fr. Delattre recorded an impression which concurred with Lavigerie's judgment, in
a personal letter to one of his oldest friends in France (AL, B3,
512, Delattre to Abbé Catteville, 3 November 1881):

> The Arabs around us are little concerned with events.
> Provided that they do not have to fight; that their taxes
> are not too high; that they can tranquilly labor and tend
> their lands, make their harvests, and sell their barley;
> that is all they ask. The government which offers them
> these advantages will be to their taste, and if the French
> occupation will better their condition . . . they will
> accept it willingly.
>
> I speak here of the Arabs around us who customarily
> find themselves in rapport with the Europeans and see
> them often. As for the Arabs of the interior, a nomadic
> people who freely travel from one place to another with
> arms and baggage, it is another affair. It is they who
> from time to time come to attack by surprise the army
> of occupation and to make of it their victims. . . . The
> officers who come to visit Carthage are all astonished
> to be able to walk about so peacefully in the midst of
> the people who surround us, to enter so freely into
> their villages. Is that the effect already of our pres-
> ence here for six years?

The answer to Delattre's question is perhaps rather that Tunisians are by nature gentle and friendly.

37. Vincennes, 30H1, "Mission Sandherr," 14 December 1881; AL, "Diaire," 29 October 1881.

38. Quotation from AE, T 63:303, Roustan to Barthélemy, 23 October 1881; AL, "Diaire," 29 October 1881; Baunard, 2:167-68; Ganiage, L'expansion, p. 79; Brogan, p. 163; Ferry, pp. 52, 53.

39. C. Alfred Perkins, "French Catholic Opinion and Imperial Expansion, 1880-1886," p. 69; Goyau, "Le Cardinal Lavigerie," 26:788; Grussenmeyer, 2:24.

40. C. Alfred Perkins, pp. 71, 7, 69.

41. AE, T 63:164, Roustan to Courcel, 11 October 1881; AL, B3, 97, Lavigerie to Roustan, 10 December 1881; Baunard, 2:178; extensive material and quotation from Ganiage, "L'Enfida," pp. 374-77.

42. AE, T 64:79-87, Lavigerie to Courcel, 5 November 1881; the first draft is found in AL, B3, 96.

43. AE, T 64:79-87, Lavigerie to Courcel, 5 November 1881. The emphasis is Lavigerie's.

44. Ibid.

45. AE, T 64:270-71, cable from Gambetta to Roustan, 18 November 1881.

46. AE, T 64:275, Roustan to ministry, 19 November 1881.

47. AE, T 65:91, Logerot to Roustan, 11 December 1881.

48. AE, T 66:212-14, Roustan to Gambetta, 26 January 1882.

49. AE, T 66:327-28, Lavigerie to Roustan, 18 February 1882.

50. Goyau, "Le Cardinal Lavigerie," 26: 791, 792.

51. See Betts, pp. 126-32.

52. AE, T 64:290-97, Lavigerie to Charmetant, 19 November 1881.

53. Goyau, "Le Cardinal Lavigerie," 26: 788, 789.

54. AL, "Charmetant au Cardinal" 2:5038 / C4, 521, 4 December 1881.

55. AL, "Charmetant au Cardinal" 2:5039 / C4, 522, 17 December 1881.

56. AL, 36:3142(104) / T, 542, Lavigerie to "My Dear Friend,"

24 December 1881. The identity of the addressee as Gambetta is confirmed by a reference in AL, 36:529 / C4, 171, Lavigerie to
Charmetant, 26 December 1881.

57. Ibid. "Life and property were so insecure that natives
registered as protected subjects of the European powers," Keith
Eubank, Paul Cambon, Master Diplomatist, p. 16. With regard to
Leland Louis Bowie's works on the importance of the protégé system
in undermining the authority of the Sultan of Morocco, see ch. 3,
note 10.

58. Ibid. With regard to Land Policy in Colonial Algeria during
the first two decades of French control, see John Ruedy's book,
cited in bibliography. The beys took French money and jewels over
and under the table for most of the protectorate's seventy-five
years. There was no effective opposition to Habib Bourguiba's abolition of the monarchy on 25 July 1957.

59. AE, T 62:147-49, Lavigerie to Courcel, 12 September 1881;
T 66:209-10, Roustan to Gambetta, 26 January 1882; T 66:241-42,
Lavigerie to "My Dear Friend," 4 February 1882; Goyau, "Le Cardinal
Lavigerie," 26:789; AL, "Charmetant au Cardinal" 2:5045 / C4, 528,
11 February 1882.

60. AL, 36:1399 / C4, 168, Lavigerie to "My Dear Friend," 20
December 1881.

61. Ibid. The order of the original text of this letter has been
changed.

62. Ibid.

63. AL, "Charmetant au Cardinal" 2:5039 / C4, 522, 17 December
1881.

64. AL, "Charmetant au Cardinal" 2:5040 / C4, 523, 31 December
1881.

65. AL, "Charmetant au Cardinal" 2:5038 / C4, 521, 4 December
1881.

66. AE, SS 1071:183-87, Desprez to Barthélemy, 9 October 1881.

67. AL, "Charmetant au Cardinal" 2:5036 / C4, 519, 27 November
1881.

68. AL, "Charmetant au Cardinal" 2:5038 / C4, 521, 4 December 1881.

69. AL, 36:525 / C4, 165, Lavigerie to Charmetant, 10 December 1881, original emphasis.

70. Préville, pp. 324, 325.

71. AE, SS 1072:187, Desprez to Quai d'Orsay, 4 March 1882; AL, "Charmetant au Cardinal" 2:5042 / C4, 525 of 15 January 1882, 5045 / C4, 528 of 11 February 1882, and 5047 / C4, 530 of 26 February 1882.

72. Montclos, Toast, p. 180.

73. Quotation from AL, B3, 102, Lavigerie to Roustan, 5 April 1882; Billing, pp. 384-86; APF, Barbaria 21:858-60, Lavigerie to Simeoni, 4 April 1882, including clipping from L'Avvenire de Sardegna, 31 March 1882.

74. AE, T 66:30-34, Roustan to Gambetta, 7 January 1882; T 70:76-79, Cambon to Duclerc, 10 November 1882; Ganiage, L'expansion, p. 296.

75. AE, T 66:298-304, Conrad to Jauréguiberry, 7 February 1882.

76. Ibid.; AE, T 66:244-45, Conrad to Jauréguiberry, 31 January 1882; AL, B3, 520, Delattre to Catteville, 24 May 1883. Besides being the key to the assimilation program, the Maltese appealed to French leaders as prospective settlers. Their small islands could not support their prolific population. The director of the French consulate at Malta, M. Marie, recommended them as "industrious, sober, and thrifty," the sort of immigrants the French needed for Tunisia. A French company, the Société Marseillaise, already had definite plans for introducing them, but Marie urged caution lest a premature scheme inflate the settlers' expectations. Such a program of enlarging the Maltese community in Tunisia was sound, but it should be followed gradually. AE, Correspondance politique, Angleterre, Poste consulaire de Malte (M), 66: 246-50, 254-55, and 256-61, reports of Marie to Freycinet, dated 8, 23, and 23 May 1882; M 66:276-77, Bureau des Affaires Tunisiennes to Marie, 30 June 1882.

77. Cussac, pp. 107, 108; Goyau, "Le Cardinal Lavigerie," 26:

795, 796; Grussenmeyer, 2:52; Mercui, pp. 315, 316; AN, F19, 2487, "Mgr. Lavigerie," 100; AL, B3, 102, Lavigerie to Roustan, 5 April 1882; "Charmetant au Cardinal" 2:5052 / C4, 535, 23 April 1882. De Rameau, the Spanish consul, snubbed the new cardinal by not coming to the ceremony at Carthage. Lavigerie wrote to the nuncio at Madrid, Mgr. Rampolla, that His Catholic Majesty ought to transfer him. APT, LCL, 2001, Lavigerie to Rampolla, n.d.

78. AL, "Charmetant au Cardinal" 2:5050 / C4, 533, 2 April 1882; 37:3142 / T, 556, cable from Lavigerie to Charmetant, 15 April 1882; Mercui, pp. 315, 316; AE, T 66:30-34, Roustan to Gambetta, 7 January 1882; T 70:76-79, Cambon to Declerc, 10 November 1882. Several clippings from the extensive press coverage given to Lavigerie's cardinalate are assembled together in AN, F19, 2487, "Mgr. Lavigerie," items 109-24. See in particular item 122, La Justice of 23 May 1882.

79. Quotation from Paul Cambon, Correspondance, pp. 184-86; Ward, "'The Diplomat Pope,'" pp. 58, 59.

80. AE, M 66:303-8, Marie to Freycinet, 21 July 1882; AN, F19, 2487, "Mgr. Lavigerie," 143, Français, 21 July 1882.

81. AL, B3, 16, circular letter to clergy of Tunis, 4 August 1884; AN, F19, 2487, "Algérie," 11, substitute for procurator of the republic to minister of cults, 1 September 1884; quotation from F19, 2487, "Cambon," Cambon to "My Dear Friend," 7 August 1884.

82. AL, 36:1400 / C4, 170, Lavigerie to Charmetant, 24 December 1881.

83. AL, 37:534 / C4, 178, Lavigerie to Charmetant, 17 January 1882.

84. AL, 36:529 / C4, 171, Lavigerie to Charmetant, 26 December 1881.

85. Paul Cambon, Correspondance, p. 215.

CHAPTER VI

1. Both Paul Cambon (1843-1924) and his brother Jules (1845-1935) served the Third Republic as prefect of the Nord before going to North Africa. They worked above party and class, advancing French

interests by their tactful efforts. Paul Cambon went from Tunis to
the embassy in Madrid, then to Constantinople, and finally to London
where he was ambassador from 1898 to 1920. Paul Cambon's name is
associated with the Entente Cordiale which he negotiated with
Britain. Jules Cambon was governor general of Algeria, and thereafter ambassador to Washington, Madrid, and Berlin (1907-14). Petit
Robert 2, p. 324.

2. AL, "Charmetant au Cardinal" 2:5048 / C4, 531, 12 March 1882.

3. Keith Eubank provides many interesting details concerning
Cambon's service in Tunisia in ch. 2. Quotation is from p. 14.

4. Paul Cambon, Correspondance, 25 July 1882.

5. Baron d'Estournelles de Constant wrote an article titled
"Les Débuts d'un protectorat: La France en Tunisie," Revue des Deux
Mondes 79 (1887): 785-819, see pp. 787, 788. He wrote another work,
La Politique française en Tunisie, under the pseudonym P.H.X. See
p. 326. D'Estournelles de Constant (1852-1924) became a deputy,
senator, and recipient of the Nobel Peace Prize (1909). Petit Robert 2,
p. 615.

6. Paul Cambon, Correspondance, p. 168.

7. Par un Diplomate [Henri Cambon], Paul Cambon, Ambassadeur de
France, p. 54.

8. AE, T 70:11-14, Cambon to Duclerc, 1 November 1882; Paul
Cambon, Correspondance, pp. 169, 170; Paul Cambon, "Lettres," pp.
129, 137, 138.

9. AL, 37:1405 / C4, 197, Lavigerie to Charmetant, 21 October
1882.

10. Ibid.; APT, LCL, 93, Lavigerie to Pope, 14 December 1882;
AE, T 69:423-25, d'Estournelles to Duclerc, 10 October 1882; T 69:467,
d'Estournelles to Duclerc, 18 October 1882; Baunard, 2:228-29, Paul
Cambon, "Lettres," pp. 137, 138; Ganiage, L'expansion, p. 277.

11. Quotation from AE, T 70:11-14, Cambon to Duclerc, 1 November
1882; Martel, 1:284. Turkey proposed to send the new bey a firman of
investiture, but Duclerc refused even to discuss it. Cayci, pp. 103,
104.

12. Paul Cambon, "Lettres," pp. 141, 142; Eubank, pp. 18-21,
26; Ganiage, L'expansion, p. 80.

13. Paul Cambon, Correspondance, p. 218; Paul Cambon, "Lettres,"
pp. 377, 380, 381.

14. The Italian consular jurisdiction was suspended by a protocol of 25 January 1884, negotiated at Rome and ratified the following summer. Other governments represented at Tunis, not including
the United States, followed Britain and Italy. The Financial Commission soon disappeared, and the conversion of 1884 reduced the
interest on the bey's debt. Rigorous control of revenue and expendi-
ture put the Tunisian budget in balance, with a surplus in reserve.
A sizeable civil list kept the bey and the royal family - "a nursery
of successors" - dependent on the French. Eubank, pp. 22, 23;
Ganiage, L'Expansion, p. 294; Ministero degli Affari Esteri, Indici
del Archivio Storico, 6, Ministero degli Affari Esteri del Regno
d'Italia, 1861-1887, p. 184; Ling, Tunisia, pp. 47, 252 note 8;
d'Estournelles, "Débuts," pp. 792-94.

15. Diplomate, Paul Cambon, pp. 59. 60; Soumille, "Les Européens,"
p. 295n; AL, "Charmetant au Cardinal" 2:5091 / C4, 575, 8 August 1883;
37:3139(158) / AC, 250, Lavigerie to Charmetant, 24 December 1884.
The Alliance Israélite Universelle was founded in 1860. The name of
its first president, Adolphe Crémieux, is identified with the 1870
decree which gave French citizenship to Jews in Algeria. In Tunisia
and Morocco the Alliance Israélite saw Gallicization as the "way to
foster enlightened Judaism." In Tunisia, where the Livournais (Grana)
supported Italy, the organization sought to bring the larger native
group of middle-class Jews over to the side of France. A regional
committee had been established at Tunis in 1865, and the bey initially opposed its program. Eventually the Alliance Israélite established
schools at Tunis for boys (1878) and girls (1882), mixed schools at
Sousse and Mahdia (1883), another at Sfax (1909), and an agricultural
school at Djedeideh (1903). Roland, "The Alliance Israélite Universelle
and French Policy in North Africa, 1860-1918," abstract, pp. 52,
135-44.

16.   AN, F19, 2487, "Mgr. Lavigerie," 180, <u>La Paix</u>, 22 April 1884; "Mgr. Lavigerie," 194, <u>Le Temps</u>, 21 April 1884.

17.   AN, F19, 2487, "Cambon," letters of Cambon to "My Dear Friend" (Flourens?) dated 13 February and 7 August 1884; Baunard, 2:260-69; C. Alfred Perkins, p. 69; AL, 28:3139(172) / AC, 263, Lavigerie to "Minister" (Cambon?), 19 April 1884.

18.   AN, F19, 2487, Cambon to "My Dear Friend" (Flourens?), 7 August 1884.

19.   Baunard, 2:260-69; AL, 37:3139(158) / AC, 250 / B3, 37, Lavigerie to Charmetant, 24 December 1884.

20.   Baunard, 2:260-69; Soumille, "Les Européens," p. 67; AL, "Charmetant au Cardinal" 3:5127 / C4, 615 of 15 February 1885, 5130 / C4, 618 of 17 March, and 5131 / C4, 618 bis of 24 March 1885; 38:1580(8) / A11, 222 and 1580(9) / A11, 224, Lavigerie to Charmetant, 28 February and 14 March 1885; 28:3139(174) / AC, 264, Lavigerie to Cambon or Ferry, 16 March 1885.

21.   Vincennes, 30H1: "Mission Sandherr," 28 May and 2 June 1881; quotation from AL, 36:3142(104) / T, 542, Lavigerie to "My Dear Friend" (Gambetta), 24 December 1881. The emphasis is Lavigerie's.

22.   Vincennes, 30H1, "Mission Sandherr," 5 October 1881; AL, 37: 3139(171)/AC, 261, Lavigerie to Charmetant, 27 March 1884; Archives Nationales, Premier Ministère, Tunis (ANT), Série Historique, Carton 10, Dossier 95, 5/6726, Chancellery of Consulate of France at Tunis, Excerpt of minutes, 17 September 1881, and subsequent documents relating to diverse claims against Mustapha ben Ismael and his wife. Dossier 96 contains many inventories. Dossier 115, 3/6846 is a letter to the French consulate, 13 May 1883, regarding claims for restitution of properties taken by Mustapha.

23.   Quotation from AL, 28:3139(172) / AC, 262, Lavigerie to Minister (Cambon), 19 April 1884; 37:3160(45) / C4, 240, Lavigerie to Charmetant, 19 April 1884; APT, LCL, 176, Lavigerie to "perhaps a journalist," 19 April 1884; ANT, Série Historique, Carton 10, Dossier 96, 34/3809, Ali Bey to Cambon, ca. 18 April 1884.

24.   AL, 37:3160(45) / C4, 240, Lavigerie to Charmetant, 19 April

1884.

25. Ibid.; AL, "Charmetant au Cardinal" 3:5111 / C4, 598, 4
May 1884; APT, LCL, 180, Lavigerie to Spezzafumo, 6 April 1884; LCL,
175, 181, 182, Lavigerie to Mustapha, d'Estournelles, and Tournier,
all dated 9 April 1884; ANT, Série Historique, Carton 10, Dossier
96, 44/6818, bey's proxy of 29 July 1886; Dossier 115, 3/6846,
letter to French consulate, 13 May 1883, regarding claim for restitution of property taken by Mustapha; Dossier 115, 6898, minister
to lawyer Durier, 12 May 1887, referring to agreement between
Mustapha and bey; Dossier 115, 119/6968, lawyer Cardozo to secretary
general of Tunisian government, 23 March 1890, refers to court judgment of 18 July 1885.

26. D'Estournelles, "Les Débuts," p. 813; Eubank, pp. 24-33;
Dwight L. Ling, "Paul Cambon, Coordinator of Tunisia," Historian 19
(1957): 436-55; G. Valbert, "Le Régime du protectorat en Tunisie,"
Revue des Deux Mondes 78 (1886): 193-204. Boulanger's popularity
soared quickly in the 1880s. In 1889 he almost seized power in a
coup d'etat, but lost his nerve. He shot himself on the grave of
his mistress in 1891. Langer, Encyclopedia, p. 639.

27. APT, LCL, 448 and 449, Lavigerie to Boulanger, 1 July and
17 October 1885; AL, "Charmetant au Cardinal" 3, 5163 / C4, 645,
7 February 1886.

28. AL, 37:572 / C4, 262, Lavigerie to Charmetant, 22 November
1884.

29. AL, 37:571 / C4, 261, Lavigerie to Charmetant, 22 November
1884.

30. APT, LCL, 100, Lavigerie to Jacobini, 16 May 1884.

31. AL, 28:3142(115) / T, 580, Lavigerie to Brisson April-May
1885.

32. AL, 38:1426 / C4, 314, Lavigerie to Charmetant, 9 July 1885.

33. APT, LCL, 139, Lavigerie to Brincat, 28 June 1886.

34. "The creation of a corps of civil controllers permitted
[Massicault], with the support of the Ministry of War and the chiefs
of the Corps of Occupation, to reabsorb the 'Arab Bureaus' which the

organisms of the Intelligence Service had spontaneously and neces-
sarily become. The reduction of the Corps of Occupation to a division, then to a brigade, had equally weakened the influence of the
military authority," Martel, 1:353. Kenneth P. Perkins ("Pressure
and Persuasion," pp. 76, 77) discusses the restrained and constructive role of the Intelligence Service officers in southern Tunisia:
"Force no longer dominated their relations with the tribes. They
were strong, but the Tunisians saw that strength used, not against
themselves, but against their traditional enemies [marauding Tri-
politanian nomads]. Finally, the officers attempted to mix, or
associate, European with local practices, avoiding the Algerian
error of trying to supplant the latter with the former."

35. APT, LCL, 2027, Lavigerie to Massicault, 15 December 1886.

36. Tournier, "Le Cardinal Lavigerie," pp. 853-61.

37. APT, LCL, 902, Lavigerie to Rampolla, late October 1887.

38. Tournier, "Le Cardinal Lavigerie," p. 854; quotation from
Claude Liauzu, "Les précurseurs du mouvement ouvrier: Les Libertaires
en Tunisie à la fin du XIXe siècle," Cahiers de Tunisie 81-82 (1973):
153-82, pp. 165, 170.

39. Abbé Félix Klein, Le Cardinal Lavigerie et ses oeuvres
d'Afrique, pp. 295, 296.

40. APT, LCL, 902, Lavigerie to Rampolla, late October 1887.

41. AE, Correspondance politique, Tunisie, Nouvelle Série (TNS),
122:50-52, Massicault to Foreign Minister Flourens, 18 April 1887.

42. Préville attributes this remark to Maccio (pp. 223, 224).
Goyau says it was his successor Raibaudi (Un Grand missionnaire,
p. 174).

43. AN, F19, 2487, "Mgr. Lavigerie," 160 and 189, clippings of
Le Monde, 7 December 1882 and 7 August 1883. Lavigerie and his
priests were amiable and generous in their personal relations with
British and Italian adversaries. The British consul wrote a poignant
letter to Fr. Delattre on the death of his daughter. Thomas Reade's
wife and children were Catholic, and he asked Delattre to come around
and comfort them. AL, B3, 591, Reade to Delattre, 7 July 1884.

44. Goyau, "Le Cardinal Lavigerie," 26:803.

45. Enrico Serra, "Francesco Crispi ed il problema tunisino," Storia e Politica 5, no. 1 (January-March 1966): 25-65; Marsden, British Diplomacy, pp. 89-101.

46. Lavigerie had previously urged his own government to detach Italy from the Triplice by encouraging her conquest of Tripoli. He likewise had recommended the development of Spanish interests in Morocco as a counter to German influence there. Tournier, Action politique, p. 269.

47. AN, F19, 2487 contains a score of clippings from the press coverage given to this awkward incident in "Mgr. Lavigerie," items 281-302. Items 292 and 301 are taken from Matin, 29 November 1888, and Univers, 2 December 1888. Martel, 1:414-17.

48. AL, B3, 122, rough draft of Lavigerie's 1889 reply.

49. Kittler, pp. 196-202; Renault, 1:345-47, 2:73. Lavigerie found himself in a controversy with the Turkish minister to Brussels. Caratheodory-Effendi protested the cardinal's reference to slavery as the logical result of Islam's concept of a world divided into believers and infidels. European newspapers accused Lavigerie of turning a work of humanity into a religious crusade. Renault, 2:363-77. An American mission journal also criticized the cardinal for behaving as if Protestants previously had contributed little to the fight against African slavery before he majestically stepped forward to reorganize it under Catholic auspices. See Rev. J. C. Bracq, "Cardinal Lavigerie and his Anti-slavery Work," The Missionary Review of the World 8/3 (October 1890): 721-25.

50. Renault, 2:12-14. In the Tunisia of Ahmad Bey the practice of slavery had been milder than in some other places. Customarily the bey's black slaves were freed upon his death. Ahmad abolished the Tunis slave market in 1841, and he officially abolished the institution of slavery in 1846 - two years before abolition in Algeria. Brown, pp. 47, 321-25. Brown notes that in 1842 a slave family who feared being sold separately claimed legal sanctuary in the French shrine at Carthage. The consul, de Lagau, persuaded them to go to

the French consulate, where the problem was worked out. Brown observes that "the native Tunisian population had integrated the newly
completed Saint Louis Chapel into their own conception of religious
buildings" (p. 324).

51. Préville, ch. 15; Martel, 1:481; AE, TNS 123:35, foreign
minister to Premier-War Minister Freycinet, 9 April 1891; TNS 123:72-
77, interior minister to foreign minister, June 1891; TNS 123: 216,
217, Freycinet to foreign minister, 27 October 1891; TNS 124:47,
no signature nor date; APT, LCL: 278, 279, 280, three letters supporting Jules Cambon's appointment to Algeria, Lavigerie to President
Sadi Carnot, Paul Cambon, and former Governor General Tirman, 17
February 1891.

52. Tournier, Action politique, part 2, ch. 1; Ward, "Franco-
Vatican Relations," pp. 123, 124.

53. AE, TNS 123:10-15, Massicault to Foreign Minister Ribot,
26 January 1891. Whenever Lavigerie used this phrase in reference
to his episcopal colleagues, he denied coining it.

54. Préville, p. 280.

55. James E. Ward, "The Algiers Toast: Lavigerie's Work or
Leo XIII's?" Catholic Historical Review 51, no. 2 (July 1965): 173-91;
Pierre Soumille, conversation at Dijon, August 1971.

56. Goyau, "Le Cardinal Lavigerie," 26: 172, 173n. The aftermath
of the Toast had serious financial consequences for the White Fathers.
The Society's historians and confreres remember many anecdotes about
the episode, not all of which have been printed. Frs. François
Renault and Leonard Marchant related some of them in conversations
at Rome, Spring 1969.

57. Baunard, 2:180.

CHAPTER VII

1. AL, B3, 11, Lavigerie to Simeoni, 25 December 1881, also
found in APF, Barbaria 21:810-11.

2. Soumille, "Les Européens," p. 22.

3. AL, B3, 11 / APF, Barbaria 21:810-11, cited above.

4. Henri Cambon, Histoire, p. 268.

5. Pons, p. 250.

6. Macken, pp. 45-55; P.H.X., pp. 452-55; Henri Cambon, Histoire, pp. 270, 271; Claude Liauzu and Pierre Soumille, "La Gauche française en Tunisie au printemps 1906: Le Congrès républicain, radical et socialiste de Tunis," Le Mouvement Social 86 (January-March 1974): 55-78, p. 61; AE, TNS 307: folio 97, Machuel's report of 14 March 1887; quotation from AL, 38:3160(74) / C4, 299, Lavigerie to Charmetant, 8 April 1885; ANT, Série E, Carton 271, "Ecoles diverses de Tunis," folio 1, "Ecole congregations religieuses," last folder no. 3468: several documents concerning the arrangements for paying Tunisian government salaries to religious teachers.

7. P.H.X., p. 454. Le Reveil Tunisien condemned religious instuction in the Collège Saint-Charles, as well as in the Collège Sadiki and in the government-assisted schools of the Alliance Israélite Universelle. This anticlerical paper went so far as to call Machuel Lavigerie's puppet. Roland, "The Alliance Israélite Universelle," pp. 284, 285.

8. APF, Barbaria 21:921-22, Lavigerie to Simeoni, 21 October 1882; Mercui, p. 321.

9. AL, B3, 115, Lavigerie to foreign minister, 12 October 1885.

10. Upon the assassination of President Sadi Carnot in 1894, the college was renamed Lycée Carnot. It remains one of the most prestigious lycées in Tunisia.

AL, B3, 115, Lavigerie to foreign minister, 12 October 1885; 38:1600(3) / C4:324 bis, Lavigerie to Charmetant, 6 November 1885; 28:3165(6) / B5:127, Lavigerie to minister of public instruction, 24 January 1886; AN, F19, 2487, "Mgr. Lavigerie," 337, clipping of L'Univers, 8 October 1889; ANT, Série E, carton 270, "Lycée Carnot-Divers"; Baunard, 2: 418, 419.

11. Mgr. Charles Lavigerie, "Lettre Circulaire de Mgr. L'Archevêque d'Alger au clergé de son diocèse relativement à sa nomination d'administrateur apostolique de la Tunisie," dated Rome, 29 July 1881, p. 9.

12. AE, TNS 122:129-32, Lavigerie, circular to Archdiocese of Carthage, Easter Octave 1890; AL, "Diaire," 27 November 1881; quotation from APT, LCL, 543, Lavigerie to Massicault, 1890, not sent.

13. AE, T 60:300, "Draft requested by Mgr. Lavigerie, 19 August 1881"; finished copy is found in AL, B3, 45, copy of circular of Barthélemy to Flourens, 8 September 1881; AL, B3, 8, Lavigerie to Bishops of France, 6 September 1881; B3, 87, "Note on the installation of a French clergy and the preparation of a French diocese at Tunis," 1881.

14. Cussac, pp. 108-11; Henri Cambon, Histoire, pp. 270, 271; P.H.X., pp. 452-55; APT, LCL, 496, Lavigerie to superior general of the Brothers of the Christian Schools, 24 August 1881.

15. Archivio Segreto Vaticano, Vatican City (ASV), Segretaria di Stato, Rubric 280 (1884), 60228, Lavigerie to Pope, 19 April 1884, quoting from St. Leo IX's Letter to Bishops Peter and John; AN, F19, 6212, "Clergé tunisienne: 87-88," Cambon to Freycinet, 16 March 1886; Goyau, "Le Cardinal Lavigerie," 26:798.

16. ASV, Rubric 280 (1884), 60228, cited above.

17. Paul Cambon, Correspondance, pp. 209-11; Tournier, "Le Cardinal Lavigerie," pp. 850-53; Ward, "Franco-Vatican Relations," pp. 38-40.

18. AE, SS 1079:47, Béhaine to ministry, 29 June 1884; AL, B3, 109, "Note confidentielle," 17 January 1884; B3, 47, Cambon to Lavigerie, 25 July 1884; B3, 13, Lavigerie to Simeoni, 19 April 1884; ASV, Rubric 280 (1884), 60228, cited above; Goyau, 26:800; Mercui, p. 333.

19. AE, SS 1079: 198-99 and 247-48, dispatches of Béhaine to Ferry, dated 8 September and 9 October 1884; AL, B3, 112, Lavigerie to Flourens, 12 July 1884; B3, 532, Delattre to Catteville, 3 August 1884; AN, F19, 2487, "31 Lettres," 31, Lavigerie to Flourens, 9 July 1884.

20. AN, F19, 2487, "Algérie," 12, Cambon to Foreign Ministry, 1 November 1884; F19, 2487, "Mgr. Lavigerie," 200, minister of cults to Cambon, 5 November 1884; ASV, Rubric 280 (1884), 58872, Lavigerie

to Jacobini, 12 August 1884, also found in AL, B3, 14; 280 (1884),
59840, Lavigerie to Jacobini, 1 October 1884, also found in AL, B3,
18; 280 (1884), 59861, cable from Lavigerie to Jacobini, 29 October
1884; 280 (1884), 59907, Jacobini to Deguerry, 4 November 1884; 280
(1884), 59861, Jacobini to Lavigerie, 5 November 1884; Baunard,
2:253; Grussenmeyer, 2:393. The White Fathers used to say that the
Archbishop of Carthage and Algiers always had one foot in France
and the other in his grave.

21.   ASV, Rubric 280 (1884), 60228, Lavigerie to Jacobini, 19
November 1884. The emphasis is Lavigerie's.

22.   Ibid., Jacobini to Lavigerie, 1 December 1884.

23.   APT, LCL, 563, Lavigerie to Simeoni, 10 December 1884.

24.   APT, LCL, 563, 557, 551, 555, and 556, Lavigerie to Simeoni,
10 and 20 December 1884, 2, 17 and 17 February 1885. In LCL, 555
Lavigerie asked Simeoni to address correspondence to him care of
"Carthage, Tunisia," lest his mail be routed by way of Cartagena,
Spain. Grussenmeyer, 2: 149, 150.

25.   APT, LCL, 941, "Note on the Curé of Sfax," 2 July 1884; LCL,
942, Lavigerie to Reade, 5 August 1884; LCL, 944, Lavigerie to Pope,
2 December 1884: LCL, 950, Lavigerie to Pope, 3 December 1884.

26.   APT, LCL, 950, cited above.

27.   APT, LCL, 952, Lavigerie to Pope, 8 February 1885; LCL, 953,
Lavigerie to Jacobini, 20 March 1885; LCL, 959, Lavigerie to Buhagiar,
21 December 1886; LCL, 966, Lavigerie to Jacobini, n.d.; LCL, 120,
Lavigerie to Rampolla, 1 August 1890; Renault, 1: 227, 228.

28.   Pons, pp. 261, 262.

29.   Jourdan was Bishop of Rosea, coincidentally the title in
partibus of Mgr. Sutter. AE, TNS 122:56-57, Lavigerie to Flourens,
25 July 1887; TNS 122:58-61, Lavigerie to Jusserand, 16 August 1887;
TNS 122:74-75, cults minister to Flourens, 12 September 1887; APT,
LCL, 896, Lavigerie to Massicault, 25 July 1887; LCL, 898, Lavigerie
to Flourens, 25 July 1887; AL, 37:543 / C4:192, Lavigerie to
Charmetant, 25 April 1882.

30.   APT, LCL, 148, draft on the "Coadjuterie de Carthage," n.d.;

LCL, 882, 883, Lavigerie to Jourdan, 1 and 20 July 1887.

31. APT, LCL, 905, "Draft of a letter (not sent) of Mgr. Lavigerie to Cardinal Rampolla, 30 April 1889."

32. Cussac, p. 142.

33. AE, TNS 122:86, excerpt, Journal Officiel Tunisien, 3 November 1887.

34. AE, TNS 122:96-97, decree of the Council of State, 9 February 1888; APT, LCL, 905, "Draft of a letter (not sent) of Mgr. Lavigerie to Cardinal Rampolla, 30 April 1889"; LCL, 907, Lavigerie to Jourdan, 2 March 1889; LCL, 593, Lavigerie to Burtin, 15 February 1889; LCL, 141, Lavigerie to Jourdan, not sent, March 1889.

35. AE, TNS 122:102-3, Massicault to foreign minister, 17 May 1889; APT, LCL, 904, Lavigerie to Rampolla, 1 March 1889; Henri Brunschwig, French Colonialism, 1871-1914, p. 168.

36. AE, TNS 122:102-4, Massicault to foreign minister, 17 May 1889.

37. Bouniol, p. 58; Pons, p. 262; APT, LCL, 150, Lavigerie to Pope, 7 November 1891; LCL, 143, Lavigerie to Tournier, Gazaniol, and Paloméni, 22 March 1892.

38. Tournier, "Le Cardinal Lavigerie," pp. 863, 864; quotation from AE, TNS 122:133, Massicault to foreign minister, 9 May 1890.

39. Tournier, "Le Cardinal Lavigerie," pp. 863, 864.

40. Henri Cambon, Histoire, p. 269. The Basilica of Saint-Louis is now a Tunisian state museum. Although the altar stones are gone, the massive bells remain in place. The view from the roof is panoramic, but beware the soft floor under the bells. Next door, the old Chapelle Saint-Louis has been torn down. Delattre's archeological collection is spread out in the garden in front of the former seminary, which is now restored as a museum. Adjacent archeological diggings are roped off from public access.

41. AE, TNS 122:141-42, "Note pour le ministre," 8 May 1890; TNS 122:145-46, and 177-80, Massicault to foreign minister, 7 and 17 May 1890.

42. AE, TNS 122:153-58, Lavigerie to foreign minister and

minister to Massicault, 10 May 1890; Henri Cambon, Histoire, p. 271.

43. AE, TNS 122:177-80, Massicault to foreign minister, 17 May
1890; TNS 122:186-87, Lavigerie to Pope, 19 May 1890.

44. Billing, pp. 384-86. See Pierre Soumille, "Le Cimetière
européen de Bab-El-Khadra a Tunis: Etude historique et sociale,"
Cahiers de Tunisie 19, nos. 75-76 (1971): 129-82.

45. APT, LCL, 928, Lavigerie to Cambon, 28 June 1883.

46. APT, LCL, 929.

47. APT, LCL, 927, Lavigerie to Cambon, 10 July 1885.

48. Soumille, "Le Cimetière," pp. 143. 144.

49. Ibid. pp. 141-45; Soumille, "Les Européens," p. 503; AE,
TNS 122:193-95, Massicault to foreign minister, 20 June 1890; TNS
122:215-16, residence to foreign minister, 24 October 1890; TNS
122:217-19, Gazaniol to delegate at residence, 19 October 1890; TNS
123:25-26, Massicault to Foreign Minister Ribot, 13 May 1891.

50. AE, TNS 123:108-14, Lavigerie to Massicault, 19 June 1891,
also found in AL, B3, 123.

51. APT, LCL, 43, Lavigerie to Simeoni, 19 October 1883; LCL,
44, 45, scraps of letters, n.d. (3 December 1883?); LCL, 46,
Lavigerie to Capuchin general and Lavigerie to Simeoni, 5 December
1883; LCL, 51, Lavigerie to "Eminent Lord," 3 August 1888; Anselme
des Arcs, p. 134.

52. AE, TNS 123:167-70, memoir from Fr. Antonio da Recchio,
Capuchin secretary general of missions, to Simeoni, 30 June 1891;
APT, LCL, 48, Lavigerie to Simeoni 27 March 1887; LCL, 49, Lavigerie
to Capuchin superior general, 27 April 1887; LCL, 10, Lavigerie to
Fr. Barnabas, reply to letter of 24 September 1888; AE, TNS 122:50-52,
Massicault to foreign minister, 18 April 1887; TNS 123:80-81,
Regnault to Quai d'Orsay, 16 June 1891; Henri Cambon, Histoire,
p. 272. Because of the Capuchin proposal to withdraw in the late
1880s Lavigerie wrote to the superior general of the Lazarist order
requesting that a Lazarist community of Italian priests be established
in Tunisia under a French superior. The Lazarists' refusal noted
that they faced the same shortage of personnel which affected the

Capuchins. Pons, pp. 258, 259.

53. AE, TNS 123:106-7, Massicault to Foreign Minister Ribot, 23 June 1891.

54. APT, LCL, 624, Lavigerie to Gazaniol, 18 January 1891; LCL, 4, Lavigerie to Capuchin superior general, n.d.

55. AE, TNS 123:167-70, cited above. This memoir leaked to the press and became the Capuchin order's white paper on the expulsion.

56. AE, SS 1105:215, Ribot to Béhaine, 17 June 1891; SS 1105:220, Béhaine to Ribot, 19 June 1891.

57. AE, TNS 123:108-14, Lavigerie to Massicault, 19 June 1891. This letter was enclosed with Massicault's report to Foreign Minister Ribot of 23 June, TNS 123:106-7. See also TNS 123:78, Regnault to Quai d'Orsay, 16 June 1891.

58. Ibid.

59. APT, LCL, 54, Lavigerie to Tournier, 18 June 1891; AE, SS 1105:234-36, Béhaine to Ribot, 19 June 1891; TNS 123: 83-89, 93-102, and 130-35, Regnault (delegate at residence) to Ribot, 17, 19, and 29 June 1891. L'Unione of Tunis treated this story on the front page in nos. 50-52 of 21, 25, and 28 June 1891.

60. AE, TNS 123:108-14, Lavigerie to Massicault, 19 June 1891.

61. AE, TNS 123:105, Ribot to Regnault, 20 June 1891; TNS 123:140-41, Regnault to Quai d'Orsay, 5 July 1891; TNS 123:189-92, clipping from L'Unione, 23 July 1891; SS 1105:322, Béhaine to Ribot, 8 July 1891; TNS 123:161 and 164, Regnault to Quai d'Orsay, 11 and 16 July 1891; TNS 123:215, clipping from L'Unione, 22 October 1891; APT, LCL, 60 and 62, Lavigerie to Tournier, 6 and 10 July 1891.

62. AE, TNS 123:130-35, Regnault to Ribot, 29 June 1891.

63. AL, B3, 121, Lavigerie to foreign minister, 18 April 1890; B3, 123, Lavigerie to Massicault, 19/20 June 1891, already cited; AN, F19, 2487, "Mgr. Lavigerie," 346, Le Monde, 18 October 1889; Grussenmeyer, 2: 285-304, 309-12, 391, 392; Paul Lesourd, "Aperçus historiques sur les missions des Pères Blancs," Revue d'Histoire des Missions (Paris) 12 (1935): 348-85, pp. 364, 365; APT, LCL, 540, notes of Lavigerie to Massicault, 18 November 1890(?). The Domain

of Thibar, which produces wine and "Thibarine" liqueur, was managed
by White Fathers headed by Fr. Dubus until its complete Tunisifica-
tion in 1975. La Presse (Tunis), 22 April and 13 August 1975.

CHAPTER VIII

1. Henri Cambon, Histoire, p. 299.

2. AL, B3, 11, Lavigerie to Simeoni, 25 December 1881; Fr. Gerald
Lachance, conversation at Rome, 3 March 1969.

3. APT, LCL, 93, Lavigerie to Pope, Christmas Report, 14 December 1882.

4. AE, TNS 122:69-72, Massicault to Flourens, 5 September 1887;
Goyau, "Le Cardinal Lavigerie," 26:775; Préville, pp. 136-39.

5. AE, TNS 122:69-72, cited above; APT, LCL, 78 "Mémoire," 1888.

6. Baunard, 1:496; AL, "Charmetant au Cardinal" 1:4927 / C4,
398 of 1 October 1875, quotation from 4940 / C4, 411 of 2 May 1877.

7. AL, B3, 257 and 266, Lavigerie to Delattre, letters of 8 July
1875 and 30 November 1878.

8. AL, B3, 210 (1), Lavigerie to Bresson, 15 June 1875; B3, 259,
Lavigerie to Delattre, 7 September 1875; B3, 349, Roustan to Bresson,
23 August 1875; B3, 583, Delattre to Charmetant, 5 April 1881;
Mercui, p. 205; Lavigerie, "Saint-Louis et son tombeau," p. 15;
L'Union, 4 September 1875; Goyau, "Le Cardinal Lavigerie," 26:775.

9. AL, 35:428 / C4, 42, Lavigerie to Charmetant, 27 August 1875;
38:3160(109) / C4, 353, Lavigerie to Charmetant, 25 April 1886;
quotation from "Charmetant au Cardinal" 3:5171 / C4, 649(4), 10 May
1886.

10. AL, "Charmetant au Cardinal" 1:4966 / C4, 440 of 8 December
1878 and 4979 / C4, 453 of 5 March 1879; 35:1381 / C4, 87, Lavigerie
to Charmetant, 18 March 1879; Baunard, 2: 235, 236.

11. AL, 37:1402 / C4, 180, Lavigerie to Charmetant, 22 February
1882.

12. AE, T 60:127-29, Roustan to Barthélemy, 8 July 1881; AL,
"Charmetant au Cardinal" 2:5069 / C4, 552, 19 November 1882.

13. AE, T 60:300, "Draft requested by Mgr. Lavigerie 19 August

1881"; finished copy is found in AL, B3, 45, copy of circular of
Barthélemy to Flourens, 8 September 1881; AL, B3, 8, Lavigerie to
Bishops of France, 6 September 1881; Bulletin du diocèse de Reims,
8 October 1881, quoted in C. Alfred Perkins, p. 69; Goyau, "Le
Cardinal Lavigerie," 26:788; Grussenmeyer, 2:24.

14. AE, T 59:147, ministry to Roustan, 2 June 1881; T 65:225-26,
Ministry of Post and Telegraph to Gambetta, 24 December 1881; T
70:37-38, Cambon to Duclerc, 3 November 1882; AL, B3, 87, cited
above; B3, 240 and 246, Lavigerie to Deguerry, 29 August and 12
September 1881; B3, 87, "Note on the installation of a French clergy
and the preparation of a French diocese at Tunis," 1881.

15. AL, B3, 92, "L'Oeuvre de Françisation," previously cited.

16. AE, T 60:127-29, Roustan to Barthélemy, 8 July 1881.

17. AE, T 65:293-94, Lavigerie to "Dear Friend," 31 December
1881; quotation from T 66:30-34, Roustan to Gambetta, 7 January
1882.

18. AL, "Charmetant au Cardinal" 2:5046 / C4, 529, 19 February
1882.

19. AL, B3, 11, Lavigerie to Simeoni, 25 December 1881.

20. AE, T 66:30-34, Roustan to Gambetta, 7 January 1882; T
66:57-60, Lavigerie to Gambetta, 10 January 1882, also found in AL,
B3, 98.

21. AE, T 66:57-60 / AL, B3, 98, cited above.

22. Henri Cambon, Histoire, p. 268.

23. AE, T 65:293-94, Lavigerie to "My Dear Friend," 31 December
1881; T 66:330-35, Lavigerie to Roustan, 15 February 1882; ASV,
Rubric 261 (1884): protocol 60520, list of nearly one hundred subventions to diverse religious, educational, and hospital overseas
establishments under the patronage of France.

24. AN, F19, 2487, "31 Lettres," 24, Lavigerie to Flourens,
29 April 1882; "Mgr. Lavigerie," 106, Humbert to Flourens, 1 May
1882; ASV, Rubric 280 (1884): 60228, Lavigerie to Pope, 19 April
1884; AE, T 69:33, ministry to Cambon, 9 August 1882; AL, B3, 6,
Lavigerie to Simeoni, 24 July 1881; Baunard, 2: 236, 237; Guérin,

pp. 76, 77.

25. Acomb, pp. 236, 237; AE, T 68:172, Lavigerie to Freycinet, 27 May 1882; T 68:177, Humbert to justice minister, 30 May 1882; AL, B3, 103, "Note sur l'organisation du personnel ecclésiastique en Tunisie," 17 May 1882; AN, F19, 2487, "Mgr. Lavigerie," 126, Flourens to Noirot, 19 June 1882; F19, 2487, "31 Lettres," 26, Lavigerie to Flourens, 4 July 1882.

26. Baunard, 2:233-35.

27. AL, B3, 104, Lavigerie to Duclerc, 2 December 1882; AN, F19, 2487, "Mgr. Lavigerie," items 153 and 163, clippings of Le Constitutionnel, 20 November 1882, and La Solidarité, 8 December 1882; Missions d'Alger (Saint-Cloud: Belin) 45:1-6 (January 1883), open letter of Lavigerie to Mgr. Dauphin, 2 December 1882.

28. AL, B3, 104, Lavigerie to Duclerc, 2 December 1882; B3, 105, Lavigerie to Fallières, 13 December 1882.

29. AE, T 70:456, Duclerc to Duvau, 23 December 1882; AL, B3, 106, Lavigerie to Challemel-Lacour, 27 June 1883; "Charmetant au Cardinal" 2:5041 / C4, 524, 10 January 1882; AN, F19, 2487, "Algérie," 6, "Lettre a MM. les Membres de la Commission du Budget du Sénat au Sujet de la Suppression des Bourses dans les Séminaires de l'Algérie," 29 November 1883.

30. Acomb, p. 237.

31. Tournier, Action politique, pp. 149, 150; APT, LCL, 471, Lavigerie to general, 25 August 1882; AN, F19, 2487, folder "Ecclésiastiques français à Tunis, Secours de 500 francs chacun par arrêté du 5 Janvier 1885," Lavigerie to minister of cults, 2 October 1884; F19, 2487, "Algérie," 9, Lavigerie to minister of cults, 15 August 1884, also found in AL, B3, 113; F19, 6212, personnel list attached to letter of Lavigerie to Ministry of Cults, 9 July 1885; Lavigerie to minister of cults, 1 May 1886; Baunard, 2: 240, 253.

32. AN, F19, 6212, "Clergé tunisienne '87-88," Goblet to Lavigerie, 15 April 1886; Cambon to Freycinet, 16 March 1886; Flourens to Floquet, 21 November 1888.

33. AL, AC818, list of "Aumôneries Militaires en dehors de

paroisses."

34. AE, SS 1073:212, Monbel to Duclerc, 5 September 1882; SS
1076:174-86, Béhaine to Ferry, 23 June 1883; SS 1078: 23-24, Ferry
to Béhaine, 9 January 1884; quotation from Ward, "Franco-Vatican
Relations," p. 41; Montclos, Toast, p. 122; AL, 38:588 bis / C4,
320, Lavigerie to Charmetant, 6 August 1885; 38:1419 / C4, 276 bis,
Lavigerie to Charmetant, 17 January 1885. Among Curia cardinals
there was jealousy at the suggestion that Lavigerie might eventually
succeed Simeoni as prefect of Propaganda. AL, 38:575B / C4, 278,
Lavigerie to Charmetant, 28 January 1885. A word at the Quai d'Orsay
later confirmed Lavigerie's suspicion that Béhaine had influenced
the Brisson cabinet's decision in 1885 to refuse him the use of a
navy vessel to go to the Holy Land. AL, "Charmetant au Cardinal"
3:5146 / C4, 629, 9 August 1885.

35. AE, SS 1079:88-89, Ferry to Béhaine, 19 July 1884; quotation
from ASV, Rubric 261 (1884): 60857, Embassy of France to the Holy
See, "Project of an arrangement," 6 July 1884; Baunard, 2: 250, 251,
291. Puyol was fired in 1891. AN, F19, 6236, "Etablissements
Etrangères," letter of 11 February 1891.

36. Mercui, p. 347.

37. Quotation from AL, B3, 114, Lavigerie to Cambon (in the
third person), 20 December 1884; AN, F19, 2487, "31 Lettres," 30,
Lavigerie to Flourens, 5 June 1884; F19, 2487, "Mgr. Lavigerie,"
202; Tournier, Action politique, p. 207n; Préville, pp. 138, 139.

38. Picot, p. 16.

39. AN, F19, 2487, "Mgr. Lavigerie," 515, pamphlet titled
"Conférence donnée dans l'Eglise de la Madeleine" (Paris: Oeuvre des
Ecoles d'Orient, 1885); Grussenmeyer, 2:261-69; Goyau, "Le Cardinal
Lavigerie," 26:802.

40. AN, F19, 2487, "Algérie," 15, Jules Cambon to minister of
interior and cults, 29 May 1885.

41. Ibid.; AN, F19, 2487, "Algérie," 17, minister of interior
and cults to Ferry, 4 June 1885; Baunard, 2:276.

42. Acomb, p. 243; AN, F19, 2487, "Algérie," 21, memo in Cults

Ministry files titled "Elections 1885"; F19, 6212, "Clergé tunisienne
'87-88"; Baunard, 2: 276, 305-7.

43. Baunard, 2:305-7.

44. Acomb, pp. 237, 238; Goyau, "Le Cardinal Lavigerie," 26:802.
The horse's name was "Tunis."

45. AN, F19, 6212, "Clergé tunisienne '87-88," Goblet to
Lavigerie, 10 February 1887, and clipping from Justice of 29 January
1887, article by Léon Millot; Baunard, 2:424-26; Missions d'Alger
62:35-40 (March 1887); A. Debidour, L'Eglise catholique et l'Etat
sous la Troisième République, 1870-1906, 1: 1870-1889, pp. 133, 134;
AN, TNS 122:19, Lavigerie to Freycinet, 9 October 1886; TNS 122:46-47,
Massicault to Foreign Minister Flourens, 7 March 1887; APT, LCL,
535, Lavigerie to Flourens, 14 February 1887. The French Reformed
pastor and leaders of the Jewish community in Tunisia were well
aware of French and Tunisian government aid to Lavigerie's archdiocese. Roland, "The Alliance Israélite Universelle," pp. 228, 229.

46. AE, TNS 124:24-30, Massicault to Foreign Minister Ribot,
11 April 1892; TNS 123:51-53, Massicault to Ribot, 22 May 1891; APT,
LCL, 78, "Mémoire Justificatif" 1888; LCL, 543, Lavigerie to
Massicault (not sent), 1890.

47. Baunard, 2: 236, 237; AL, B3, 108, "Lettres Tunisiennes,"
15 January 1884; AN, F19, 2487, "31 Lettres," 27, Lavigerie to
Flourens, 12 October 1883.

48. Henri Cambon, Histoire, p. 269; Grussenmeyer, 2:164-70.

49. Cussac, pp. 139-41; APT, LCL, 153, Lavigerie to Canon Thevin,
26 February 1886; LCL, 156, Lavigerie to Empress Eugénie, n.d.
(1886); LCL, 163, Lavigerie to Mlle Louise Roustan, 4 July 1886.

50. Cussac, pp. 139-41.

51. AE, TNS 122:114-18, Massicault to foreign minister, 14 April
1890. Pons states that Lavigerie appointed twenty Canons of Carthage
quickly (p. 254).

52. AL, B3, 101, Lavigerie to Roustan, 20 February 1882; Baunard,
2:179; Grussenmeyer, 2:312-15; AL, "Charmetant au Cardinal" 2:5048
/ C4, 531, 12 March 1882.

53. AL, 37:3160(37) / C4, 220, Lavigerie to Charmetant, 4 January 1884.

54. Ibid.

55. AL, "Charmetant au Cardinal" 2:5077 / C4, 561, 12 January 1883; APT, LCL, 2044, 2045, Minutes of the Tunisian Lottery Council, 3 August 1885.

56. AL, AC360, Sainte-Marie to Lavigerie, 31 August 1875; quotation from B3, 210(14), Lavigerie to Bresson, 3 June 1880. Other examples are B3, 56, 69, 210 (items 1, 5, 7 bis, and 8), 280, 318, 334, 336, 338, 387, and 453.

57. AL, B3, 25, Roustan to Lavigerie, 27 December 1876.

58. AL, B3, 220, Lavigerie to Bresson, 27 April 1881.

59. AL, "Charmetant au Cardinal" 2:5024 / C4, 507, 28 April 1881; 36:1574(5) / T, 479 and 935(47) / T, 480, Lavigerie to Charmetant, 20 and 24 April 1881.

60. Many details of the celebrated "Affaire de L'Enfida" are presented in Jean Ganiage's excellent article, previously cited. Lavigerie's tangential involvement is revealed in AL, B3, 227, "Lavigerie: Instructions to Bresson, 9 June 1881, 'Note on the Enfida'"; AL, "Charmetant au Cardinal" 2:5024 / C4, 507, 28 April 1881.

61. Mercui, p. 378; AL, "Charmetant au Cardinal" 2:5024 / C4, 507, 28 April 1881; 36:935(46) / T, 478, 935(47) / T, 480, 935(49) / T, 483, 935(51) / T, 521, and 517 / C4, 149, Lavigerie to Charmetant, 19, 24, and 27 April, 1 and 7 May 1881; AL, B3, 221, 224, and 225, letters of Lavigerie to Bresson of 3 May, 2 and 7 June 1881. See also B3, 227.

62. AL, B3, 227, "Instructions to Bresson . . . on the Enfida," cited above. New parishes in Tunisia are listed in Grussenmeyer, 2:125.

63. ANT, Armoire 6 (42-II), Carton 64, "Culte Catholique-Enseignement Laique," dossier 758:6, documents concerning confiscation by eminent domain; dossier 758:8, documents concerning enclaves at La Marsa and Sidi Bou Said. Dr. Abdeljelil Temimi helped cull and

translate Arabic documents.

64. APT, LCL, 2046, Lavigerie to chargé d'affaires, 27 November 1885.

65. AE, TNS 122:15, La Justice, 22 September 1886; Arthur Christopher Benson, ed., The Life of Edward White Benson, 2:418.

66. Ibid.; APT, LCL, 540, Notes of Lavigerie to resident, 18 November 1890(?).

67. Préville, pp. 245, 246; Debidour, 1: 133, 134.

68. Renault, 1:218n; Mercui, pp. 158-60. After "Father General" Deguerry's other disagreements with the founder this was the last straw. He left the Society.

69. APT, LCL, 17, Testament of Cardinal Lavigerie, 8 June 1890. Lavigerie's brother Félix found it amusing to hear from an Algerian shop clerk that "he enriches his family," Préville, pp. 245, 246. A nephew attempted to challenge Lavigerie's will, according to Fr. René Dionne of the Archives Lavigerie, conversation of summer 1972.

70. Bouniol, p. 59; Pottier, p. 328.

71. APT, LCL, 173, Lavigerie to Delattre, 6 August 1892.

72. Louis Bertrand, Le Sang des races, p. 6; anecdote of the White Fathers, July 1972.

CHAPTER IX

1. Soumille, "Les Européens," p. 135.

2. Conversation of 3 July 1972 with Fr. René Dionne of the Archives Lavigerie. Fr. Dionne was working with the Linvinhac Letters, which contained many apologies for what Linvinhac considered to be his inadequate efforts. His unjustified humility contrasted sharply with the imperiousness of his predecessor. Mercui, pp. 437-39; Pons, pp. 256, 257.

3. Jules Cambon, "Souvenirs," Revue d'Histoire des Missions, p. 3.

4. AE, TNS 124:80-82, Rouvier to Foreign Ministry, cable of 5 January 1893.

5. AE, TNS 124:87-90, Jules Cambon to Foreign Minister Ribot,

11 January 1893.

6. AE, TNS 124:120-23, Jules Cambon to Foreign Minister Develle, 6 May 1893.

7. AE, TNS 124:62-68, "Confidential, Urgent Note," 28 December 1892; TNS 124:80-82, cited above.

8. AE, TNS 124:87-90, Jules Cambon to Foreign Minister Ribot, 11 January 1893.

9. AE, TNS 124:80-82, cited above.

10. Ibid.; AE, TNS 124:62-68, cited above; TNS 124:75, "Note de M. J. Montet, January 1893"; TNS 124:132-34, documents and instruments between Cardinal-Secretary of State Rampolla and Béhaine concerning the See of Carthage, 7 November 1893.

11. AE, TNS 124:132-34, cited above. In 1926 Archbishop Lemaître obtained an increase of the French government's support to 1.8 million francs per year. Pons, p. 264.

12. Pierre Soumille's research on "Les Européens" discloses that at Tunis during the period 1893-1901 only 1.4 percent of those who died received civil burials (p. 532). Soumille gives considerable attention to the importance of Lavigerie's legend during the years right after his death. See pp. 164-81, 222-37. Other material appears on pp. iii, 58-66, 99, 102, 103, 213, 217, 240, 254, 256, 261, 503-37. See also Pons, p. 264.

13. Liauzu and Soumille, "La Gauche française," pp. 61, 62.

14. Ling, _Tunisia_, p. 117. A picture postcard shows the placement of the "Statue du Cardinal Lavigerie, No. 4 Tunis," Cie. des Arts Photoméchaniques, Paris.

15. Ling, _Tunisia_, p. 91; Soumille, "Les Européens," p. 14n; _La Presse_ (Tunis), 15 October 1974, p. 1, "Le President Bourguiba: En dépit des tentatives de dépersonalisation la Tunisie est démeurée une terre de l'Islam."

16. Conversations with White Fathers at Rome, 1969.

17. X.X.X., "L'Eglise en Tunisie," _Annuaire de L'Afrique du Nord 1964_ (Aix-en-Provence: Le Centre de Recherche sur l'Afrique Méditerranéene, 1964), pp. 63-71.

18. Ibid.

19. Montclos, Saint-Siège, p. 598.

20. Pierre Soumille, "L'Idée de race chez les européens de
Tunisie dans les années 1890-1910," Revue d'Histoire Maghrébine 5
(January 1976): 59-65, p. 65.

21. Evangelical Protestants began sustained mission work in the
1880s. George Pearse, an Englishman, set up a mission in Kabylia in
1880 while French Methodists, Swedish Lutherans and Baptists, and
others went to North Africa in the eighties and nineties. The
Methodist Episcopal Church got involved in the early 1900s. By 1897
these missionaries and helpers totalled twenty-one in Tunisia and
eighteen in Algeria. They did not enjoy a good rapport with the
White Fathers except occasionally on the local, personal level.
The French authorities were not hospitable, but they permitted
teaching and medical stations. Generally, the Evangelical Protestants
had more freedom of action in the protectorate than in Algeria,
where they suffered intervals of denunciation and restriction.
During the second and third decades of the twentieth century the
French authorities were more cooperative, and the Protestants led
several hundred Muslims to embrace Christianity. Neither Protestant
nor Catholic natives were numerous nor steadfast enough to endure
as a permanent Christian community after independence. See Willie
Normann Heggoy, "Fifty Years of Evangelical Missionary Movement in
North Africa," pp. 22-36, 51-54, 99-153, 303, 354, and elsewhere.

22. Rouvier wanted to bring the factious Jewish community together
under one consistory affiliated with the Paris Consistory. Neither
the Alliance Israélite nor the French residence could bring this
about before 1921. Roland, "The French Role in the Modernization of
Jewish Community Organizations in North Africa, 1880-1918," pp. 16-23.

23. AL, B3, 90, cited above.

24. AN, F19, 2487, "Algérie," 33, secretary general of the prefecture to minister of cults, 17 July 1888.

25. Alexander Sedgwick, The Third French Republic, 1870-1914,
p. 98.

26.   Paul Cambon, "Lettres," p. 374.

27.   Renault, 1: 355, 356.

28.   AL, "Charmetant au Cardinal," 3:5118 / C4, 604, 23 July 1884.

29.   AL, 38:3160(119) / C4, 362 bis, Lavigerie to Charmetant, 13 July 1886; Renault, 1:356-58. Fr. François Renault was very generous with advice in a conversation at Rome on 4 February 1969. He was then completing his Sorbonne thesis on <u>Lavigerie, l'esclavage africaine, et l'Europe</u>. He had begun his research assuming that Lavigerie favored French involvement in central Africa as an imperialist power. Fr. Renault stated that several years of research changed that opinion.

30.   Fr. Jacques Durant of the <u>Service Historique</u> is also preparing a thesis for the Sorbonne. He expressed this opinion in a conversation at Rome, 9 April 1969.

31.   Taken from Jules Cambon, "Souvenirs," <u>Revue des Deux Mondes</u>, p. 289. The complete address on "The Mission of France" is in Lavigerie, <u>Oeuvres choisies</u> 1: ch. 2.

32.   Jules Cambon, "Souvenirs," <u>Revue d'Histoire des Missions</u>, p. 3; Fr. Leonard Marchant, conversation at Rome, spring 1969.

Sources

The basic collection of documents for this research was the Archives
Lavigerie of the White Fathers' headquarters in Rome. The B3 series
on Tunisia includes 600 items ranging from Broglie's 1873 reply to
Lavigerie's first suggestion of recovering Saint-Louis, to the cardinal's pathetic letter to Massicault in 1891 after the government's
refusal to provide passage to Algiers on the "Hirondelle." Many of
these documents are the secretary's original draft, and a number of
letters are written in Lavigerie's own hand. Frequently sections
which Lavigerie crossed out of the first draft reveal thoughts not
found in the final copy. The B3 collection also includes several
hundred letters written by Delattre, Bresson, Deguerry, and other
priests stationed at Saint-Louis. These day-to-day accounts as well
as the "Diaire de Saint-Louis / Saint-Charles" provide a vivid picture of the White Fathers' early years at Carthage. The Lavigerie
collection also contains microfilms of many documents still in the
Archives de la Prélature at Tunis. The White Fathers have typed
copies of all the series of Lavigerie correspondence, and the carbon
copies have been reorganized and bound in chronological order. The
letters between Lavigerie and Fr. Charmetant were particularly valuable.

A wealth of official correspondence is at Paris in the Quai
d'Orsay, Archives Nationales, and War Ministry archives. Examination
of the French Foreign Ministry Correspondance consulaire et
commerciale disclosed nothing, but the Correspondance politique,
Tunis, vols. 49-70 (the crucial years 1880-82), reveals much about
Lavigerie's relations with the government. The second series,
Tunisie, Nouvelle Série, is organized topically rather than

chronologically, and it contains much of value. The Correspondance
politique of the French embassy to the Holy See details the triangu-
lar diplomacy of the government, the Vatican, and Lavigerie. Other
reports from consuls in Malta and Beyrouth place the cardinal's
activities in better perspective.

The archives of the Army Ministry at Vincennes just outside Paris
contain reconnaissance files gathered before the 1881 invasion as
well as considerable material on army intelligence activities.
Lavigerie's contact, Captain Sandherr, left a large file of raw
notes. The personnel dossier on Sandherr was quite interesting to
read in view of his later part in the Dreyfus Affair.

Forty cartons of the Ministry of Cults archives in the F19 series
of the Archives Nationales were examined, and seven of them contained
much relevant material amid bureaucratic trivia. The ministry's
personnel dossier on Lavigerie (F19, 2487) includes a valuable folio
of hundreds of news clippings; several dozen very important letters
of.Paul Cambon, Flourens, and other officials illuminate Lavigerie's
relationship with the government. Documents in other Cults Ministry
cartons treat the March Decrees and the Eastern Religious Protectorate.

The Archives de la Prélature at Tunis contain three cartons of
"Lettres du Cardinal Lavigerie" dealing with Church politics in
France as well as diocesan affairs in Tunisia. Archbishop (in
partibus) Michel Callens and his secretary, Mgr. Paul Labbe, were
most hospitable during my visit to Tunis in June 1972. Mgr. Labbe
brought me the Lavigerie letters as well as other materials such as
diocesan yearbooks and printed pastoral letters. During the same
trip to Tunis I also visited the Bibliothèque Nationale and the
Archives Nationales. These two facilities are small compared to
European collections, and the warm personal interest of their staffs
makes working there pleasant as well as professionally rewarding.
Dr. Abdeljelil Temimi at the AN was particularly helpful. The
friendliness and hospitality of Tunisian people in general make a
visit to their country most enjoyable.

Except for the Lavigerie papers, sources in Rome were relatively
limited. The Italian Foreign Ministry archives at the Farnesina
contain many consular reports from Tunis regarding the commercial
rivalry which preceded Bardo. But initial examination of this collection disclosed no trace of Lavigerie, although several reports
from Italian intelligence agents and friendly British diplomats
made this preliminary search profitable.

Both the Vatican and Propaganda Fide archives reserve all material
after the pontificate of Pius IX (d. February 1878), but it was possible to examine selected Church documents of the 1880s. Lavigerie's
letters concerning the restoration of Carthage (traced by Fr. Charles
Burns of the Archivio Segreto Vaticano) were communicated to me as
part of a large carton of papers containing many other revealing
items of diplomatic correspondence between Paris and Rome. Most of
these significant papers did not relate to Lavigerie and Tunisia,
but the casualness with which Vatican archivists set this lavish
collection on my desk indicated that they were sharing what they
had. The Tunisian correspondence of the Propaganda Fide archives
for the years 1878-82 is bound in "Scritture Riferite nei Congressi,"
Barbaria, vol. 21. It is often possible there for a researcher to
examine letters from the beginning of Leo XIII's pontificate by
requesting access to earlier material sewn together with them. Confidential letters from Lavigerie and from the Capuchins to Cardinal-
Prefect Simeoni at the Propaganda filled a few gaps which remained
in the historical account reconstructed from the other sources.

PRINTED PRIMARY SOURCES

The two volumes of <u>Oeuvres choisies de son Eminence, le Cardinal
Lavigerie, Archevêque d'Alger</u> (1884) contain many of his North
African public letters, discourses, and memorials. Excerpts from
the <u>Oeuvres choisies</u> are part of an autobiographical work which
Lavigerie published under the name of the vicar general of the
Archdiocese of Algiers, A.-C. Grussenmeyer, <u>Vingt-cinq années
d'épiscopat en France et en Afrique: Documents biographiques sur</u>

S. E. le Cardinal Lavigerie, 2 vols. (1888). The White Fathers'
periodical Missions d'Alger printed many articles written by the
founder. Another journal, Revue d'Histoire des Missions, in 1925
printed Fr. Joseph Mazé's excellent analysis of Lavigerie's mission
ecclesiology, attributed to "Un Père Blanc," "Les Idées principales
du Cardinal Lavigerie sur l'évangélisation de l'Afrique." More recently Fr. Xavier de Montclos edited a short anthology of letters
and statements, Le Cardinal Lavigerie: La mission universelle de
l'Eglise (1968). It includes an introduction and commentary on
Lavigerie's opinions regarding the Church's role, organization,
problems, and personnel.

Paul Cambon's Correspondance, 1 (1940) and a briefer collection
entitled "Lettres de Tunisie" (Revue des Deux Mondes, May 1931) contain many letters written during his assignment in the regency;
several of them relate confidential discussions with Lavigerie. The
French resident's son, Henri Cambon, devotes a chapter of his
Histoire de la Régence de Tunis (1948) to the history of the Christian
Church there from its first century to Lavigerie's revival.

PRINTED SECONDARY SOURCES

The first important biography, Le Cardinal Lavigerie, was written
at the request of the White Fathers by Mgr. Louis Baunard. The first
of several editions of this two-volume study appeared in 1896.
Baunard relied on Church documents available at the time, but others
were lost. In 1908 Abbé Jules Tournier discovered important additional letters, on which he based his 1913 Sorbonne thesis, Le
Cardinal Lavigerie et son action politique (1863-1892). This study
of church-state relations within the métropole gives some attention
to the cardinal's concern with French expansion. Tournier had previously published a few letters relating to overseas policy.
Fr. J. Mercui, Les Origines de la Société des Missionnaires d'Afrique,
is an "official history" privately printed for the White Fathers in
1929. Mercui notes a few inaccuracies in Baunard's "authorized
history."

Dozens of other biographies have appeared over the years. Georges
Goyau's series of articles, "Le Cardinal Lavigerie" in the Revue des
Deux Mondes (1925-26) appeared also in book form as Un Grand missionnaire: Le Cardinal Lavigerie (1925). Goyau provides much in the way
of background and anecdotes not found in other biographies. Two
good recent studies have appeared in English: Glenn D. Kittler con-
tinues the history of the White Fathers after Lavigerie's death
until the Algerian War in The White Fathers (1957). William Burridge
has published Destiny Africa: Cardinal Lavigerie and the Making of
the White Fathers (1966).

Editions E. de Boccard has published specific studies by White
Fathers of the Service Historique. Xavier de Montclos, Lavigerie,
le Saint-Siège, et l"Eglise, 1846-1878 (1965), treats Lavigerie's
ecclesiology from its formation at the Seminary of Saint-Sulpice.
Another work by de Montclos, Le Toast d'Alger: Documents 1890-1891
(1966), provides material relating to the ralliement. Fr. François
Renault, Lavigerie, l'esclavage africain, et l'Europe, 1868-1892,
2 vols. (1971), is an excellent study of the slave trade and the
cardinal's efforts to organize opposition against it.

The complicated issues of French anticlericalism, the Eastern
Religious Protectorate, and a papal diplomacy keyed to the Roman
Question, are treated very effectively in Professor James E. Ward's
dissertation (Cornell University, 1962), "Franco-Vatican Relations
1878-1892: The Diplomatic Origins of the Ralliement." Ward has developed several aspects of this research more thoroughly in articles.

Several researchers in the history of Tunisia have produced excellent studies during the last two decades. Leon Carl Brown provides
an excellent treatment of the social and political structure of
Tunisia in the mid-nineteenth century in The Tunisia of Ahmad Bey,
1837-1855 (1974). Brown considers Ahmad's perception of the regency's
predicament in a changing world, and he evaluates the bey's efforts
to reform a governmental machine and a society resistant to change.

One of the most active French researchers in Tunisian history is
Professor Jean Ganiage of the Sorbonne. Several articles published

during the 1950s provide a wealth of detailed information on the
regency during the nineteenth century, particularly with regard to
demography and economic history. Extensive footnotes contain much
biographical material on individuals and families in the European
colony. His book, Les Origines du protectorat français en Tunisie,
1861-1881 (1959) reflects monumental research, particularly concerning the Franco-Italian commercial rivalry.

Pierre Soumille spent five years in Tunisia doing research on the
history and social structure of the European population. In addition
to his numerous articles, Soumille published Européens de Tunisie et
questions religieuses, 1892-1901 (1975), a well-written and encyclo-
pedic collection of details on Europeans under the early protectorate.

ARCHIVE SOURCES
(Footnote abbreviations in parentheses)

Archives Lavigerie, White Fathers of Africa Generalate, Rome (AL).
  Series B3, Tunisia, items 1-608.
  Vols. 3(1), 3(2), and 3(3), Letters "De Charmetant au Cardinal,"
      30 December 1871 to 12 January 1892, typed copies numbered
      4901-5180, taken from Series C4, items 396-657.
  Vol. 28, Letters "Aux Authorités de la France," through 1892,
      typed copies of items from other series.
  Vols. 35-38, Letters "Au Père Charmetant," 186?-1889, typed
      copies of items from other series.
  "Diaire de Saint-Louis de Carthage, 1875-1881," and second cahier,
      "Diaire de Saint-Charles, 1881-1886" ("Diaire").
  Microfilms of Archives de la Prélature-Tunis.
      Series AC359 and AC360, "Tunisie-relations, affaires étrangères
      avant protectorat."
      Series AC818 to AC826, "Correspondance personnelle, Roustan."
Archives du Ministère des Affaires Etrangères, Quai d'Orsay, Paris
          (AE), Correspondance politique.
  Angleterre, Poste consulaire de Malte (M), vol. 66, 1879-1883.
  Rome, Saint-Siège (SS), vols. 1067-74, January 1880 to December

1882; vol. 1079, June-December 1884; vol. 1105, May-July
1891.

Tunis (T), vols. 49-70, 1880-82.

Tunisie, Nouvelle Série (TNS), vols. 122-124, "Cultes Catholique
et Protestant," 1886-98; vol. 307, "Instruction Publique,
Antiquités, Beaux-Arts," January 1886 to November 1888.

Turquie, Poste consulaire de Beyrouth (B), vols. 27, 28, 1882-84.

France, Ministère des Armées, Service Historique de l'Armée, Château
de Vincennes, Val de Marne (Vincennes).

Section Outre-Mer, Tunisie, Series 3H, "Fonds Tunisie, 1831-1920."

Sub-Series 30H, "Avant le protectorat."

31H, "Archives de l'expédition de 1881-1882."

32H, "Correspondances diverses de 1881 à 1914."

Archives Nationales, Paris (AN).

F19 Series of the Ministry of Cults:

2487, Personnel dossier on Lavigerie.

3105, Military chaplains, Algeria and Tunis.

3219, French clerics at Tunis.

6075, Execution of the March Decrees.

6212, Folders on Tunisia.

6236, "Etablissements Etrangères."

6243, Folder on the French Religious Protectorate in the Orient.

Archives de la Prélature-Tunis (APT).

"Lettres du Cardinal Lavigerie" (LCL), Cartons I-III.

Archives Nationales, Premier Ministère, Tunis (ANT).

Série E, primarily concerning "Education Nationale": cartons
260-264, 269-271, 295 (dossier 4), 296 (dossiers 1, 2),
500-503.

Série Historique, material concerning beylical litigation against
former Prime Minister Mustapha ben Ismael, carton 10: dossiers
95, 96, 115, 116, 116 bis, 117.

Armoire 6 (42-II), carton 64: dossiers 755-78, "Culte Catholique-
Enseignement Laïque."

Archivio Segreto Vaticano, Vatican City (ASV).

Segreteria di Stato, Rubric 261 (1884), and Rubric 280 (1884),
    locality C.
Archivio Storico, Ministero degli Affari Esteri, Rome (Farnesina).
    "Archivi di Gabinetto, 1861-1887."
        Busta 233, "Affari d'Africa in genere, 1886-1887" (mislabeled,
        should read "1868-1887").
Archivo Storico della Sacra Congregazione de Propaganda Fide, Piazza
        di Spagna, Rome (APF).
    "Scritture Riferite nei Congressi," Barbaria, vols. 20, 21,
        1867-82.

PRINTED PRIMARY SOURCES

Anselme des Arcs, R. P. Mémoires pour servir à l'histoire de la
    mission des Capucins dans la Régence de Tunis, 1624-1865. Rome,
    Archives Générales de l'Ordre des Capucins, 1889.
Benson, Arthur Christopher, ed. The Life of Edward White Benson.
    2 vols. London: Macmillan, 1899.
Billing, le Baron Robert de. Le Baron Robert de Billing, Vie, notes,
    correspondance. Paris: Savine, 1895.
Cambon, Jules (brother of Paul). "Souvenirs sur le Cardinal Lavigerie."
    Revue des Deux Mondes 32 (1926): 277-89.
——— "Souvenirs sur le Cardinal Lavigerie." Revue d'Histoire des
    Missions (Paris) 3 (1926): 1-6.
Cambon, Paul. Correspondance, 1870-1924. Edited by Henri Cambon (son).
    3 vols. Paris: Grasset, 1940, 1946. Vol. 1, 1870-1898.
——— "Lettres de Tunisie." Edited by Henri Cambon. Revue des Deux
    Mondes 3 (May 1931): 127-50, 373-98.
D'Estournelles de Constant. "Les Débuts d'un protectorat: La France
    en Tunisie." Revue des Deux Mondes 79 (1887): 785-819.
Ferrata, Cardinal Dominique. Mémoires. 3 vols. Rome: Cuggiani, 1920.
Ferry, Jules. Les Affaires de Tunisie: Discours de M. Jules Ferry,
    publiés avec préface et notes à l'appui par M. Alfred Rambaud.
    Paris: Hetzel, n.d. [1882].
Freycinet, Charles de. Souvenirs, 1878-1893. 4th ed. Paris: Delagrave,
    1913.

Grussenmeyer, A.-C. Vingt-cinq années d'épiscopat en France et en
   Afrique: Documents biographiques sur S.E. le Cardinal Lavigerie.
   2 vols. Algiers, 1888.

Journal officiel (Paris).

Lavigerie, Charles, Mgr. De l'Utilité d'une Mission Archéologique
   Permanente à Carthage: Lettre à M. le Secrétaire Perpétuel de
   l'Académie des Inscriptions et Belles-Lettres par l'Archevêque
   d'Alger. Algiers: Jourdan, April 1881.

——— "Lettre Circulaire de Mgr. L'Archevêque d'Alger au clergé de
   son diocèse relativement à son nomination d'administrateur
   apostolique de la Tunisie." Algiers: Jourdan, 1881, dated Rome,
   29 July 1881.

——— "Missions d'Afrique." Annales de la Propagation de la Foi
   53 (1881): 182-218.

——— Oeuvres choisies de son Eminence, le Cardinal Lavigerie,
   Archevêque d'Alger. 2 vols. Paris: Poussielgue, 1884.

——— "Saint-Louis, roi de France, et son tombeau sur les ruines
   de Carthage, Lettre de Mgr. l'Archevêque d'Alger aux missionnaires
   de son diocèse." Paris: Belin, 1875, dated Algiers, 20 August
   1875.

La Presse (Tunis), "Le President Bourguiba: En dépit des tentatives
   de dépersonalisation la Tunisie est démeurée une terre de l'Islam."
   15 October 1974.

Missions d'Alger. Saint Cloud: Belin.

Tournier, J., ed. "Le Cardinal Lavigerie et la politique coloniale
   de la France en Afrique (documents inédits)." Correspondant 210
   (10 March 1912): 833-64.

L'Union. Paris.

L'Unione. Tunis.

SECONDARY SOURCES

Acomb, Evelyn M. The French Laic Laws, 1879-1889. New York: Columbia
   University Press, 1941.

Baudrillart, Alfred. "Le Cardinal Lavigerie, apôtre de l'Evangile."
   Revue d'Histoire des Missions 3 (1926): 7-29.

Baunard, Mgr. Le Cardinal Lavigerie. 2 vols. Paris: Gigord, 1922.

Bertrand, Louis. "Le Centenaire du Cardinal Lavigerie." Revue des Deux Mondes 30 (1925): 578-608.

———— Le Sang des races. Paris: Ollendorff, n.d. (preface dated 1920).

Betts, Raymond F. Assimilation and Association in French Colonial Theory, 1890-1914. New York, Columbia University Press, 1961.

Bouniol, J., ed. The White Fathers and their Missions. London: Sands, 1929.

Bowie, Leland Louis. The Impact of the Protégé System in Morocco, 1880-1912. Ohio University Papers in International Studies, Africa Series, no. 11. Athens, 1970.

———— "The Protégé System in Morocco, 1880-1904." Ph. D. dissertation, University of Michigan, 1970.

Bracq, Rev. J. C. "Cardinal Lavigerie and his Anti-slavery Work." The Missionary Review of the World 13 (October 1890): 721-25.

Brogan, Denis W. The Development of Modern France, 1870-1939. London: Hamish Hamilton, 1967.

Brown, L. Carl. The Tunisia of Ahmad Bey, 1837-1855. Princeton: Princeton University Press, 1974.

Brunschwig, Henri. French Colonialism, 1871-1914. New York: Praeger, 1966.

Burridge, William. Destiny Africa: Cardinal Lavigerie and the Making of the White Fathers. London and Dublin: Chapman, 1966.

Cambon, Henri (son of Paul Cambon). Histoire de la Régence de Tunis. Paris: Berger-Levrault, 1948.

Carthage, Le Diocèse de (Mission de Tunisie). "Notice Historique" par L'Abbé Bombard, Curé de la Cathédrale. Tunis: Imprimerie Rapide, 1899.

Cayci, Abdurrahman. La Question tunisienne et la politique ottomane, 1881-1913. Atatürk Ünïversïtesï Yayinlari no. 31. Fen-Edebïyat Fakültesï Arastirmalari no. 13. Erzurum, 1963.

Clarke, R. F., ed. Cardinal Lavigerie and the African Slave Trade. London: Longmans, Green and Co., 1889.

Confer, Vincent. France and Algeria: The Problem of Civil and Political Reform, 1870-1920. Syracuse: Syracuse University Press, 1966.

Cooke, James J. New French Imperialism 1880-1910: The Third Republic and Colonial Expansion. Devon: David and Charles, 1973.

Cragg, Kenneth. The Call of the Minaret. New York: Oxford University Press, 1956.

Cussac, J., R. P. Un Géant de l'apostolat, le Cardinal Lavigerie. Paris: Toulouse, 1940.

Damis, John James. "The Free School Movement in Morocco, 1919-1970." Ph. D. dissertation, Fletcher School of Law and Diplomacy, 1970.

————— "The Free-School Phenomenon: The Cases of Tunisia and Algeria." International Journal of Middle East Studies 5 (1974): 434-49.

Debidour, A. L'Eglise catholique et l'Etat sous la Troisième République, 1870-1906. 2 vols. Paris: Alcan, 1906. Vol. 1, 1870-1889.

Demeerseman, A. "Au Berceau des premières réformes démocratiques en Tunisie." IBLA, 20 (1957): 1-12.

————— "Doctrine de Khéreddine en matière de politique extérieure." IBLA 21 (1958): 13-29.

————— "Un Grand témoin des premières idées modernisantes en Tunisie." IBLA 76 (1956): 349-74.

————— "Indépendence de la Tunisie et politique extérieure de Khéreddine," IBLA 21 (1958): 229-77.

Dictionnaire universel des contemporains. Paris: Hachette, 1893.

Diplomate, Par un (son Henri Cambon). Paul Cambon, Ambassadeur de France. Paris: Plon, 1937.

Eubank, Keith. Paul Cambon, Master Diplomatist. Norman: University of Oklahoma Press, 1960.

Faucon, Narcisse. La Tunisie avant et depuis l'occupation française, histoire et colonisation. Introduction by Jules Ferry. 2 vols. Paris: A. Challamel, 1893.

Fontaine, J. "Khéreddine, Réformiste ou moderniste?" IBLA 117 (1967): 75-81.

Gadille, Jacques. La Pensée et l'action politiques des évêques
    français au début de la IIIe République, 1870-1883. 2 vols.
    Paris: Hachette, 1967.
──── "La Politique de défense républicaine à l'égard de l'Eglise
    de France, 1876-1883." Bulletin de la Société d'Histoire Moderne
    1 (1967): 2-9.
Ganiage, Jean. "Une Affaire tunisienne: L'Affaire de L'Enfida, 1880-
    1882." Revue Africaine 99 (1955): 341-78.
──── "La Crise des finances tunisiennes, et l'ascension des Juifs
    de Tunis, 1860-1880." Revue Africaine 99 (1955): 153-73.
──── "Etude démographique sur les Européens de Tunisie au milieu
    de XIXe siècle." Cahiers de Tunisie 5 (1957): 167-201.
──── "Les Européens en Tunisie au milieu du XIXe siècle, 1840-1870."
    Cahiers de Tunisie 3 (1955): 388-421.
──── L'Expansion coloniale de la France sous la Troisième République,
    1871-1914. Paris: Poyot, 1968.
──── Les Origines du protectorat français en Tunisie, 1861-1881.
    Paris: Presses Universitaires de France, 1959.
Gehring, Gilbert. "Les Relations entre la Tunisie et l'Allemagne
    avant le Protectorat français." Cahiers de Tunisie 71-72 (1970):
    11-155.
Goyau, Georges. "Le Cardinal Lavigerie." Revue des Deux Mondes 26
    (1925): 310-43, 579-609, 775-807; 27 (1926): 149-86. This is a
    series of articles marking the centenary of his birth.
──── Un Grand missionnaire: le Cardinal Lavigerie. Paris: Plon,
    1925. The text is identical to the series in Revue des Deux Mondes.
Green, Arnold H., "French Islamic Policy in Tunisia, 1881-1918: A
    Preliminary Inquiry." Revue d'Histoire Maghrébine 3 (January 1975):
    5-17.
──── "The Tunisian Ulama and the Establishment of the French Pro-
    tectorate, 1881-1892." Revue d'Histoire Maghrébine 1 (January
    1974): 14-25.
Groves, Charles P. The Planting of Christianity in Africa. 4 vols.
    London: Lutterworth Press, 1948-58. Vol. 2, 1840-1878; vol. 3,
    1878-1914.

Guérin, Victor. Les Missionnaires catholiques dans le Nord de l'Afrique. Tours: Mame, 1888.

Haussonville, J.O.B. de Cléron, Cte. d'. La Colonisation officielle en Algérie. Paris: Lévy. 1883.

Hayes, Carlton J. H. A Generation of Materialism. New York: Harper, 1941.

Helmreich, Ernst, ed. A Free Church in a Free State? Boston: Heath, 1964.

Heggoy, Willy Normann. "Fifty Years of Evangelical Missionary Movement in North Africa, 1881-1931." Ph. D. dissertation, Hartford Seminary Foundation, 1960.

Hitti, Philip Khuri. History of the Arabs: From the Earliest Times to the Present. 9th ed. London: Macmillan, 1967.

——— Islam, A Way of Life. Minneapolis: University of Minnesota Press, 1970.

——— The Near East in History: A 5000 Year Story. Princeton: Van Nostrand, 1961.

Holt, P. M.; Ann K. S. Lambton; Bernard Lewis. The Cambridge History of Islam. 2 vols. Cambridge: Cambridge University Press, 1970.

Italy, Ministero degli Affari Esteri. Indici del Archivio Storico. Vol. 6, Ministero degli Affari Esteri del Regno d'Italia, 1861-1887, edited by Ruggero Moscati. Rome, 1953.

Jamali, Fadhel. Review of The Surest Path: The Political Treatise of a Nineteenth Century Muslim Statesman, by Leon Carl Brown. This is a translation of the introduction to the Surest Path to Knowledge Concerning the Condition of Countries by Khayr al-Dîn al Tûnisî. Cahiers de Tunisie 65-67 (1969): 274-76.

Jammes, François. Lavigerie. Paris: Flammarion, 1927.

Julien, Charles-André. L'Afrique du Nord en marche: Nationalismes musulmans et souveraineté française. 2d ed. Paris: René Julliard, 1953.

——— Histoire de l'Afrique du Nord: Tunisie, Algérie, Maroc. Paris: Payot, 1931.

——— Histoire de l'Algérie contemporaine. 1 vol. Paris: Presses Universitaires de France, 1964. Vol. 1, La Conquête et les débuts de la colonisation, 1827-1871.

———— L'Impérialisme colonial et les rivalités internationales, 1870-1914. Paris: 1947.

———— et al. Les Politiques d'expansion impérialiste. Paris: Presses Universitaires de France, 1949.

[Julien, Charles-André.] La Question italienne en Tunisie, 1868-1938. Paris: Jouve, 1939.

———— et al. Les Techniciens de la colonisation. Paris: 1945.

Julien, M. E. L. "Notice sur la vie et les travaux de M. Paul Cambon (1843-1924)." Paris: Institute de France, 1926. (Collected in Publications diverses, 1926.)

Kittler, Glenn D. The White Fathers. New York: Harper, 1957.

Klein, Felix, Abbé. Le Cardinal Lavigerie et ses Oeuvres d'Afrique. Paris: Poussielgue, 1890.

Lacombe, Bernard de. "Le Cardinal Lavigerie." Correspondant 200 (1909): 891-921.

Laffey, John F. "Roots of French Imperialism in the Nineteenth Century: The Case of Lyon." French Historical Studies 6 (1969): 78-92.

Langer, William L., ed. An Encyclopedia of World History. Boston: Houghton Mifflin, 1948.

———— "The European Powers and the French Occupation of Tunis, 1878-1881." American Historical Review 31 (1925): 55-78; (1926): 251-65.

Laroui, Abdallah. The History of the Maghrib: An Interpretive Essay. Translated by Ralph Manheim. Princeton: Princeton University Press, 1977.

Larousse, Pierre. Grand dictionnaire universel du XIXe Siècle, s.v. "Lavigerie." Paris, n.d.

"L'Eglise catholique en Afrique du Nord." Maghreb 5 (September-October): 27-39.

Lesourd, Paul. "Aperçus historiques sur les missions des Pères Blancs." Revue d'Histoire des Missions 12 (1935): 348-85.

Lewis, Bernard. The Arabs in History. 4th ed. London: Hutchinson, 1966.

————— ed. and trans. Islam: From the Prophet Muhammad to the
Capture of Constantinople. 2 vols. New York: Walker, 1974.

————— Islam in History: Ideas, Men, and Events in the Middle East.
London: Alcove, 1973.

————— The Middle East and the West. Bloomington: Indiana University
Press, 1964.

Liauzu, Claude. "Les Précurseurs du mouvement ouvrier: Les Libertaires
en Tunisie à la fin du XIXe siècle." Cahiers de Tunisie 81-82
(1973): 153-82.

Liauzu, Claude, and Pierre Soumille. "La Gauche française en Tunisie
au printemps 1906: Le Congrès républicain, radical et socialiste
de Tunis." Le Mouvement Social 86 (January-March 1974): 55-78.

Ling, Dwight L. "The French Invasion of Tunisia, 1881." Historian
22: 396-412.

————— "Paul Cambon, Coordinator of Tunisia." Historian 19 (1957):
436-55.

————— Tunisia from Protectorate to Republic. Bloomington: Indiana
University Press, 1967.

Macken, Richard. "Louis Machuel and Educational Reform in Tunisia
during the Early Years of the French Protectorate." Revue
d'Histoire Maghrébine 3 (January 1975): 45-55.

Marion, Raymond Joseph. "La Croix and the Ralliement." Ph. D. dissertation, Clark University, 1957.

Marsden, Arthur. Britain and the End of the Tunis Treaties, 1894-
1897. Supplement no. 1 of the English Historical Review. London:
Longmans, 1965.

————— British Diplomacy and Tunis, 1875-1902: A Case Study in
Mediterranean Policy. New York: Africana, 1971.

Martel, André. Les Confins saharo-tripolitains de la Tunisie, 1881-
1911. 2 vols. Paris: Presses Universitaires de France, 1965.

McManners, John. Church and State in France, 1870-1914. New York:
Harper, 1973.

Mercui, J. Les Origines de la Société des Missionnaires d'Afrique.
Algiers: Maison-Carrée, 1929 (private printing).

Montclos, Xavier de, ed. Le Cardinal Lavigerie: La Mission universelle de l'Eglise. Paris: Editions du Cerf, 1968.

———— Lavigerie, le Saint Siège et l'Eglise, 1846-1878. Paris:
Boccard, 1965.

———— Le Toast d'Alger: Documents 1890-1891. Paris: Boccard, 1966.

Néré, J. Review of Lavigerie, Le Saint-Siège, et l'Eglise, 1846-
1878 by Xavier de Montclos. Revue Historique 239 (April-June
1968): 444-46.

Nouvelle biographie générale. Edited by Dr. Hoefer. Paris: Firmin
Didot Frères, 1862.

O'Donnell, J. Dean, Jr. "Cardinal Charles Lavigerie: The Politics
of Getting a Red Hat." Catholic Historical Review 63, no. 2
(April 1977): 185-203.

Oliver, Roland. The Missionary Factor in East Africa. London:
Longmans, 1952.

Père Blanc, Un [Mazé, Joseph]. "Les Idées principales du Cardinal
Lavigerie sur l'évangélisation de l'Afrique." Revue d'Histoire
des Missions 2 (1925): 351-96.

Perkins, C. Alfred. "French Catholic Opinion and Imperial Expansion,
1880-1886." Ph. D. dissertation, Harvard University, 1964.

Perkins, Kenneth J. "The Bureaux Arabes and the Colons." In Proceed-
ings of the First Meeting of the French Colonial Historical
Society, edited by Alf Andrew Heggoy and Gail Carter Dendy,
pp. 96-107. Athens, Ga.: French Colonial Historical Society,
1976.

Perkins, Kenneth P. "Pressure and Persuasion in the Policies of the
French Military in Colonial North Africa." Military Affairs
40 (April 1976): 74-78.

Perraudin, Jean. "Le Cardinal Lavigerie et Léopold II." Zaïre 11
(1957): 901-32; 12 (1958): 37-64, 165-77, 275-91, 393-408.

Phillips, C. S. The Church in France, 1848-1907. London: Society
for Promoting Christian Knowledge, 1936.

P.H.X. [Baron d'Estournelles de Constant]. La Politique française
en Tunisie: Le Protectorat et ses origines, 1854-1891. Paris:
Plon, 1891.

Picot, Georges. Le Cardinal Lavigerie et ses oeuvres dans le bassin de la Méditerranée et en Afrique. Paris: Société d'Economie Sociale, 1889. Item 517 in the Cults dossier "Mgr. Lavigerie," Archives Nationales: F19, 2487.

Pons, Mgr. A[lexandre]. La Nouvelle Eglise d'Afrique, ou la catholicisme en Algérie, en Tunisie, et au Maroc depuis 1830. Tunis: Namura, 1930.

Pottier, René. "Cardinal Lavigerie." Encyclopédie Mensuelle d'Outre-Mer 1 (November 1952): 325-28.

Préville, R. P. de. Un Grand Français: Le Cardinal Lavigerie. Paris, Librairie Saint-Joseph. 1926.

Raymond, André. "Les Libéraux anglais et la question tunisienne, 1880-1881." Cahiers de Tunisie 3 (1955): 422-65.

Renault, François. Lavigerie, l'esclavage africain, et l'Europe, 1868-1892. 2 vols. Paris: Boccard, 1971.

Retif, André. "Les Evêques français et les missions au XIXe siècle." Etudes 295 (December 1952): 362-72.

Robert, Claude-Maurice. "Lavigerie L'Africain," in "Groupe des Nord-Africains." Contacts en Terres d'Afrique, special number of Terres d'Afrique, pp. 75-85. Paris: Editions C.R.E.E.R., 1946.

Robert, Paul. Dictionnaire universel des noms propres: Le Petit Robert 2. Paris: S.E.P.R.E.T., 1974.

Roland, Joan Gardner. "The Alliance Israélite Universelle and French Policy in North Africa, 1860-1918." Ph. D. dissertation, Columbia University, 1969.

———— "The French Role in the Modernization of Jewish Communal Organizations in North Africa, 1880-1918." Paper presented to Middle East Studies Association at Los Angeles, 12 November 1976.

Ruedy, John. Land Policy in Colonial Algeria: The Origins of the Rural Public Domain. Berkeley: University of California Press, 1967.

Sainte-Marie, E. de. "Essai sur l'histoire religieuse de la Tunisie." Les Missions Catholiques 8 (1876): 512; 9 (1877): 374.

Scham, Alan. Lyautey in Morocco: Protectorate Administration, 1912-1925. Berkeley: University of California Press, 1970.

Seaman, L. C. B. From Vienna to Versailles. New York: Harper, 1963.

Sedgwick, Alexander. The Ralliement in French Politics, 1890-1898. Cambridge: Harvard University Press, 1965.

———— The Third French Republic, 1870-1914. New York: Crowell, 1968.

Serra, Enrico. "Francesco Crispi ed il problema tunisino." Storia e Politica 5, no. 1 (January-March 1966): 25-65.

Serres, Victor. "Le Protectorat tunisien." L'Afrique Française 40 (1932): 329-46.

Soumille, Pierre. "Le Cimetière européen de Bab-El-Khadra à Tunis: Etude historique et sociale." Cahiers de Tunisie 19 (1971): 129-82.

———— "Les Européens de Tunisie et les questions religieuses de 1893 à 1914: Etude d'une opinion publique," Tome Premier 1893-1901. Third cycle thesis, Université de Provence (Aix-Marseille I) 1973. Citations refer to the manuscript, later published as Européens de Tunisie et questions religieuses, 1892-1901: Etude d'une opinion publique. Paris: Centre National de la Recherche Scientifique, 1975.

———— "L'Idée de race chez les européens de Tunisie dans les années 1890-1910." Revue d'Histoire Maghrébine 5 (January 1976): 59-65.

———— "Le Passé de l'Eglise Catholique en Tunisie." Echo de la Prélature 17 (24 October 1971): 11-13.

Spillmann, Gen. Georges. "Controverse entre Napoléon III et Mac-Mahon au sujet du Royaume arabe d'Algérie." Comptes Rendus Mensuels des Séances 33 (1973): 157-67.

Streit, Robert, and Johannes Dindinger. Bibliotheca Missionum. Freiburg: Verlag Herder.

Temimi, Abdeljelil. "Rôle des missionnaires dans l'expansion du christianisme en Tunisie, 1830-1881." Revue d'Histoire Maghrébine 3 (January 1975): 114, 115, 5-17.

Tomkinson, Michael. Tunisia: A Holiday Guide. 4th ed. Tonbridge and London: Ernest Benn, 1974.

Tournier, J. Le Cardinal Lavigerie et son action politique, 1863-1892. Paris: Perrin, 1913.

Turin, Yvonne. _Affrontements culturels dans l'Algérie coloniale: Ecoles, médecines, religion, 1830-1880_. Paris: Maspero, 1971.

Valbert, G. "Le Régime du protectorat en Tunisie." _Revue des Deux Mondes_ 78 (1886): 193-204.

Ward, James Edward. "The Algiers Toast: Lavigerie's Work or Leo XIII's?" _Catholic Historical Review_ 51 (1965): 173-91

———— "Franco-Vatican Relations, 1878-1892: The Diplomatic Origins of the _Ralliement_." Ph. D. dissertation, Cornell University, 1962.

———— "Leo XIII: 'The Diplomat Pope.'" _Review of Politics_ 28 (1966): 47-61.

———— "Leo XIII and Bismarck: The Kaiser's Vatican Visit of 1888." _Review of Politics_ 24 (1962): 392-414.

X.X.X. "L'Eglise en Tunisie." _Annuaire de L'Afrique du Nord 1964_, pp. 63-71. Aix-en-Provence: Le Centre de Recherche sur l'Afrique Méditerranéenne, 1964.

Index